W9-CZT-364

Select Works of Edmund Burke

Miscellaneous Writings

Select Works of Edmund Burke

A NEW IMPRINT OF THE PAYNE EDITION

VOLUME 1

Thoughts on the Cause of the
Present Discontents

The Two Speeches on America

VOLUME 2

Reflections on the
Revolution in France

VOLUME 3

Letters on a Regicide Peace

Miscellaneous Writings

Edmund Burke

SELECT WORKS OF EDMUND BURKE

MISCELLANEOUS WRITINGS

Compiled and with a Foreword and Select Bibliography

by Francis Canavan

LIBERTY FUND
INDIANAPOLIS

This book is published by Liberty Fund, Inc., a foundation established to encourage study of the ideal of a society of free and responsible individuals.

The cuneiform inscription that serves as our logo and as the design motif for our endpapers is the earliest-known written appearance of the word "freedom" (*amagi*), or "liberty." It is taken from a clay document written about 2300 B.C. in the Sumerian city-state of Lagash.

Frontispiece is a portrait of Edmund Burke by James Barry. By permission of the Board of Trinity College Dublin.

99 00 01 02 03 C 5 4 3 2 1
99 00 01 02 03 P 5 4 3 2 1

Library of Congress Cataloging-in-Publication Data

Burke, Edmund, 1729–1797.
[Selections. 1999]
Select works of Edmund Burke : a new imprint of the Payne edition / foreword and biographical note by Francis Canavan.
p. cm.
Vols. 1–3 originally published: Oxford : Clarendon Press, 1874–1878.
Includes bibliographical references.
Contents: v. 1. Thoughts on the cause of the present discontents. The two speeches on America—v. 2. Reflections on the revolution in France—v. 3. Letters on a regicide peace—[4] Miscellaneous writings.
ISBN 0-86597-162-5 (v. 1 : hc : alk. paper).—ISBN 0-86597-163-3 (v. 1 : pb : alk. paper)
1. Great Britain—Politics and government—18th century. 2. Great Britain—Colonies—America. 3. France—History—Revolution, 1789–1799. 4. Great Britain—Relations—France. I. Canavan, Francis, 1917– . II. Payne, Edward John, 1844–1904. III. Title.
JC176.B826 1999
320.9′033—dc21 97-34325

ISBN 0-86597-168-4 (*Miscellaneous Writings* : hc : alk. paper)
ISBN 0-86597-169-2 (*Miscellaneous Writings* : pb : alk. paper)

LIBERTY FUND, INC.
8335 Allison Pointe Trail, Suite 300
Indianapolis, IN 46250-1687

Contents

Editor's Foreword

In the three volumes of Liberty Fund's new edition of E. J. Payne's *Select Works of Edmund Burke* are writings in which Burke expounded his Whig theory of limited (and party) government, his views on the imperial crisis that led to American independence, and his views on the great Revolution in France, which he saw as a crisis of Western civilization. This companion volume includes writings that present Burke's views on three additional themes: representation, economics, and the defense of politically oppressed peoples. These themes are touched upon in many of his writings, but the documents selected for this volume are among the clearest examples of his thought on these subjects.

The first theme is Burke's understanding of representative government. Although he was skeptical of democracy as a form of government for any but small countries (and not optimistic even there), he did believe that government existed for the good of the whole community and must represent the interests of all its people. But, as he explained in his *Speech to the Electors of Bristol* after his election there, his idea of representation was not the radically democratic one that saw representation as a mere substitute for direct democracy and a representative as a mere agent of the local electorate whose duty it was to carry out its wishes despite his own best judgment.

As Burke said in his own words in this speech, while he surely would listen respectfully and seriously to his constituents, he rejected the idea of "*authoritative* instructions; *Mandates* issued, which the Member [of Parliament] is bound blindly and implicitly to obey, to vote, and to argue for, though contrary to the clearest conviction of his judgement and conscience."[1] (In his *Speech on the Reform of the Representation of the Commons in Parliament,* which follows this speech in the present volume, Burke explained the political theory that lies behind the view of representation that he rejected at Bristol.) Rather, he argued in his Bristol speech, a representative was to act for the interest of his constituents, to be sure, but as part of a larger national whole, in accordance with the enlightened judgment that could be exercised only at the center of government and in possession of the knowledge available there. If nothing were at issue in politics but the question of whose will should prevail, clearly the will of the electors should. But for Burke, political judgment was a matter of reason: prudent, practical reason.

This view of the function of representative government was compatible with the aristocratic theory of civil society that Burke set forth in his *Reflections on the Revolution in France* and in its sequel, *An Appeal from the New to the Old Whigs* (which may be found in Daniel Ritchie's *Further Reflections on the Revolution in France,* published by Liberty Fund). The British constitution that he admired and loved was a prescriptive one, not based upon the democratic theory of the rights of men, but legitimated by its long service to the welfare of the people. It is explained here in a speech that Burke neither delivered nor published, but which his literary executors found among his papers and included in the first set of his *Works:* the *Speech on the Reform of the Representation of the Commons in Parliament.* Burke's political theory derived the powers of government from the consent of the people, as he had explained in his early and never-completed *Tracts relative to the Laws against Popery in Ireland.* But both there and in this speech, the people's consent was demanded and controlled by their moral obligation to obey a government that served

1. See below, p. 11.

their welfare. It was not derived from Everyman's original right to govern himself in the "state of nature."

The second theme dealt with in this volume is economics. Since Burke never wrote a formal treatise on that subject, his views on it are found in relatively brief form scattered throughout his works. Two examples of them are included here.

The first is *Two Letters to Gentlemen in Bristol on the Trade of Ireland,* which Burke wrote to merchants in Bristol while he was that city's Member of Parliament. He had voted for certain relaxations of the legislation that restrained Ireland's right to export goods to Great Britain. The Bristol merchants, typically, saw Ireland's gain as their loss and wrote to protest Burke's vote as hostile to their interests. Burke replied that trade is not a zero-sum game but a two-way street, the traffic on which benefits both parties.

One must not exaggerate what Burke says in those letters and make him out to be a free-trader *tout court.* He was addressing a particular question, the trade between the two kingdoms under one crown of Great Britain and Ireland. He had no desire to have the British Parliament relinquish its power to regulate commerce within and outside the Empire. In the debate on British policy toward the American colonies, he had accepted the Navigation Acts by which Britain severely restricted American trade because the Americans derived real benefits from their membership in the Empire, and he was content to argue that the Acts were a reason for Britain not to tax the colonies. Nor did he propose opening all of Britain's possessions to international trade on even terms.

Yet we can say that he had a bias in favor of freeing trade from mercantilist restraints. After the controversy over the trade between Britain and Ireland, he wrote to a member of the Irish Parliament that his aim had been "to fix the principle of a free trade in all the parts of these islands, as founded in justice and beneficial to the whole, but principally to the seat of the supreme power."[2] The regulation of trade, however, would remain with the supreme power.

Nor should we exaggerate the import of the next document, *Thoughts and Details on Scarcity.* It, too, addresses a narrow question—whether government should subsidize the wages of agricultural laborers in a period of bad harvests—and is not a general treatise on economics. It is cast, nevertheless, in broad terms that strongly reflect Burke's Whig desire to limit the power of government, particularly over private property, which he regarded as the strong bulwark of liberty. Its meaning, therefore, cannot be limited to the question of agricultural wages, and it implies a laissez-faire theory of economics.

On the other hand, Burke was not always unwilling to have government intervene in economic matters. The next document included here, the *Speech on Fox's East India Bill,* shows that, having earlier defended the chartered rights of the East India Company against efforts to bring it under greater control by the British government, Burke had changed his mind and now advocated stripping the Company of independent power to govern the parts of India that it controlled. The interested reader may also consult the Ninth Report of the House of Commons Select Committee on India, of which Burke is the acknowledged author, for his free-market views, but should be careful not to make him out to be a Manchester liberal before his time.

The third theme is Burke's genuine concern for oppressed peoples. Burke always claimed to be a reformer, and in many ways he was one. For example, one of the actions that cost him his seat as M.P. for Bristol was his support of a bill for the relief of insolvent debtors. The documents selected here, however, demonstrate his concern for peoples outside Great

2. *Letter to Thomas Burgh, Esq.,* New Year's Day, 1780, *W&S* 9:550.

Britain but under British rule. Burke was always an imperialist but an enlightened one who believed that the Empire could and should be a blessing to all the lands that composed it. Volume 1 of this set presents the arguments he used in favor of the American colonies and against the British policy that drove them into revolt. He did not favor American independence, but when it came he accepted it gracefully and even saw a benefit to the British people in it. If the British government had succeeded in suppressing the American revolt by force, he feared, the result would have been a vast increase in the power of the Crown, and no Whig could approve of that. "We lost our Colonies"; he therefore said, "but we kept our Constitution."[3]

The other great imperial topics he dealt with were India and Ireland. The first of these is the subject of Burke's *Speech on Fox's East India Bill,* which is a lengthy indictment of the East India Company's misgovernment of India. It was followed by his *Speech on the Nabob of Arcot's Debts,* the Ninth Report of the Select Committee, and the long series of speeches in the impeachment of Warren Hastings, the Company's Governor-General of Bengal, whom the Committee failed to convict.

Whether Burke was fair to the Company and to Hastings is a matter of dispute, as is the issue of whether the prosecution of Hastings had much effect on Britain's subsequent government of India. But there is little doubt of the sincerity of Burke's conviction that, as he said in his speech on the East India bill, "Our Indian government is in its best state a grievance,"[4] or of his desire to relieve that grievance and do justice to the suffering people of India.

Burke himself was Irish and had been born into a family in which the father had conformed to the Established Church

3. *Letter to a Noble Lord* (1796), *W&S* 9:152.

4. See below, p. 126.

in order to practice law (a profession forbidden to Catholics under the Penal Laws), while his mother remained Catholic. His relatives on his mother's side were numerous, and he remained in friendly contact with them throughout his life. He had an intense sympathy with their plight under the government of what came to be called the Protestant Ascendancy, and he labored long and with considerable success to relieve Irish Catholics of their legal burdens. His *Letter to Sir Hercules Langrishe* presents a good picture of their situation as it was in 1792 and of what more he thought should be done for them. The interested reader may also consult Burke's document *On the State of Ireland,* written in the same year, and his *Tracts relative to the Laws against Popery in Ireland,* written three decades earlier, when the laws against the Catholics of Ireland were even more severe.

Finally, while Burke did not take much part in the movement to abolish the slavery of African blacks in the British colonies, he did write a document, *Sketch of the Negro Code,* that outlined a typically Burkean plan for the gradual amelioration and eventual abolition first of the slave trade and then of slavery itself. Once again, it shows Burke's genuine concern for politically oppressed peoples. He admired and defended aristocracy, but he did so as a man who truly believed that *noblesse oblige.*

That phrase, *noblesse oblige,* explains what may seem to be a contradiction in Burke's attitude toward the poor and oppressed. He strongly opposed a government policy of relieving their lot in England by subsidizing their wages in a time of poor harvests. Yet he denounced Britain's government for its policies in America, India, Ireland, and the slave-owning colonies.

But we must notice that Burke never proposed that government should support the poor in any of those instances. Even in regard to Negro slavery, his aim was gradually to abolish the slave trade and slavery while training the slaves to learn the social and economic skills necessary for freedom, to acquire property, and thus to be able to support themselves. So also in America, India, and Ireland. He wanted government to stop burdening the peoples of those countries with oppressive policies and to allow them the freedom to earn their own way. But, he thought, it was simply not the function of government to furnish them with their livelihood. Doing that in a period of hardship was a work of private charity and the Christian duty of the aristocracy of property owners, for whom "noblesse" did indeed oblige, not in justice but in charity.

Whether this policy would have been adequate after the Industrial Revolution had transformed Great Britain is a valid question. But although the Industrial Revolution got under way during Burke's latter years (perhaps as late as 1780), it did not hit its full stride until the following century. Burke did not see what it would do to the rural economic order dominated by the land-owning aristocracy, which he thought, rightly or wrongly, could handle the problem of poverty without government intervention in such questions as wages.

I have borrowed freely for the factual information in the footnotes to these documents, usually without explicit acknowledgment of the source when information could have been obtained from other sources as well. The sources I have used most frequently are the *Oxford English Dictionary;* the *Dictionary of National Biography;* The Loeb Classical Library; *The Writings and Speeches of Edmund Burke* (general ed. Paul Langford); *The Correspondence of Edmund Burke* (general ed. Thomas Copeland); Carl Cone's two-volume *Burke and the Nature of Politics;* Thomas Mahoney's *Edmund Burke and Ireland;* and *Edmund Burke: A Bibliography of Secondary Sources to 1982,* by Clara Gandy and Peter Stanlis, as well as several encyclopedias and general reference works.

Francis Canavan

Fordham University

Editor's Note

The texts used in this volume have been chosen from their original publication in accordance with William B. Todd's *Bibliography of Edmund Burke* (Godalming, Surrey: St. Paul's Bibliographies, 1982). Burke's *Speech on the Reform of the Representation of the Commons in Parliament* and *Sketch of the Negro Code,* however, were not published in Burke's lifetime and were included by his literary executors in their New Edition of *The Works of the Right Honourable Edmund Burke* (London: F. C. and J. Rivington, 16 vols., 1808–27), from vols. 10 and 9 of which, respectively, they are taken here. *Thoughts and Details on Scarcity* also did not appear in print in Burke's lifetime, but is taken here from the pamphlet under that title published by his executors prior to their publication of his *Works* (in vol. 7 of which it is reprinted).

Burke's speech at Bristol on November 3, 1774, is taken from *Mr. Burke's Speeches at His Arrival at Bristol and at The Conclusion of the Poll* (London: J. Dodsley, 2nd edition, 1775).

Two Letters from Mr. Edmund Burke to Gentlemen in the City of Bristol on the Bills Depending in Parliament Relative to the Trade of Ireland, 1st edition, was published in London by J. Dodsley in 1778.

Burke's speech on Fox's East India Bill is taken from *Mr. Burke's Speech on the 1st December 1783, upon the question for the Speaker's leaving the chair in order for the House to resolve itself into a committee on Mr. Fox's East India Bill* (London: J. Dodsley, 1st edition, 1784).

Burke's *Letter to Sir Hercules Langrishe* is taken from *A Letter from the Right Hon. Edmund Burke, M.P. in the Kingdom of Great Britain, to Sir Hercules Langrishe, Bart. M.P. on the subject of*

Roman Catholics of Ireland, and the Propriety of Admitting Them to the Elective Franchise, consistently with the Principles of the Constitution as Established at the Revolution (London: J. Debrett, 2nd edition, corrected, 1792).

Thoughts and Details on Scarcity, originally presented to the Right Hon. William Pitt, in the month of November, 1795, by the late Right Honourable Edmund Burke was first published in London in 1800 by F. and C. Rivington and J. Hatchard.

Burke's spellings (including in particular Indian and other foreign names), capitalizations, and use of italics have been retained, strange as they may seem to modern eyes.

I take this occasion to express my thanks to the staff of the Beinecke Rare Book and Manuscript Library at Yale University for providing the text of Burke's speech at Bristol, and to the staff of the Boston Athenaeum for providing the text of the two letters to gentlemen in Bristol. I owe special thanks to Ms. Carol Rosato of the Duane Library at Fordham University for her help in providing the texts of the speech on Fox's East India Bill, the letter to Sir Hercules Langrishe, and *Thoughts and Details on Scarcity.*

I also thank my friends and fellow Burke scholars Professors Peter J. Stanlis of Rockford College and Daniel E. Ritchie of Bethel College for their very helpful comments on my work for these Liberty Fund volumes.

Short Titles

The Annual Register *The Annual Register* (began publication by J. Dodsley in London in 1758, under Burke's editorship, and continues publication to the present day).

Corr. 1844 Burke, Edmund, *Correspondence of the Right Honourable Edmund Burke between the Year 1744, and the Period of his Decease, in 1797,* eds. Charles William Wentworth-Fitzwilliam, 5th Earl Fitzwilliam, and Sir Richard Bourke. 4 vols. (London: Francis and John Rivington, 1844).

Corr. Copeland, Thomas W., gen. ed., *The Correspondence of Edmund Burke.* 10 vols. (Chicago and Cambridge: University of Chicago Press and Cambridge University Press, 1958–78).

Parliamentary History *The Parliamentary History of England from the Norman Conquest in 1066 to the year 1803,* ed. W. Cobbett. 36 vols. London: T. C. Hansard, 1806–20).

Works *The Works of the Right Honourable Edmund Burke.* A New Edition. 16 vols. (London: F. C. and J. Rivington, 1808–27).

W&S Langford, Paul, gen. ed., *The Writings and Speeches of Edmund Burke.* 12 vols. (Oxford: Clarendon Press, 1981–).

Select Works of Edmund Burke

Miscellaneous Writings

Speech to the Electors of Bristol

[November 3, 1774]

Burke was elected in 1765 to the House of Commons from the borough of Wendover, which was "owned" by Lord Verney (its voters were his tenants and did his bidding). But in 1774, Lord Verney told Burke that financial difficulties prevented him from renominating the impecunious Burke in that year's election. At the last moment, however, after the public poll (which went on for days) had already begun in Bristol, Britain's second most important port, Joseph Harford and Richard Champion, merchants of that city, nominated Burke for one of Bristol's two seats. Burke rushed to Bristol and delivered a speech on his arrival there. What is printed here, however, is Burke's speech at the conclusion of the poll, after he had been elected. It has become the classic exposition of a certain view of the role of an elected representative.

To understand some of the things that Burke says in this speech, one will need a bit of historical background. In those days, each parliamentary constituency elected two members of Parliament. Bristol's previous incumbents had been Lord Clare (a courtesy title, since, if he had been a nobleman, he could not have sat in the Commons), a Whig, and Matthew Brickdale, a Tory. But the Whigs were dissatisfied with Lord Clare, who had gone over to the court party, and thought they could take Brickdale's seat as well in the 1774 election.

Their first nominee was Henry Cruger, Jr., who came of a prominent commercial family. Some of the Crugers had emigrated to New

York, and Henry's uncle, John Cruger, was the Speaker of the New York Assembly when that body elected Edmund Burke in 1770 as the colony's agent at the British royal court. Burke was acquainted with him through official correspondence, and he was still the Speaker at the time of the election in Bristol.

His nephew, Henry Cruger, was a political radical, as radicalism was reckoned in that day, and some of his faction of the Whigs had sounded out Burke for the second candidacy. When the two of them met in Burke's home in Beaconsfield, however, it became clear that they had important differences in political philosophy, and Cruger declined to stand for election with Burke. Burke's last-minute nomination was the result of Lord Clare's suddenly withdrawing on the day the poll opened, because he had been assured of a safe seat in another constituency. Harford and Champion, men of more moderate views than Cruger's, now nominated Burke and urged him to come at once to Bristol.

Cruger was easily elected, but Burke won only after a closely contested poll. Brickdale, following a custom of losers still practiced to the present day, sought to have the election results nullified on grounds of fraud. A large number of those who had voted, he alleged, were not freemen of Bristol and therefore not entitled to cast a vote. He petitioned the House of Commons not to seat Burke; a committee held hearings and reported in Burke's favor, and the House accepted its recommendation.

The important part of this speech, however, is Burke's declaration of the independence that an elected representative ought to enjoy in Parliament. He not only stated his view but acted on it, in ways which his Two Letters on the Trade of Ireland, *printed below, illustrate. One may well believe that on the issues on which Burke acted contrary to the wishes of his constituents, he was right and they were wrong. But the discontent he caused in them made it obvious that he could not win in the election of 1780, so he withdrew from the poll and accepted a safe seat from his parliamentary patron, Lord Rockingham, which he held until his retirement in 1794.*

Mr. Edmund Burke's Speech to the Electors of Bristol

[On his being declared by the Sheriffs, duly elected one of the Representatives in Parliament for that City, on Thursday the 3d of November, 1774]

GENTLEMEN,

I CANNOT AVOID SYMPATHIZING strongly with the feelings of the Gentleman who has received the same honour that you have conferred on me. If he, who was bred and passed his whole Life amongst you; if he, who, through the easy gradations of acquaintance, friendship, and esteem, has obtained the honour, which seems of itself, naturally and almost insensibly, to meet with those, who, by the even tenour of pleasing manners and social virtues, slide into the love and confidence of their fellow-citizens; if he cannot speak but with great emotion on this subject, surrounded as he is on all sides with his old friends; you will have the goodness to excuse me, if my real, unaffected embarrassment prevents me from expressing my gratitude to you as I ought.

I was brought hither under the disadvantage of being unknown, even by sight, to any of you. No previous canvass was made for me.[1] I was put in nomination after the poll was

1. In fact, Richard Champion and others had been working for two or three months to win support for Burke.

opened. I did not appear until it was far advanced. If, under all these accumulated disadvantages, your good opinion has carried me to this happy point of success; you will pardon me, if I can only say to you collectively, as I said to you individually, simply and plainly, I thank you—I am obliged to you—I am not insensible of your kindness.

This is all that I am able to say for the inestimable favour you have conferred upon me. But I cannot be satisfied, without saying a little more in defence of the right you have to confer such a favour. The person that appeared here as counsel for the Candidate,[1] who so long and so earnestly solicited your votes, thinks proper to deny, that a very great part of you have any votes to give. He fixes a standard period of time in his own imagination, not what the law defines, but merely what the convenience of his Client suggests, by which he would cut off, at one stroke, all those freedoms, which are the dearest privileges of your Corporation;[2] which the common law authorizes: which your Magistrates are compelled to grant; which come duly authenticated into this Court;[3] and are saved in the clearest words, and with the most religious care and tenderness, in that very act of Parliament, which was made to regulate the Elections by Freemen, and to prevent all possible abuses in making them.

I do not intend to argue the matter here. My learned Counsel has supported your Cause with his usual Ability; the worthy Sheriffs have acted with their usual equity, and I have no doubt, that the same equity, which dictates the return, will guide the final determination. I had the honour, in conjunction with many far wiser men, to contribute a very small assistance, but however some assistance, to the forming the Judicature which is to try such questions. It would be unnatu-

1. Matthew Brickdale.

2. The municipal corporation of Bristol.

3. The electorate of Bristol.

ral in me, to doubt the Justice of that Court,[1] in the trial of my own cause, to which I have been so active to give jurisdiction over every other.

I assure the worthy Freemen, and this Corporation, that, if the Gentleman perseveres in the intentions, which his present warmth dictates to him, I will attend their cause with diligence, and I hope with effect. For, if I know any thing of myself, it is not my own Interest in it, but my full conviction, that induces me to tell you—*I think there is not a shadow of doubt in the case.*

I do not imagine that you find me rash in declaring myself, or very forward in troubling you. From the beginning to the end of the election, I have kept silence in all matters of discussion. I have never asked a question of a voter on the other side, or supported a doubtful vote on my own. I respected the abilities of my managers; I relied on the candour of the court. I think the worthy sheriffs will bear me witness, that I have never once made an attempt to impose upon their reason, to surprize their justice, or to ruffle their temper. I stood on the hustings (except when I gave my thanks to those who favoured me with their votes) less like a Candidate, than an unconcerned Spectator of a public proceeding. But here the face of things is altered. Here is an attempt for a general *massacre* of Suffrages; an attempt, by a promiscuous carnage of *friends* and *foes,* to exterminate above two thousand votes, including *seven hundred polled for the Gentleman himself, who now complains,* and who would destroy the Friends whom he has obtained, only because he cannot obtain as many of them as he wishes.

How he will be permitted, in another place, to stultify and disable himself, and to plead against his own acts, is another question. The law will decide it. I shall only speak of it as it concerns the propriety of public conduct in this city. I do

1. The House of Commons.

not pretend to lay down rules of decorum for other Gentlemen. They are best judges of the mode of proceeding that will recommend them to the favour of their fellow-citizens. But I confess, I should look rather awkward, if I had been the *very first to produce the new copies of freedom,*[1] if I had persisted in producing them to the last; if I had ransacked, with the most unremitting industry, and the most penetrating research, the remotest corners of the kingdom to discover them; if I were then, all at once, to turn short, and declare, that I had been sporting all this while with the right of election: and that I had been drawing out a Poll, upon no sort of rational grounds, which disturbed the peace of my fellow-citizens for a month together—I really, for my part, should appear awkward under such circumstances.

It would be still more awkward in me, if I were gravely to look the sheriffs in the face, and to tell them, they were not to determine my cause on my own principles; nor to make the return upon those votes, upon which I had rested my election. Such would be my appearance to the court and magistrates.

But how should I appear to the *Voters* themselves? If I had gone round to the citizens intitled to Freedom, and squeezed them by the hand—"Sir, I humbly beg your Vote—I shall be eternally thankful—may I hope for the honour of your support?—Well!—come—we shall see you at the Council-house."—If I were then to deliver them to my managers, pack them into tallies, vote them off in court, and when I heard from the Bar—"Such a one only! and such a one for ever!—he's my man!"—"Thank you, good Sir—Hah! my worthy friend! thank you kindly—that's an honest fellow—how is your good family?"—Whilst these words were hardly

1. This seems to charge Brickdale with being the first of the candidates who scoured the countryside outside the city, and even places far away, for persons with a title to being freemen of Bristol and with having brought them in to vote.

out of my mouth, if I should have wheeled round at once, and told them—"Get you gone, you pack of worthless fellows! you have no votes—you are Usurpers! you are intruders on the rights of real freemen! I will have nothing to do with you! you ought never to have been produced at this Election, and the sheriffs ought not to have admitted you to poll."

Gentlemen, I should make a strange figure, if my conduct had been of this sort. I am not so old an acquaintance of yours as the worthy Gentleman. Indeed I could not have ventured on such kind of freedoms with you. But I am bound, and I will endeavour, to have justice done to the rights of Freemen; even though I should, at the same time, be obliged to vindicate the former[1] part of my antagonist's conduct against his own present inclinations.

I owe myself, in all things, to *all* the freemen of this city. My particular friends have a demand on me, that I should not deceive their expectations. Never was cause or man supported with more constancy, more activity, more spirit. I have been supported with a zeal indeed and heartiness in my friends, which (if their object had been at all proportioned to their endeavours) could never be sufficiently commended. They supported me upon the most liberal principles. They wished that the members for Bristol should be chosen for the City, and for their Country at large, and not for themselves.

So far they are not disappointed. If I possess nothing else, I am sure I possess the temper that is fit for your service. I know nothing of Bristol, but by the favours I have received, and the virtues I have seen exerted in it.

I shall ever retain, what I now feel, the most perfect and grateful attachment to my friends—and I have no enmities; nor resentment. I never can consider fidelity to engagements, and constancy in friendships, but with the highest approba-

1. A footnote in the original publication states: "Mr. *Brickdale* opened his poll, it seems, with a tally of those very kind of freemen, and voted many hundreds of them."

tion; even when those noble qualities are employed against my own pretensions. The Gentleman, who is not fortunate as I have been in this contest, enjoys, in this respect, a consolation full of honour both to himself and to his friends. They have certainly left nothing undone for his service.

As for the trifling petulance, which the rage of party stirs up in little minds, though it should shew itself even in this court, it has not made the slightest impression on me. The highest flight of such clamorous birds is winged in an inferior region of the air. We hear them, and we look upon them, just as you, Gentlemen, when you enjoy the serene air on your lofty rocks, look down upon the Gulls, that skim the mud of your river, when it is exhausted of its tide.

I am sorry I cannot conclude, without saying a word on a topick touched upon by my worthy Colleague.[1] I wish that topick had been passed by; at a time when I have so little leisure to discuss it. But since he has thought proper to throw it out, I owe you a clear explanation of my poor sentiments on that subject.

He tells you, that "the topick of Instructions[2] has occasioned much altercation and uneasiness in this City"; and he expresses himself (if I understand him rightly) in favour of the coercive authority of such instructions.

Certainly, Gentlemen, it ought to be the happiness and glory of a Representative, to live in the strictest union, the closest correspondence, and the most unreserved communication with his constituents. Their wishes ought to have great weight with him; their opinion high respect; their business unremitted attention. It is his duty to sacrifice his repose, his pleasures, his satisfactions, to theirs; and, above all, ever, and

1. Henry Cruger, Jr., who spoke before Burke at the conclusion of the poll, had pledged himself to a "radical" program.

2. Instructions given by constituents to their representatives in Parliament.

in all cases, to prefer their interest to his own. But, his unbiassed opinion, his mature judgement, his enlightened conscience, he ought not to sacrifice to you; to any man, or to any sett of men living. These he does not derive from your pleasure; no, nor from the Law and the Constitution. They are a trust from Providence, for the abuse of which he is deeply answerable. Your Representative owes you, not his industry only, but his judgement; and he betrays, instead of serving you, if he sacrifices it to your opinion.

My worthy Colleague says, his Will ought to be subservient to yours. If that be all, the thing is innocent. If Government were a matter of Will upon any side, yours, without question, ought to be superior. But Government and Legislation are matters of reason and judgement, and not of inclination; and, what sort of reason is that, in which the determination precedes the discussion; in which one sett of men deliberate, and another decide; and where those who form the conclusion are perhaps three hundred miles distant from those who hear the arguments?

To deliver an opinion, is the right of all men; that of Constituents is a weighty and respectable opinion, which a Representative ought always to rejoice to hear; and which he ought always most seriously to consider. But *authoritative* instructions; *Mandates* issued, which the Member is bound blindly and implicitly to obey, to vote, and to argue for, though contrary to the clearest conviction of his judgement and conscience; these are things utterly unknown to the laws of this land, and which arise from a fundamental Mistake of the whole order and tenour of our Constitution.

Parliament is not a *Congress* of Ambassadors from different and hostile interests; which interests each must maintain, as an Agent and Advocate, against other Agents and Advocates; but Parliament is a *deliberative* Assembly of *one* Nation, with *one* Interest, that of the whole; where, not local Purposes, not local Prejudices ought to guide, but the general

Good, resulting from the general Reason of the whole. You chuse a Member indeed; but when you have chosen him, he is not Member of Bristol, but he is a Member of *Parliament.* If the local Constituent should have an Interest, or should form an hasty Opinion, evidently opposite to the real good of the rest of the Community, the Member for that place ought to be as far, as any other, from any endeavour to give it Effect. I beg pardon for saying so much on this subject. I have been unwillingly drawn into it; but I shall ever use a respectful frankness of communication with you. Your faithful friend, your devoted servant, I shall be to the end of my life: A flatterer you do not wish for. On this point of instructions, however, I think it scarcely possible, we ever can have any sort of difference. Perhaps I may give you too much, rather than too little trouble.

From the first hour I was encouraged to court your favour to this happy day of obtaining it, I have never promised you any thing, but humble and persevering endeavours to do my duty. The weight of that duty, I confess, makes me tremble; and whoever well considers what it is, of all things in the world will fly from what has the least likeness to a positive and precipitate engagement. To be a good Member of Parliament, is, let me tell you, no easy task; especially at this time, when there is so strong a disposition to run into the perilous extremes of servile compliance, or wild popularity. To unite circumspection with vigour, is absolutely necessary; but it is extremely difficult. We are now Members for a rich commercial *City;* this City, however, is but a part of a rich commercial *Nation,* the Interests of which are various, multiform, and intricate. We are Members for that great *Nation,* which however is itself but part of a great *Empire,* extended by our Virtue and our Fortune to the farthest limits of the East and of the West. All these wide-spread Interests must be considered; must be compared; must be reconciled if possible. We are Members for a *free* Country; and surely we all know, that the machine of a free Constitution is no simple thing; but as intricate and as delicate, as it is valuable. We are Members in a great and ancient *Monarchy;* and we must preserve religiously, the true legal rights of the Sovereign, which form the Key-stone that binds together the noble and well-constructed Arch of our Empire and our Constitution. A Constitution made up of balanced Powers must ever be a critical thing. As such I mean to touch that part of it which comes within my reach. I know my Inability, and I wish for support from every Quarter. In particular I shall aim at the friendship, and shall cultivate the best Correspondence, of the worthy Colleague you have given me.

I trouble you no farther than once more to thank you all; you, Gentlemen, for your Favours; the Candidates for their temperate and polite behaviour; and the Sheriffs, for a Conduct which may give a Model for all who are in public Stations.

FINIS

Speech on the Reform of the Representation of the Commons in Parliament

[May 7, 1782]

On this day, William Pitt the Younger (1759–1806) made a motion in the House of Commons for a committee to inquire into the state of the representation of the Commons in Parliament. The geographical distribution of seats in the House of Commons had changed little in centuries (and was not to be changed until 1832). The right to send representatives to Parliament was therefore a product of history and conformed to no discernible rational pattern. Populous cities of recent growth elected no members of Parliament, while "decayed," thinly populated, old boroughs elected two; counties suffered disparities, since large counties had only two members of Parliament, just as small ones did. In addition, seats in the Commons were shamelessly bought and sold.

A demand for the reform and more even distribution of the representation of the people had been first formulated only a decade earlier. The parliamentary reform movement was at the beginning not a widely popular one; the great unrepresented towns showed no enthusiasm for it. England was still a predominantly agricultural country ruled by a landholding aristocracy, and the nation was content to have it so. Even the reformers, by and large, sought only moderate changes in the representative system, but the American, and later the French, revolutions fostered radical ideas of democracy based on the natural right of individual men to govern themselves. It was characteristic of Burke that he focussed his attention on this radical ideology and attacked it as a deadly threat to the aristocratic constitution under which England had flourished for so long.

Yet Burke, and the Rockingham Whigs whose spokesman he was, were, in their own way, reformers. As they saw the matter, the corruption of politics was due to the undue influence of the Crown on elections to and votes in Parliament. To reduce this influence, Burke had proposed his "economical reform" bill in 1780 (little of which was actually passed). It sought to eliminate many of the sinecure jobs in the royal household (which could be held by members of Parliament) and to trim the king's civil list, which the Treasury used as a campaign fund in parliamentary elections. Farther than that, however, the Rockingham Whigs refused to go.

This attitude explains both why Burke wrote his speech on Pitt's motion and why it was never delivered. The Parliamentary History of England *shows that Pitt made his motion on the 7th of May and that it was debated and rejected on that day but makes no mention of a speech by Edmund Burke. The reason probably is that on the preceding day Burke had gotten leave to introduce another economical reform bill, and his friends dissuaded him from alienating Pitt by attacking his motion, since they wanted his support for economical reform.*

Burke later wrote what is at least an initial draft of the speech he would have given, but never published it. His literary executors found it among his papers after his death and published it in volume 10 of their edition of his Works, *from which the following document is taken. Incomplete though it is, it is presented here because of the important contribution it makes to our understanding of Burke's political theory and of his idea of representation in particular.*

Speech

[On a Motion made in the House of Commons, the 7th of May 1782, for a Committee to inquire into the state of the Representation of the Commons in Parliament]

Mr. Speaker,

We have now discovered, at the close of the eighteenth century, that the Constitution of England, which for a series of ages had been the proud distinction of this Country, always the admiration, and sometimes the envy of the wise and learned in every other Nation, we have discovered that this boasted Constitution, in the most boasted part of it, is a gross imposition upon the understanding of mankind, an insult to their feelings, and acting by contrivances destructive to the best and most valuable interests of the people. Our political architects have taken a survey of the fabrick of the British Constitution. It is singular, that they report nothing against the Crown, nothing against the Lords; but in the House of Commons every thing is unsound; it is ruinous in every part. It is infested by the dry rot, and ready to tumble about our ears without their immediate help. You know by the faults they find, what are their ideas of the alteration. As all government stands upon opinion, they know that the way utterly to destroy it is to remove that opinion, to take away all reverence, all confidence from it; and then, at the first blast of publick discontent and popular tumult, it tumbles to the ground.

In considering this question, they, who oppose it, oppose it on different grounds; one is, in the nature of a previous question; that some alterations may be expedient, but that this is not the time for making them. The other is, that no essential alterations are at all wanting: and that neither *now,* nor at *any* time, is it prudent or safe to be meddling with the fundamental principles, and ancient tried usages of our Constitution—that our Representation is as nearly perfect as the necessary imperfection of human affairs and of human creatures will suffer it to be; and that it is a subject of prudent and honest use and thankful enjoyment, and not of captious criticism and rash experiment.

On the other side, there are two parties, who proceed on two grounds, in my opinion, as they state them, utterly irreconcileable. The one is juridical, the other political. The one is in the nature of a claim of right, on the supposed rights of man as man; this party desire the decision of a suit. The other ground, as far as I can divine what it directly means, is, that the Representation is not so politically framed as to answer the theory of its institution. As to the claim of *right,* the meanest petitioner, the most gross and ignorant, is as good as the best; in some respects his claim is more favourable on account of his ignorance; his weakness, his poverty and distress, only add to his titles; he sues in *forma pauperis;*[1] he ought to be a favourite of the Court. But when the *other* ground is taken, when the question is political, when a new Constitution is to be made on a sound theory of government, then the presumptuous pride of didactick ignorance is to be excluded from the counsel in this high and arduous matter, which often bids defiance to the experience of the wisest.

1. In the character of a pauper, which confers permission to sue without liability for costs.

The first claims a personal representation, the latter rejects it with scorn and fervour. The language of the first party is plain and intelligible; they, who plead an absolute right, cannot be satisfied with anything short of personal representation, because all *natural* rights must be the rights of individuals; as by *nature* there is no such thing as politick or corporate personality; all these ideas are mere fictions of Law, they are creatures of voluntary institution; men as men are individuals, and nothing else.[1] They therefore, who reject the principle of natural and personal representation, are essentially and eternally at variance with those, who claim it. As to the first sort of Reformers, it is ridiculous to talk to them of the British Constitution upon any or upon all of its bases; for they lay it down, that every man ought to govern himself, and that where he cannot go himself he must send his Representative; that all other government is usurpation, and is so far from having a claim to our obedience, it is not only our right, but our duty, to resist it. Nine tenths of the Reformers argue thus, that is on the natural right.[2] It is impossible not to make some reflection on the nature of this claim, or avoid a comparison between the extent of the principle and the present object of the demand. If this claim be founded, it is clear to what it goes. The House of Commons, in that light, undoubtedly is no representative of the people as a collection of individu-

1. Burke here states the political theory of the radical reformers. He himself would not deny that the constitution of a civil society is a convention. But he would deny that there is a gulf between nature and convention; rather, convention, when properly made, complements and implements nature. Burke sees man as by nature a social and political animal whose nature requires civil society and therefore requires a conventional constitution that corresponds to the needs of human nature. Civil society is thus natural to man but exists in conventional and variable forms.

2. Most of the parliamentary reformers were in fact much more moderate in their proposals, but the most radical of them argued in these terms, as Thomas Paine was to do in his *The Rights of Man,* his reply to Burke's *Reflections on the Revolution in France.*

als. Nobody pretends it, nobody can justify such an assertion. When you come to examine into this claim of right, founded on the right of self-government in each individual, you find the thing demanded infinitely short of the principle of the demand. What! one *third* only of the Legislature,[1] and of the Government no share at all? What sort of treaty of partition is this for those, who have an inherent right to the whole? Give them all they ask, and your grant is still a cheat; for how comes only a third to be their younger childrens fortune in this settlement? How came they neither to have the choice of Kings, or Lords, or Judges, or Generals, or Admirals, or Bishops, or Priests, or Ministers,[2] or Justices of Peace? Why, what have you to answer in favour of the prior rights of the Crown and Peerage but this—our Constitution is a prescriptive Constitution; it is a Constitution, whose sole authority is, that it has existed time out of mind.[3] It is settled in these *two* portions against one, legislatively; and in the whole of the judicature, the whole of the federal[4] capacity, of the executive, the prudential and the financial administration, in one alone. Nor was your House of Lords and the prerogatives of the Crown settled on any adjudication in favour of natural rights, for they could never be so partitioned. Your King, your Lords, your Judges, your Juries, grand and little, all are prescriptive; and what proves it, is, the disputes not yet concluded, and never near becoming so, when any of them first originated. Prescription is the most solid of all titles, not only

1. The House of Commons was only one part of the tripartite lawmaking body composed of King, Lords, and Commons.

2. Burke conceived of Church and State as one unified whole, of which the King (in Parliament, of course) was the head.

3. For a treatment of this much discussed sentence, see Canavan, *Edmund Burke: Prescription and Providence,* chap. 6, "Time Out of Mind."

4. The power of a national government to conduct relations with the governments of other nations and to make compacts or treaties (*foedera*) with them.

to property, but, which is to secure that property, to Government.[1] They harmonize with each other, and give mutual aid to one another. It is accompanied with another ground of authority in the constitution of the human mind, presumption. It is a presumption in favour of any settled scheme of government against any untried project, that a nation has long existed and flourished under it. It is a better presumption even of the *choice* of a nation, far better than any sudden and temporary arrangement by actual election. Because a nation is not an idea only of local extent, and individual momentary aggregation, but it is an idea of continuity, which extends in time as well as in numbers, and in space. And this is a choice not of one day, or one set of people, not a tumultuary and giddy choice; it is a deliberate election of ages and of generations; it is a Constitution made by what is ten thousand times better than choice, it is made by the peculiar circumstances, occasions, tempers, dispositions, and moral, civil, and social habitudes of the people, which disclose themselves only in a long space of time. It is a vestment, which accommodates itself to the body. Nor is prescription of government formed upon blind unmeaning prejudices—for man is a most unwise, and a most wise, being. The individual is foolish. The multitude, for the moment, is foolish, when they act without deliberation; but the species is wise, and when time is given to it, as a species it almost always acts right.

The reason for the Crown as it is, for the Lords as they

1. Prescription is a title to the ownership of property which arises out of long-continued and uncontested possession and overrides all earlier claims to the property. It makes it impossible, after the period required for prescription has elapsed, to revive old claims to the property. Then it is no longer enough to produce documents proving that A's great-great-grandfather got the property by fraud from B's great-great-grandfather. Similarly, Burke holds, the long-continued existence of a constitution under which a people has lived and flourished makes it immune to claims based on every man's right to govern himself in the state of nature and therefore to vote for representatives when he enters civil society.

are, is my reason for the Commons as they are, the Electors as they are. Now, if the Crown and the Lords, and the Judicatures, are all prescriptive, so is the House of Commons of the very same origin, and of no other. We and our Electors have their powers and privileges both made and circumscribed by prescription, as much to the full as the other parts; and as such we have always claimed them, and on no other title. The House of Commons is a legislative body corporate by prescription, not made upon any given theory, but existing prescriptively—just like the rest. This prescription has made it essentially what it is, an aggregate collection of three parts, Knights, Citizens, Burgesses.[1] The question is, whether this has been always so, since the House of Commons has taken its present shape and circumstances, and has been an essential operative part of the Constitution; which, I take it, it has been for at least five hundred years.

This I resolve to myself in the affirmative: and then another question arises, whether this House stands firm upon its ancient foundations, and is not, by time and accidents, so declined from its perpendicular as to want the hand of the wise and experienced architects of the day to set it upright again, and to prop and buttress it up for duration; whether it continues true to the principles, upon which it has hitherto stood; whether this be *de facto* the Constitution of the House of Commons, as it has been since the time, that the House of Commons has, without dispute, become a necessary and an efficient part of the British Constitution?[2] To ask whether a thing, which has always been the same, stands to its usual principle, seems to me to be perfectly absurd; for how do you know the principles but from the construction? and if that

1. The House of Commons was composed of knights, who represented shires (counties); citizens, who represented cities; and burgesses, who represented boroughs.

2. That the Constitution had so "declined from its perpendicular" was Pitt's argument in the speech in which he introduced his motion.

remains the same, the principles remain the same. It is true, that to say your Constitution is what it has been, is no sufficient defence for those, who say it is a bad Constitution. It is an answer to those, who say that it is a degenerate Constitution. To those, who say it is a bad one, I answer, look to its effects. In all moral machinery the moral results are its test.

On what grounds do we go, to restore our Constitution to what it has been at some given period, or to reform and re-construct it upon principles more conformable to a sound theory of government? A prescriptive Government, such as ours, never was the work of any Legislator, never was made upon any foregone theory. It seems to me a preposterous way of reasoning, and a perfect confusion of ideas, to take the theories, which learned and speculative men have made from that Government, and then supposing it made on those theories, which were made from it, to accuse the Government as not corresponding with them. I do not vilify theory and speculation—no, because that would be to vilify reason itself. *Neque decipitur ratio, neque decipit unquam.*[1] No; whenever I speak against theory, I mean always a weak, erroneous, fallacious, unfounded, or imperfect theory; and one of the ways of discovering, that it is a false theory, is by comparing it with practice. This is the true touchstone of all theories, which regard man and the affairs of men—does it suit his nature in general; does it suit his nature as modified by his habits?

The more frequently this affair is discussed, the stronger the case appears to the sense and the feelings of mankind. I have no more doubt than I entertain of my existence, that this very thing, which is stated as an horrible thing, is the means of the preservation of our Constitution, whilst it lasts; of curing it of many of the disorders, which, attending every

1. "Reason is never deceived nor ever deceives." The Latin phrase, attributed to Manilius, is found on the title page of Jean LeClerc's *Logica: sive Ars Ratiocinandi* (London, 1692), which was part of the curriculum at Trinity College, Dublin, when Burke was a student there.

species of institution, would attend the principle of an exact local representation, or a representation on the principle of numbers.[1] If you reject personal representation, you are pushed upon expedience; and then what they wish us to do is, to prefer their speculations on that subject to the happy experience of this Country of a growing liberty and a growing prosperity for five hundred years. Whatever respect I have for their talents, this, for one, I will not do. Then what is the standard of expedience? Expedience is that, which is good for the community, and good for every individual in it. Now this expedience is the *desideratum,*[2] to be sought either without the experience of means, or with that experience. If without, as in case of the fabrication of a new Commonwealth, I will hear the learned arguing what promises to be expedient: but if we are to judge of a Commonwealth actually existing, the first thing I inquire is, what has been *found* expedient or inexpedient? And I will not take their *promise* rather than the *performance* of the Constitution.

* * *[3] But no, this was not the cause of the discontents. I went through most of the Northern parts—the Yorkshire Election was then raging; the year before, through most of the Western Counties—Bath, Bristol, Gloucester—not one word, either in the towns or country, on the subject of representation; much on the Receipt Tax, something on Mr. Fox's ambition; much greater apprehension of danger from thence than from want of representation. One would think that the ballast of the ship was shifted with us, and that our Constitution had the gunnel under water. But can you fairly and

1. Representation in the House of Commons was of communities, each of which, regardless of size, had two members of Parliament.

2. The object desired.

3. The blank space here may indicate either that Burke had not finished writing his speech when he laid it aside or that a page or pages had disappeared from it by the time his literary executors found the document among his papers.

distinctly point out what one evil or grievance has happened, which you can refer to the Representative not following the opinion of his Constituents? What one symptom do we find of this inequality? But it is not an arithmetical inequality, with which we ought to trouble ourselves. If there be a moral, a political equality, this is the *desideratum* in our Constitution, and in every Constitution in the world. Moral inequality is as between places and between classes. Now I ask, what advantage do you find, that the places, which abound in representation, possess over others, in which it is more scanty, in security for freedom, in security for justice, or in any one of those means of procuring temporal prosperity and eternal happiness, the ends, for which society was formed? Are the local interests of Cornwall and Wiltshire, for instance, their roads, canals, their prisons, their police, better than Yorkshire, Warwickshire, or Staffordshire? Warwick has Members; is Warwick, or Stafford, more opulent, happy, or free, than Newcastle, or than Birmingham? Is Wiltshire the pampered favourite, whilst Yorkshire, like the child of the bond-woman, is turned out to the desert? This is like the unhappy persons, who live, if they can be said to live, in the Statical Chair;[1] who are ever feeling their pulse, and who do not judge of health by the aptitude of the body to perform its functions, but by their ideas of what ought to be the true balance between the several secretions. Is a Committee of Cornwall, &c thronged, and the others deserted? No. You have an equal representation, because you have men equally interested in the prosperity of the whole, who are involved in the general interest and the general sympathy; and, perhaps, these places, furnishing a superfluity of publick agents and administrators, (whether in strictness they are Representatives or not, I do not mean to inquire, but they are agents and administrators,)

1. A weighing chair designed to determine the amount of weight a sick person had lost by perspiration.

will stand clearer of local interests, passions, prejudices and cabals, than the others, and therefore preserve the balance of the parts, and with a more general view, and a more steady hand, than the rest. * * * * *

In every political proposal we must not leave out of the question the political views and object of the proposer; and these we discover, not by what he says, but by the principles he lays down. I mean, says he, a moderate and temperate reform;[1] that is, I mean to do as little good as possible. If the Constitution be what you represent it and there be no danger in the change, you do wrong not to make the reform commensurate to the abuse. Fine reformer indeed! generous donor! What is the cause of this parsimony of the liberty, which you dole out to the people? Why all this limitation in giving blessings and benefits to mankind? You admit that there is an extreme in liberty, which may be infinitely noxious to those, who are to receive it, and which in the end will leave them no liberty at all. I think so too; they know it, and they feel it. The question is then, what is the standard of that extreme? What that gentleman, and the Associations,[2] or some parts of their phalanxes, think proper? Then our liberties are in their pleasure; it depends on their arbitrary will how far I shall be free. I will have none of that freedom. If, therefore, the standard of moderation be sought for, I will seek for it. Where? Not in their fancies, nor in my own: I will seek for it where I know it is to be found, in the Constitution

1. In proposing his motion, Pitt had said that he and others had on many occasions "maintained the necessity that there was for a calm revision of the principles of the constitution, and a moderate reform of such defects as had imperceptibly and gradually stole in to deface, and which threatened at last totally to destroy the most beautiful fabric of government in the world." *Parliamentary History of England* 22:1416.

2. Societies that advocated parliamentary reform, beginning with the Society of Supporters of the Bill of Rights, which adopted a series of resolutions in June 1771, including one that demanded full and equal representation of the people.

I actually enjoy. Here it says to an encroaching prerogative, Your sceptre has its length, you cannot add an hair to your head, or a gem to your Crown, but what an eternal Law has given to it. Here it says to an overweening peerage, Your pride finds banks, that it cannot overflow: here to a tumultuous and giddy people, There is a bound to the raging of the Sea. Our Constitution is like our Island, which uses and restrains its subject Sea; in vain the waves roar. In that Constitution I know, and exultingly I feel, both that I am free, and that I am not free dangerously to myself or to others. I know that no power on earth, acting as I ought to do, can touch my life, my liberty, or my property. I have that inward and dignified consciousness of my own security and independence, which constitutes, and is the only thing, which does constitute, the proud and comfortable sentiment of freedom in the human breast. I know too, and I bless God for my safe mediocrity; I know that, if I possessed all the talents of the gentlemen on the side of the House I sit, and on the other, I cannot by Royal favour, or by popular delusion, or by oligarchical cabal, elevate myself above a certain very limited point, so as to endanger my own fall, or the ruin of my Country. I know there is an order, that keeps things fast in their place; it is made to us, and we are made to it. Why not ask another wife, other children, another body, another mind?

The great object of most of these Reformers is to prepare the destruction of the Constitution, by disgracing and discrediting the House of Commons. For they think, prudently, in my opinion, that if they can persuade the nation, that the House of Commons is so constituted as not to secure the publick liberty; not to have a proper connexion with the publick interests, so constituted, as not either actually or virtually[1] to be the Representative of the people, it will be easy to prove,

1. Burke defines "virtual representation" in his *Letter to Sir Hercules Langrishe,* below, p. 240.

that a Government, composed of a Monarchy, an Oligarchy chosen by the Crown, and such a House of Commons, whatever good can be in such a system, can by no means be a system of free government.

The Constitution of England is never to have a quietus; it is to be continually vilified, attacked, reproached, resisted; instead of being the hope and sure anchor in all storms, instead of being the means of redress to all grievances, itself is the grand grievance of the nation, our shame instead of our glory. If the only specifick plan proposed, individual personal representation, is directly rejected by the person, who is looked on as the great support of this business, then the only way of considering it is a question of convenience. An honourable gentleman prefers the individual to the present. He therefore himself sees no middle term whatsoever, and therefore prefers of what he sees the individual; this is the only thing distinct and sensible, that has been advocated. He has then a scheme, which is the individual representation; he is not at a loss, not inconsistent—which scheme the other right honourable Gentleman reprobates. Now what does this go to, but to lead directly to anarchy? For to discredit the only Government, which he either possesses or can project, what is this but to destroy all government; and this is anarchy. My right honourable friend, in supporting this motion, disgraces his friends and justifies his enemies, in order to blacken the Constitution of his Country, even of that House of Commons, which supported him.[1] There is a difference between a moral or political exposure of a publick evil, relative to the administration of government, whether in men or systems, and a declaration of defects, real or supposed, in the

1. The speaker referred to must be Charles James Fox, whom Burke calls "my right honourable friend," and who had spoken in this debate in favor of "equal representation," *Parliamentary History* 22:1452–53. The strong language Burke uses here about his friend and close political associate may foreshadow the complete break between them over the French Revolution.

fundamental Constitution of your Country. The first may be cured in the individual by the motives of religion, virtue, honour, fear, shame, or interest. Men may be made to abandon also false systems, by exposing their absurdity or mischievous tendency to their own better thoughts, or to the contempt or indignation of the publick; and after all, if they should exist, and exist uncorrected, they only disgrace individuals as fugitive opinions. But it is quite otherwise with the frame and Constitution of the State; if that is disgraced, patriotism is destroyed in its very source. No man has ever willingly obeyed, much less was desirous of defending with his blood, a mischievous and absurd scheme of government. Our first, our dearest, most comprehensive relation, our Country, is gone.

It suggests melancholy reflections, in consequence of the strange course we have long held, that we are now no longer quarrelling about the character, or about the conduct of men, or the tenour of measures; but we are grown out of humour with the English Constitution itself; this is become the object of the animosity of Englishmen. This Constitution in former days used to be the admiration and the envy of the world; it was the pattern for politicians; the theme of the eloquent; the meditation of the philosopher in every part of the world. As to Englishmen, it was their pride, their consolation. By it they lived, for it they were ready to die. Its defects, if it had any, were partly covered by partiality, and partly born by prudence. Now all its excellencies are forgot, its faults are now forcibly dragged into day, exaggerated by every artifice of representation. It is despised and rejected of men;[1] and every device and invention of ingenuity, or idleness, set up in opposition or in preference to it. It is to this humour, and it is to the measures growing out of it, that I set myself (I hope not alone) in the most determined opposition. Never before did we at any time in this Country meet upon the theory of our

1. An allusion to Isaiah 53:3.

frame of Government, to sit in judgment on the Constitution of our Country, to call it as a delinquent before us, and to accuse it of every defect and every vice; to see whether it, an object of our veneration, even our adoration, did or did not accord with a pre-conceived scheme in the minds of certain gentlemen. Cast your eyes on the journals of Parliament. It is for fear of losing the inestimable treasure we have, that I do not venture to game it out of my hands for the vain hope of improving it. I look with filial reverence on the Constitution of my Country, and never will cut it in pieces, and put it into the kettle of any magician, in order to boil it, with the puddle of their compounds, into youth and vigour. On the contrary, I will drive away such pretenders; I will nurse its venerable age, and with lenient arts extend a parent's breath.

Two Letters to Gentlemen in Bristol on the Trade of Ireland

[April 23 and May 2, 1778]

After the British defeat at Saratoga in 1777, Lord North's administration came to believe that concessions would have to be made not only to the rebellious American colonies but to Ireland as well. Great Britain and Ireland at this time were legally distinct kingdoms, under a common crown, but with separate legislatures and governing bodies (though in fact the British government kept the Irish one firmly under its thumb). Ireland chafed under the restrictions that British legislation placed on the export of Irish goods to Great Britain, and was becoming restive. Lord North therefore acquiesced when Earl Nugent (an Irish lord and member of the British House of Commons) introduced bills in the Commons in April 1778 to eliminate or reduce some of these restrictions on Irish trade. Burke enthusiastically supported them, even though he and his party, the Rockingham Whigs, were in opposition to the government.

The response from the manufacturing and trading cities of England was an angry one, not least from Burke's constituency of Bristol, which was then the second greatest port of the kingdom. His constituents let him know that by his support of these measures in favor of freeing Irish trade, he was in danger of losing his seat at the next election, as in fact he did in 1780, though not entirely for this reason.

One of the letters of protest sent to Burke was from Samuel Span, Master of the Society of Merchant Adventurers of Bristol. Another was from Harford, Cowles and Co., a firm of iron manufacturers.

*Burke wrote replies to these letters and published them in this pamphlet on May 12, 1778. In it he rejected the mercantilist assumption that trade was a zero-sum game in which what Ireland gained Britain necessarily lost. His strategy, however, was typically Burkean, as he explained in a letter after the struggle was over (*Works *9:235–36): "I was in hopes that we might obtain, gradually, and by parts, what we might attempt at once and in the whole without success; that one concession would lead to another; and that the people of England, discovering, by a progressive experience, that none of the concessions actually made were followed by the consequences they had dreaded, their fears from what they were yet to yield would considerably diminish. But that, to which I attached myself the most particularly, was to fix* the principle *of a free trade in all the ports of these Islands, as founded in justice, and beneficial to the whole; but principally to this, the seat of the supreme power."*

To Samuel Span, Esq; Master of the Society of Merchants Adventurers of Bristol

Sir,

I am honoured with your letter of the 13th, in answer to mine, which accompanied the resolutions of the House relative to the trade of Ireland.

You will be so good as to present my best respects to the Society, and to assure them, that it was altogether unnecessary to remind me of the interest of the constituents. I have never regarded any thing else, since I had a seat in parliament. Having frequently and maturely considered that interest, and stated it to myself in almost every point of view, I am persuaded, that, under the present circumstances, I cannot more effectually pursue it, than by giving all the support in my power to the propositions which I lately transmitted to the Hall.[1]

The fault I find in the scheme is, that it falls extremely short of that liberality in the commercial system, which, I trust, will one day be adopted. If I had not considered the present resolutions, merely as preparatory to better things,

1. Of the Society of Merchant Adventurers of Bristol.

and as a means of shewing experimentally, that justice to others is not always folly to ourselves, I should have contented myself with receiving them in a cold and silent acquiescence. Separately considered, they are matters of no very great importance. But they aim, however imperfectly, at a right principle. I submit to the restraint to appease prejudice: I accept the enlargement, so far as it goes, as the result of reason and of sound policy.

We cannot be insensible of the calamities which have been brought upon this nation by an obstinate adherence to narrow and restrictive plans of government.[1] I confess, I cannot prevail on myself to take them up, precisely at a time, when the most decisive experience has taught the rest of the world to lay them down. The propositions in question did not originate from me, or from my particular friends. But when things are so right in themselves, I hold it my duty, not to enquire from what hands they come. I opposed the American measures upon the very same principle on which I support those that relate to Ireland. I was convinced, that the evils which have arisen from the adoption of the former, would be infinitely aggravated by the rejection of the latter.

Perhaps Gentlemen are not yet fully aware of the situation of their country, and what its exigencies absolutely require. I find that we are still disposed to talk at our ease, and as if all things were to be regulated by our good pleasure. I should consider it as a fatal symptom, if, in our present distressed and adverse circumstances, we should persist in the errors which are natural only to prosperity. One cannot indeed sufficiently lament the continuance of that spirit of delusion, by which, for a long time past, we have thought fit to measure our necessities by our inclinations. Moderation, prudence, and equity, are far more suitable to our condition, than lofti-

1. The revolt of the American colonies and the entry of France into the war on the American side.

ness, and confidence, and rigour. We are threatened by enemies of no small magnitude, whom, if we think fit, we may despise, as we have despised others; but they are enemies who can only cease to be truly formidable, by our entertaining a due respect for their power. Our danger will not be lessened by our shutting our eyes to it; nor will our force abroad be encreased by rendering ourselves feeble, and divided at home.

There is a dreadful schism in the British nation. Since we are not able to reunite the empire, it is our business to give all possible vigour and soundness to those parts of it which are still content to be governed by our councils. Sir, it is proper to inform you, that our measures *must be healing.* Such a degree of strength must be communicated to all the members of the state, as may enable them to defend themselves, and to co-operate in the defence of the whole. Their temper too must be managed, and their good affections cultivated. They may then be disposed to bear the load with chearfulness, as a contribution towards what may be called with truth and propriety, and not by an empty form of words, *a common cause.* Too little dependence cannot be had, at this time of day, on names and prejudices. The eyes of mankind are opened; and communities must be held together by an evident and solid interest. God forbid, that our conduct should demonstrate to the world, that Great Britain can, in no instance whatsoever, be brought to a sense of rational and equitable policy, but by coercion and force of arms!

I wish you to recollect, with what powers of concession, relatively to commerce, as well as to legislation, his Majesty's Commissioners to the United Colonies have sailed from England within this week.[1] Whether these powers are sufficient for their purposes, it is not now my business to examine. But

1. A commission led by the Earl of Carlisle had just sailed for America in an attempt at reconciliation with the colonies. The effort failed because the colonies were no longer interested in reconciliation.

we all know, that our resolutions in favour of Ireland are trifling and insignificant, when compared with the concessions to the Americans. At such a juncture, I would implore every man, who retains the least spark of regard to the yet remaining honour and security of this country, not to compel others to an imitation of their conduct; or by passion and violence, to force them to seek in the territories of the separation,[1] that freedom, and those advantages, which they are not to look for whilst they remain under the wings of their ancient government.

After all, what are the matters we dispute with so much warmth? Do we in these resolutions *bestow* any thing upon Ireland? Not a shilling. We only consent to *leave* to them, in two or three instances, the use of the natural faculties which God has given to them, and to all mankind. Is Ireland united to the crown of Great Britain for no other purpose, than that we should counteract the bounty of Providence in her favour? And in proportion as that bounty has been liberal, that we are to regard it as an evil, which is to be met with in every sort of corrective? To say that Ireland interferes with us, and therefore must be checked, is, in my opinion, a very mistaken, and a very dangerous principle. I must beg leave to repeat, what I took the liberty of suggesting to you in my last letter, that Ireland is a country, in the same climate, and of the same natural qualities and productions, with this; and has consequently no other means of growing wealthy in herself, or, in other words, of being useful to us, but by doing the very same things which we do, for the same purposes. I hope that in Great Britain we shall always pursue, without exception, *every* means of prosperity; and of course, that Ireland *will* interfere with us in something or other; for either, in order to *limit* her, we *must restrain* ourselves, or we must fall into that shocking conclusion, that we are to keep our yet remaining depen-

1. The reference is to Irish emigration to America.

dency, under a general and indiscriminate restraint, for the mere purpose of oppression. Indeed, Sir, England and Ireland may flourish together. The world is large enough for us both. Let it be our care, not to make ourselves too little for it.

I know it is said, that the people of Ireland do not pay the same taxes, and therefore ought not in equity to enjoy the same benefits with this. I had hopes, that the unhappy phantom of a compulsory *equal taxation* had haunted us long enough. I do assure you, that until it is entirely banished from our imaginations, (where alone it has, or can have any existence) we shall never cease to do ourselves the most substantial injuries. To that argument of equal taxation, I can only say, that Ireland pays as many taxes, as those who are the best judges of her powers,[1] are of opinion she can bear. To bear more she must have more ability; and in the order of nature, the advantage must *precede* the charge. This disposition of things, being the law of God, neither you nor I *can* alter it. So that if you will have more help from Ireland, you must *previously* supply her with more means. I believe it will be found, that if men are suffered freely to cultivate their natural advantages, a virtual equality of contribution will come in its own time, and will flow by an easy descent, through its own proper and natural channels. An attempt to disturb that course, and to force nature, will only bring on universal discontent, distress and confusion.

You tell me, Sir, that you prefer an union with Ireland[2] to the little regulations which are proposed in Parliament. This union is a great question of state, to which, when it comes properly before me in my parliamentary capacity, I shall give an honest and unprejudiced consideration. However, it is a

1. The Irish Parliament.

2. In 1800, after Burke's death, an Act of Union abolished the Irish Parliament and joined Ireland and Great Britain in one United Kingdom with one Parliament.

settled rule with me, to make the most of my *actual situation;* and not to refuse to do a proper thing, because there is something else more proper, which I am not able to do. This union is a business of difficulty; and on the principles of your letter, a business impracticable. Until it can be matured into a feasible and desirable scheme, I wish to have as close an union of interest and affection with Ireland, as I can have; and that, I am sure, is a far better thing than any nominal union of government.

France, and indeed most extensive empires, which by various designs and fortunes have grown into one great mass, contain many Provinces that are very different from each other in privileges and modes of government; and they raise their supplies in different ways; in different proportions; and under different authorities; yet none of them are for this reason, curtailed of their natural rights; but they carry on trade and manufactures with perfect equality. In some way or other the true balance is found; and all of them are properly poised and harmonised. How much have you lost by the participation of Scotland in all your commerce?[1] The external trade of England has more than doubled since that period; and I believe your internal (which is the most advantageous) has been augmented at least fourfold. Such virtue there is in liberality of sentiment, that you have grown richer even by the partnership of poverty.

If you think, that this participation was a loss, commercially considered, but that it has been compensated by the share which Scotland has taken in defraying the public charge—I believe you have not very carefully looked at the public accounts. Ireland, Sir, pays a great deal more than Scotland; and is perhaps as much, and as effectually united to England as Scotland is. But if Scotland, instead of paying

1. By the Act of Union of 1707, England gave up its commercial exclusiveness and Scotland gave up its legislative independence.

little, had paid nothing at all, we should be gainers, not losers by acquiring the hearty co-operation of an active intelligent people, towards the increase of the common stock; instead of our being employed in watching and counteracting them, and their being employed in watching and counteracting us, with the peevish and churlish jealousy of rivals and enemies on both sides.

I am sure, Sir, that the commercial experience of the merchants of Bristol, will soon disabuse them of the prejudice, that they can trade no longer, if countries more lightly taxed, are permitted to deal in the same commodities at the same markets. You know, that in fact, you trade very largely where you are met by the goods of all nations. You even pay high duties, on the import of your goods, and afterwards undersell nations less taxed, at their own markets; and where goods of the same kind are not charged at all. If it were otherwise, you could trade very little. You know, that the price of all sorts of manufacture is not a great deal inhanced, (except to the domestic consumer) by any taxes paid in this country. This I might very easily prove.

The same consideration will relieve you from the apprehension you express, with relation to sugars, and the difference of the duties paid here and in Ireland. Those duties affect the interior consumer only; and for obvious reasons, relative to the interest of revenue itself, they must be proportioned to his ability of payment; but in all cases in which sugar can be an *object of commerce,* and therefore (in this view) of rivalship, you are sensible, that you are at least on a par with Ireland. As to your apprehensions concerning the more advantageous situation of Ireland, for some branches of commerce, (for it is so but for some) I trust you will not find them more serious. Millford Haven, which is at your door, may serve to shew you, that the mere advantage of ports is not the thing which shifts the seat of commerce from one part of the world to the other. If I thought you inclined to take up this matter on local considerations, I should state to you, that I do not know any part of the kingdom so well situated for an advantageous commerce with Ireland as Bristol; and that none would be so likely to profit of its prosperity as our city. But your profit and theirs must concur. Beggary and bankruptcy are not the circumstances which invite to an intercourse with that or with any country; and I believe it will be found invariably true, that the superfluities of a rich nation furnish a better object of trade than the necessities of a poor one. It is the interest of the commercial world that wealth should be found every where.

The true ground of fear, in my opinion is this; that Ireland, from the vitious system of its internal polity, will be a long time before it can derive any benefit from the liberty now granted, or from any thing else. But as I do not vote advantages, in hopes that they may not be enjoyed, I will not lay any stress upon this consideration. I rather wish, that the Parliament of Ireland may, in its own wisdom, remove these impediments, and put their country in a condition to avail itself of its natural advantages. If they do not, the fault is with them, and not with us.

I have written this long letter, in order to give all possible satisfaction to my constituents with regard to the part I have taken in this affair. It gave me inexpressible concern to find, that my conduct had been a cause of uneasiness to any of them. Next to my honour and conscience, I have nothing so near and dear to me as their approbation. However, I had much rather run the risque of displeasing than of injuring them; if I am driven to make such an option. You obligingly lament, that you are not to have me for your advocate; but if I had been capable of acting as an advocate in opposition to a plan so perfectly consonant to my known principles, and to the opinions I had publicly declared on an hundred occasions, I should only disgrace myself, without supporting with the smallest degree of credit or effect, the cause you wished me to undertake. I should have lost the only thing which can make such abilities as mine of any use to the world now or hereafter; I mean that authority which is derived from an opinion, that a member speaks the language of truth and sincerity; and that he is not ready to take up or lay down a great political system for the convenience of the hour; that he is in parliament to support his opinion of the public good, and does not form his opinion in order to get into parliament, or to continue in it. It is in a great measure for your sake, that I wish to preserve this character. Without it, I am sure, I should be ill able to discharge, by any service, the smallest part of that debt of gratitude and affection, which I owe you for the great and honourable trust you have reposed in me. I am, with the highest regard and esteem,

SIR,
Your most obedient and humble Servant,

E. B.
Beaconsfield,
23d April, 1778

Copy of a Letter to Mess. ******* ****** and Co. Bristol

Gentlemen,

It gives me the most sensible concern to find, that my vote on the resolutions relative to the trade of Ireland, has not been fortunate enough to meet with your approbation. I have explained at large the grounds of my conduct on that occasion in my letters to the Merchants Hall:[1] but my very sincere regard and esteem for you will not permit me to let the matter pass without an explanation, which is particular to yourselves, and which, I hope, will prove satisfactory to you.

You tell me, that the conduct of your late member[2] is not much wondered at; but you seem to be at a loss to account for mine; and you lament, that I have taken so decided a part *against* my constituents.

This is rather an heavy imputation. Does it then really appear to you, that the propositions, to which you refer, are, on the face of them, so manifestly wrong, and so certainly injurious to the trade and manufactures of Great Britain, and particularly to yours, that no man could think of proposing, or supporting them, except from resentment to you, or from

1. The preceding letter in this pamphlet and an earlier one dated April 9, 1778.

2. Lord Nugent, who introduced the Irish trade bills in this session of Parliament, had earlier been one of Bristol's members of Parliament.

some other oblique motive? If you suppose your late member, or if you suppose me, to act upon other reasons than we choose to avow, to what do you attribute the conduct of the *other* members, who in the beginning almost unanimously adopted those resolutions? To what do you attribute the strong part taken by the ministers, and along with the ministers, by several of their most declared opponents? This does not indicate a ministerial jobb; a party design; or a provincial or local purpose. It is therefore not so absolutely clear, that the measure is wrong, or likely to be injurious to the true interests of any place, or any person.

The reason, gentlemen, for taking this step, at this time, is but too obvious and too urgent. I cannot imagine, that you forget the great war, which has been carried on with so little success (and, as I thought, with so little policy) in America; or that you are not aware of the other great wars which are impending. Ireland has been called upon to repel the attacks of enemies of no small power, brought upon her by councils, in which she has had no share. The very purpose and declared object of that original war, which has brought other wars, and other enemies on Ireland, was not very flattering to her dignity, her interest, or to the very principle of her liberty. Yet she submitted patiently to the evils she suffered from an attempt to subdue to *your* obedience, countries whose very commerce was not open to her. America was to be conquered, in order that Ireland should *not* trade thither; whilst the miserable trade which she is permitted to carry on to other places has been torn to pieces in the struggle. In this situation, are we neither to suffer her to have any real interest in our quarrel, or to be flattered with the hope of any future means of bearing the burthens which she is to incurr in defending herself against enemies which we have brought upon her?

I cannot set my face against such arguments. Is it quite fair to suppose, that I have no other motive for yielding to them, but a desire of acting *against* my constituents? It is for *you,* and for *your* interest, as a dear, cherished, and respected part of a valuable whole, that I have taken my share in this question. You do not, you cannot suffer by it. If honesty be true policy with regard to the transient interest of individuals, it is much more certainly so with regard to the permanent interests of communities. I know, that it is but too natural for us to see our own *certain* ruin, in the *possible* prosperity of other people. It is hard to persuade us, that every thing which is *got* by another is not *taken* from ourselves. But it is fit, that we should get the better of these suggestions, which come from what is not the best and soundest part of our nature, and that we should form to ourselves a way of thinking, more rational, more just, and more religious. Trade is not a limited thing; as if the objects of mutual demand and consumption, could not stretch beyond the bounds of our jealousies. God has given the earth to the children of men, and he has undoubtedly, in giving it to them, given them what is abundantly sufficient for all their exigencies; not a scanty, but a most liberal provision for them all. The Author of our nature has written it strongly in that nature, and has promulgated the same law in his written word,[1] that man shall eat his bread by his labour; and I am persuaded, that no man, and no combination of men, for their own ideas of their particular profit, can, without great impiety, undertake to say, that he *shall not* do so; that they have no sort of right, either to prevent the labour, or to withhold the bread. Ireland having received no *compensation,* directly or indirectly, for any restraints on their trade, ought not, in justice or common honesty, be made subject to such restraints. I do not mean to impeach the right of the parliament of Great Britain, to make laws for the trade of Ireland. I only speak of what laws it is right for Parliament to make.

It is nothing to an oppressed people, to say that in part

1. Genesis 3:19.

they are protected at our charge. The military force which shall be kept up in order to cramp the natural faculties of a people, and to prevent their arrival to their utmost prosperity, is the instrument of their servitude not the means of their protection. To protect men, is to forward, and not to restrain their improvement. Else, what is it more, than to avow to them, and to the world, that you guard them from others, only to make them a prey to yourself. This fundamental nature of protection does not belong to free, but to all governments; and is as valid in Turkey as in Great Britain. No government ought to own that it exists for the purpose of checking the prosperity of its people, or that there is such a principle involved in its policy.

Under the impression of these sentiments, (and not as wanting every attention to my constituents, which affection and gratitude could inspire,) I voted for these bills which give you so much trouble. I voted for them, not as doing complete justice to Ireland, but as being something less unjust than the general prohibition which has hitherto prevailed. I hear some discourse, as if in one or two paltry duties on materials, Ireland had a preference; and that those who set themselves against this act of scanty justice, assert that they are only contending for an *equality*. What equality? Do they forget, that the whole woollen manufacture of Ireland, the most extensive and profitable of any, and the natural staple of that kingdom, has been in a manner so destroyed by restrictive laws of ours, and (at our persuasion, and on our promises) by restrictive laws of *their own*,[1] that in a few years, it is probable, they will not be able to wear a coat of their own fabric. Is this equality? Do gentlemen forget, that the understood faith upon which

1. "In 1699 the Irish Parliament, on government initiative, imposed heavy export duties on Irish woolen goods . . . , on the understanding that the Irish linen industry would be encouraged; and in the same year, 1699, the English Parliament forbade the export of Irish wool to foreign countries." *W&S* 9:516, n. 1.

they were persuaded to such an unnatural act, has not been kept; but a linen-manufacture has been set up, and highly encouraged, against them? Is this equality? Do they forget the state of the trade of Ireland in beer, so great an article of consumption, and which now stands in so mischievous a position with regard to their revenue, their manufacture, and their agriculture? Do they find any equality in all this? Yet if the least step is taken towards doing them common justice in the lightest articles for the most limited markets, a cry is raised, as if we were going to be ruined by partiality to Ireland.

Gentlemen, I know that the deficiency in these arguments is made up (not by you, but by others) by the usual resource on such occasions, the confidence in military force, and superior power. But that ground of confidence, which at no time was perfectly just, or the avowal of it tolerably decent, is at this time very unseasonable. Late experience has shewn, that it cannot be altogether relied upon; and many, if not all our present difficulties, have arisen from putting our trust in what may very possibly fail; and if it should fail, leaves those who are hurt by such a reliance, without pity. Whereas honesty and justice, reason and equity, go a very great way in securing prosperity to those who use them; and in case of failure, secure the best retreat, and the most honourable consolations.

It is very unfortunate, that we should consider those as rivals, whom we ought to regard as fellow-labourers in a common cause. Ireland has never made a single step in its progress towards prosperity, by which you have not had a share; and perhaps the greatest share, in the benefit. That progress has been chiefly owing to her own natural advantages; and her own efforts, which, after a long time, and by slow degrees, have prevailed in some measure over the mischievous systems which have been adopted. Far enough she is still from having arrived even at an ordinary state of perfection; and if our jealousies were to be converted into politics, as systematically as some would have them, the trade of Ireland would vanish out of the system of commerce. But, believe me, if Ireland is beneficial to you, it is so not from the parts in which it is restrained, but from those in which it is left free, though not left unrivalled. The greater its freedom, the greater must be your advantage. If you should lose in one way, you will gain in twenty.

Whilst I remain under this unalterable and powerful conviction, you will not wonder at the *decided* part I take. It is my custom so to do, when I see my way clearly before me; and when I know, that I am not misled by any passion, or any personal interest; which in this case, I am very sure, I am not. I find that disagreeable things are circulated among my constituents; and I wish my sentiments, which form my justification, may be equally general with the circulation against me. I have the honour to be, with the greatest regard and esteem,

Gentlemen,
Your most obedient and humble servant,

E. B.
Westminster,
May 2, 1773

Thoughts and Details on Scarcity

[November 1795]

This document is the nearest thing to a formal treatise on economics that Edmund Burke ever wrote. Even so, it was not meant as a full treatment of the subject but was a lengthy memorandum to the Prime Minister, William Pitt, on an immediate question of policy. Burke was alarmed by a project for governmental subsidy of the wages of agricultural laborers during a time of poor harvests. His memorandum was therefore very much an ad hoc document, addressed to a temporary situation.

Burke thought well enough of it, however, to plan to expand it into a fuller work. But in the year and a half that remained of his life, he was a sick and dying man, and more urgently concerned with the folly of British overtures toward peace with Revolutionary France. He never managed to write more than several disjointed pages of his proposed economic treatise, and the memorandum was not published until after his death, by his literary executors, French Laurence and Walker King.

They had it published in 1800 with a lengthy preface by themselves. It is included here for their explanation of the circumstances in which Burke wrote the memorandum and of their editing and interpolation in Burke's text of the fragments of his planned expansion of it that they found among his papers.

Thoughts and Details on Scarcity

[Originally Presented to The Right Hon. William Pitt, in the Month of November, 1795]

PREFACE

Beaconsfield, *Nov.* 1, 1800

The wisdom, which is canonized by death, is consulted with a sort of sacred veneration. A casual remark, or an incidental maxim in some ancient author, an interesting narrative, or a pointed anecdote from the history of past times, even though they bear but a remote and general application to the exigency of our own immediate situation, are caught up with eagerness, and remembered with delight. But how much more important is the instruction which we may derive from the posthumous opinions of those who, having been most eminent in our own times for superior talents and more extensive knowledge, have formed their observation on circumstances so similar to our own, as only not to be the same, yet who speak without influence from the little prejudices and passions, to which accident, folly, or malevolence may have given birth in the present moment.

The late Mr. Burke, in the estimation of those who were most capable of judging, stood high, both as a scientific and a practical farmer. He carried into his fields the same penetrating, comprehensive, and vigorous mind, which shone forth so conspicuously in all his exertions on the stage of public life. Wherever he was, in whatever he was engaged, he was alike assiduous in collecting information, and happy in combining, what he acquired, into general principles. All that the ancients have left us upon husbandry was familiar to him, and he once encouraged and set on foot a new edition of those valuable writers; but, though he might occasionally derive new hints even from those sources, he preferred the authority of his own hind[1] to that of Hesiod or Virgil, of Cato or Columella. He thought for himself upon this, as upon other subjects; and not rejecting sound reforms of demonstrated errors, he was, however, principally guided by the traditionary skill and experience of that class of men, who, from father to son, have for generations laboured in calling forth the fertility of the English soil. He not only found in agriculture the most agreeable relaxation from his more serious cares, but he regarded the cultivation of the earth, and the improvement of all which it produces, as a sort of moral and religious duty. Towards the close of his life, when he had lost his son, in whom all his prospects had long centered, after lamenting, in an elegant allusion to Virgil, that the trees, which he had been nursing for many years, would now afford no shade to his posterity, he was heard to correct himself, by adding, "Yet be it so: I ought not therefore to bestow less attention upon them—they grow to God."

Agriculture, and the commerce connected with, and dependent upon it, form one of the most considerable branches of political economy; and as such, Mr. Burke diligently studied them. Indeed, when he began to qualify himself for the exalted rank which he afterwards held among statesmen, he laid a broad and deep foundation; and to an accurate research into the constitution, the laws, the civil and military

1. Farmhand.

history of these kingdoms, he joined an enlightened acquaintance with the whole circle of our commercial system. On his first introduction, when a young man, to the late Mr. Gerard Hamilton, who was then a Lord of Trade, the latter ingenuously confessed to a friend still living, how sensibly he felt his own inferiority, much as he had endeavoured to inform himself, and aided as he was by official documents, inaccessible to any private person. He was also consulted, and the greatest deference was paid to his opinions by Dr. Adam Smith, in the progress of the celebrated work on the Wealth of Nations.

In Parliament, Mr. Burke very soon distinguished himself on these topics. When the first great permanent law for regulating our foreign corn-trade[1] was under the consideration of the House in 1772, he was one of its principle supporters, in a speech admired at the time for its excellence, and described as abounding with that knowledge in oeconomics, which he was then universally allowed to possess, and illustrated with that philosophical discrimination, of which he was so peculiarly a master. About the same time, too, he zealously promoted the repeal of the statutes against *forestallers;*[2] a measure not lightly and hastily proposed or adopted in the liberal impulse of an unguarded moment, but the result of various investigations made by the House, or in different committees, during six years of scarcity and high prices; a measure which, although two Bills of a contrary tendency had formerly been introduced and lost, so approved itself, at length, to the reason of all, that it was ordered to be brought in, without a single dissentient voice. Yet, though such was his early pre-eminence in these pursuits, to the last hour of his life, as his fame spread wider and wider over Europe, he

1. Corn, as a general term, includes all the cereals, wheat, rye, barley, oats, maize, rice, etc.

2. To "forestall" is to intercept goods before they reach the public market, to buy them up privately and keep them off the market with a view to raising the price. Until 1772 it had been forbidden by law.

availed himself of the advantage which this afforded him, to enlarge the sphere of his enquiries into the state of other countries, that he might benefit his own. The consequence of all was, he every day became more firmly convinced, that the unrestrained freedom of buying and selling is the great animating principle of production and supply.

The present publication records Mr. Burke's most mature reflections on these interesting subjects; the more valuable, because the sentiments which he delivered on the occasions already mentioned, have not been preserved to us, either by himself or by others. He was alarmed by the appearance of the crop in 1795, even before the harvest. In the autumn of that year, when the produce of the harvest began to be known, the alarm became general. Various projects, as in such cases will always happen, were offered to Government; and, in his opinion, seemed to be received with too much complaisance. Under this impression, anxious as he ever was, even in his retirement, and in the midst of his own private affliction, for the publick safety and prosperity, he immediately addressed to Mr. Pitt[1] a Memorial, which is the groundwork of the following tract. Afterwards, considering the importance of the matter, and fearing a long cycle of scarcity to come, he intended to have dilated the several branches of the argument, and to have moulded his "Thoughts and Details" into a more popular shape. This he purposed to have done in a series of letters on rural oeconomics, inscribed to his friend Mr. Arthur Young. It may be remembered, that he even announced this design in an advertisement.[2] But his attention was irresistibly called another way. His whole

1. William Pitt the Younger, First Lord of the Treasury (Prime Minister) since 1784.

2. In December 1795, "it was announced that a letter from Burke to Young on agricultural wages would shortly appear." *W&S* 9:119, headnote. This was a more precise description of the subject of the memorandum than "rural oeconomics," as this Preface calls it.

mind was engrossed by the change of policy which discovered itself in our councils at that period,[1] when forgetting the manly arts, by which alone great nations have ever extricated themselves from momentous and doubtful conflicts, we descended, against the remonstrances of our allies, to the voluntary and unnecessary humiliation of soliciting a peace, which, in his judgment, the animosity of our insolent enemy was not then disposed to grant, and which, if offered, we could not then have accepted, without the certainty of incurring dangers much more formidable than any that threatened us from the protraction of the war. He hastened to raise and re-inspirit the prostrate genius of his country. In a great measure he succeeded, and was still employed in the pious office, when Divine Providence took him to receive the reward of those, who devote themselves to the cause of virtue and religion. After his decease, two or three detached fragments only of the first letter to Mr. Young were found among his papers. These could not be printed in that imperfect state, and they seemed too precious to be wholly thrown aside. They have been inserted, therefore, in the Memorial, where they seemed best to cohere. The first and largest of these interpolations reaches from the middle of the sixth to the bottom of the 18th page; the second commences near the bottom of the 20th, and ends a little below the middle of the 24th; and the last, occupying about three pages and a half, forms the present conclusion.[2]

The Memorial had been fairly copied, but did not appear to have been examined or corrected, as some trifling errors of the transcriber were perceptible in it. The manuscript of the fragments was a rough draft from the Author's own hand,

1. The overtures for peace with Revolutionary France that occasioned Burke's *Letters on a Regicide Peace,* for which see volume 3.

2. These interpolations have been placed in brackets for the convenience of the reader.

much blotted and very confused. It has been followed with as much fidelity as was possible, after consulting those who were most accustomed to Mr. Burke's manner of writing. Two or three chasms in the grammar and sense, from the casual omission of two or three unimportant words at a distance, have been supplied by conjecture. The principal alteration has been the necessary change of the second for the third person, and the consequent suppression of the common form of affectionate address, where Mr. Young is named. That gentleman alone can have reason to complain of this liberty, inasmuch as it may seem to have deprived him of that, which in some sort was his property, and which no man would have known better how to value. But, it is hoped, he will pardon it, since in this manner alone these *golden fragments* (to borrow a favourite phrase of critics and commentators) could have been made, as they were designed to be, of general utility. To the reader no apology is due, if the disquisitions thus interwoven may seem a little disproportioned to the summary statements of the original Memorial. Their own intrinsic worth and beauty will be an ample compensation for that slight deformity; though perhaps in such a composition, as this professes to be (and the title is Mr. Burke's own) nothing of the kind could have been fairly regarded as an irregular excrescence, had it been placed by himself, where it now stands.

The Memorial, which was indeed communicated to several members of the King's Government, was believed at the time to have been not wholly unproductive of good. The enquiry, which had been actually begun, into the quantity of corn in hand,[1] was silently dropped. The scheme of public granaries, if it ever existed, was abandoned. In Parliament the Ministers maintained a prudent and dignified forbearance; and repressed in others, or where they could not entirely controul, interposed to moderate and divert, that rest-

1. See note on p. 77.

less spirit of legislation, which is an evil that seems to grow up, as the vehemence of party-contention abates. The consistency and good sense of the Commons defeated an attempt, which was made towards the close of the sessions, to revive against forestallers of one particular description, some portion of the exploded laws.

Last year, on the approach of our present distresses, the same excellent temper of mind seemed to prevail in Government, in Parliament, and among the people. There was no proposal of taking stock, no speculation of creating a new establishment of royal purveyors to provide us with our daily dole of bread. The corn merchants were early assured that they should not again have to contend with the competition of the Treasury,[1] in the foreign market. A Committee of the House of Commons ventured to dissuade the stopping of the distilleries[2] in a report, very closely coinciding with the reasoning of Mr. Burke. Little or no popular declamation was heard on the miseries of "the labouring poor"; not a single petition was presented, or motion made, against forestallers. The least objectionable of the experiments suggested, to encrease the supply or lessen the consumption, were adopted. It is hardly worthy of mention, as an exception, that a Parliamentary charter was granted to a company of very worthy and well-meaning persons, who, on the notion of a combination (which, by the way, they totally failed in proving) among the trades that supply the capital with bread, opened a subscription for undertaking to furnish nearly one-tenth of the consumption. They were contented to do this with limited profits, merely as humane badgers and jobbers, charitable millers,

1. The purchase of grain abroad by the British government to feed the poor at home.

2. In June 1795, the distillation of spirits from wheat, barley, or malt was prohibited until February 1796 in order to increase the supply of those grains to feed the population; in December 1796, the prohibition was extended to February 1797. *W&S* 9:141, n. 1.

sentimental mealmen,[1] and philanthropic bakers. But distrusting a little their own sufficiency for their new business, they naturally desired to be exempted from the operation of the bankrupt laws; and their bill was carried by a very small majority, consisting of partners in the firm. All this while, under trials much more severe than in the former dearth, the inferior classes displayed a patience and resignation, only to be equalled by the alacrity and zeal, which the higher and middle orders every where manifested, to relieve the necessities of their poorer neighbours in every practicable mode.

The present is a season of ferment and riot. The old cry against forestallers has been raised again with more violence than ever. It has been adjudged, for the first time, it is presumed, since the repealing act of 1772, that they are still liable to be punished by the common law, with fine and imprisonment at least, if not with whipping and the pillory, according to the notion which the judge may entertain of their crime.

The interpreters of the law must expound it, according to their conscientious judgments, as it is; and the doctrine is not quite new. It has certainly been suggested in grave books since the repeal. Yet men of sober minds have doubted, and will doubt, whether in the whole code of customs and usages, derived to us from our ancestors, there can be found any one part so radically inapplicable to the present state of the country, as their Trade law; which, formed before commerce can be said to have existed, on mixed considerations, of police for the prevention of theft and rapine, and of protection to

1. Badger: one who buys corn and other commodities and carries them elsewhere to sell—more broadly, an itinerant middleman between producers and consumers; jobber: a piece-worker, one employed by the job—more broadly, a middleman, broker, or small trader or salesman; mealman: one who deals in meal, the edible part of any grain or pulse ground to a powder, e.g., oatmeal, Indian cornmeal.

the interest of the Lord in the rights of toll and stallage,[1] permitted no transaction of bargain and sale in any kind of commodity, but openly at a market, or a fair, and more anciently still, with the addition of witnesses also before the magistrate, or the priest; which knew of no commercial principle, but that of putting, in every instance, the grower, the maker, or the importer, native and foreigner alike, at the mercy of the consumer, and for that purpose prohibited every intermediate profit, and every practice by act, by word, or by writing, that could enhance the price; by which, if the dragging of the mouldering records into day be not a mere robbery of the moths and worms, should a gentleman encourage fishermen, brewers, and bakers to settle on his estate, it may be pronounced a *forestallage* of the next town, and a silk merchant, should he *ask* too much for his raw and organzine[2] (the unfortunate Lombard in the assize-book only asked, he did not get it from the poor *silkewemen*)[3] may be punished by a heavy fine; which cannot now be partially in force against one set of dealers, and abrogated by disuse with regard to all others; which, if generally applied for a single term, without the interposition of that wisdom of Parliament, over which this resort to the common law is by some regarded as a triumph, would more effectually clog, distress, and ruin our foreign and domestic commerce in all its branches, than a confederacy of the whole world against us in many years.

1. Toll: a charge levied by a lord for the privilege of bringing goods to a market for sale; stallage: a charge for the privilege of setting up a stall at a fair or market.

2. Raw: raw silk, drawn from the cocoons by the process of reeling; organzine: the strongest and best kind of silk thread, formed of several strands twisted together in the direction contrary to that in which their component filaments are twisted.

3. An old spelling for women engaged in the manufacture, use, or sale of silk.

Be the late convictions, however, what they may, in legal merits; their practical effects have been much to be deplored. Gross minds distorted them into authorities to prove, that there was plenty in the land, and that the arts of greedy and unfeeling men alone intercepted the bounty of Providence. Meetings were called; non-consumption agreements were signed, to fix a compulsory price, and associations were formed, chiefly in cities and great towns, to prosecute those, without whom cities and great towns can never be regularly fed. There is no weak, no wild, no violent project, which did not find countenance in some quarter or other. The fall of the market immediately after the harvest, and the subsequent rise, though the natural effects of obvious causes, encreased the public agitation; and the multitude began to pursue their usual course of providing in the shortest way for their instant wants, or of terrifying, or punishing those, whom they had been taught to consider as their oppressors; unconscious or unconcerned that they were thus only preparing for themselves a tenfold aggravation of their own future sufferings. The eyes of all were now turned towards Parliament, not for a train of judicious measures, which, if it be possible, may hereafter again equalize the production with the consumption of the country, but for an immediate supply; as if the omnipotence of Parliament could restore a single grain that has been injured by the most contemptible insect.

At such a juncture, however unfavourable it may be to the popularity of this little tract, the publication of it was felt to be a duty. He who wrote it, ever set that consideration before him as the first motive of all his actions. While he lived, he never ceased, publickly and privately, to warn his country and her rulers, against every danger which his wisdom foresaw. He now gives to her and them, this solemn warning from his grave.

THOUGHTS AND DETAILS ON SCARCITY

Of all things, an indiscreet tampering with the trade of provisions is the most dangerous, and it is always worst in the time when men are most disposed to it: that is, in the time of scarcity. Because there is nothing on which the passions of men are so violent, and their judgment so weak, and on which there exists such a multitude of ill-founded popular prejudices.

The great use of Government is as a restraint; and there is no restraint which it ought to put upon others, and upon itself too, rather than on the fury of speculating under circumstances of irritation. The number of idle tales spread about by the industry of faction, and by the zeal of foolish good-intention, and greedily devoured by the malignant credulity of mankind, tends infinitely to aggravate prejudices, which, in themselves, are more than sufficiently strong. In that state of affairs, and of the publick with relation to them, the first thing that Government owes to us, the people, is *information;* the next is timely coercion: the one to guide our judgment; the other to regulate our tempers.

To provide for us in our necessities is not in the power of Government. It would be a vain presumption in statesmen to think they can do it. The people maintain them, and not they the people. It is in the power of Government to prevent much evil; it can do very little positive good in this, or perhaps in any thing else. It is not only so of the state and statesman, but of all the classes and descriptions of the Rich—they are the pensioners of the poor, and are maintained by their superfluity. They are under an absolute, hereditary, and indefeasible dependance on those who labour, and are miscalled the Poor.

The labouring people are only poor, because they are numerous. Numbers in their nature imply poverty. In a fair distribution among a vast multitude, none can have much. That class of dependant pensioners called the rich, is so extremely small, that if all their throats were cut, and a distribution made of all they consume in a year, it would not give a bit of bread and cheese for one night's supper to those who labour, and who in reality feed both the pensioners and themselves.

But the throats of the rich ought not to be cut, nor their magazines plundered; because, in their persons they are trustees for those who labour, and their hoards are the banking-houses of these latter. Whether they mean it or not, they do, in effect, execute their trust—some with more, some with less fidelity and judgment. But on the whole, the duty is performed, and every thing returns, deducting some very trifling commission and discount, to the place from whence it arose. When the poor rise to destroy the rich, they act as wisely for their own purposes as when they burn mills, and throw corn into the river, to make bread cheap.

When I say, that we of the people ought to be informed, inclusively I say, we ought not to be flattered: flattery is the reverse of instruction. The *poor* in that case would be rendered as improvident as the rich, which would not be at all good for them.

Nothing can be so base and so wicked as the political canting language, "The Labouring *Poor.*" Let compassion be shewn in action, the more the better, according to every man's ability, but let there be no lamentation of their condition. It is no relief to their miserable circumstances; it is only an insult to their miserable understandings. It arises from a total want of charity, or a total want of thought. Want of one kind was never relieved by want of any other kind. Patience, labour, sobriety, frugality, and religion, should be recommended to them; all the rest is downright *fraud.* It is horrible to call them "The *once happy* labourer."

Whether what may be called moral or philosophical happiness of the laborious classes is increased or not, I cannot say. The seat of that species of happiness is in the mind; and there are few data to ascertain the comparative state of the mind at any two periods. Philosophical happiness is to want little. Civil or vulgar happiness is to want much, and to enjoy much.

If the happiness of the animal man (which certainly goes somewhere towards the happiness of the rational man) be the object of our estimate, then I assert, without the least hesitation, that the condition of those who labour (in all descriptions of labour, and in all gradations of labour, from the highest to the lowest inclusively) is on the whole extremely meliorated, if more and better food is any standard of melioration. They work more, it is certain; but they have the advantage of their augmented labour; yet whether that increase of labour be on the whole a *good* or an *evil,* is a consideration that would lead us a great way, and is not for my present purpose. But as to the fact of the melioration of their diet, I shall enter into the detail of proof whenever I am called upon: in the mean time, the known difficulty of contenting them with any thing but bread made of the finest flour, and meat of the first quality, is proof sufficient.

I further assert, that even under all the hardships of the last year, the labouring people did, either out of their direct gains, or from charity, (which it seems is now an insult to them) in fact, fare better than they did, in seasons of common plenty, 50 or 60 years ago; or even at the period of my English observation, which is about 44 years. I even assert, that full as many in that class, as ever were known to do it before, continued to save money; and this I can prove, so far as my own information and experience extend.

It is not true that the rate of wages has not encreased with the nominal price of provisions. I allow it has not fluctuated with that price, nor ought it; and the Squires of Norfolk[1] had

1. Burke may have mistakenly written Norfolk when he meant Suffolk, where the Justices of the Peace recommended that the wages of laborers should be adjusted in proportion to the price of corn. *W&S* 9:122–23.

dined, when they gave it as their opinion, that it might or ought to rise and fall with the market of provisions. The rate of wages in truth has no *direct* relation to that price. Labour is a commodity like every other, and rises or falls according to the demand. This is in the nature of things; however, the nature of things has provided for their necessities. Wages have been twice raised in my time, and they bear a full proportion, or even a greater than formerly, to the medium of provision during the last bad cycle of twenty years. They bear a full proportion to the result of their labour. If we were wildly to attempt to force them beyond it, the stone which we had forced up the hill would only fall back upon them in a diminished demand, or, what indeed is the far lesser evil, an aggravated price of all the provisions, which are the result of their manual toil.

[There is an implied contract, much stronger than any instrument or article of agreement, between the labourer in any occupation and his employer—that the labour, so far as that labour is concerned, shall be sufficient to pay to the employer a profit on his capital, and a compensation for his risk; in a word, that the labour shall produce an advantage equal to the payment. Whatever is above that, is a direct *tax;* and if the amount of that tax be left to the will and pleasure of another, it is an *arbitrary tax.*

If I understand it rightly, the tax proposed on the farming interest of this kingdom,[1] is to be levied at what is called the discretion of justices of peace.

1. The reference is to the so-called Speenhamland system, which inspired Burke to write this memorandum to William Pitt. In 1782, Parliament had enacted Gilbert's Act, which authorized local governments to grant allowances in aid of wages. Subsidizing the wages of the poor was not even then a new departure in English law. On this basis, in 1795 the magistrates of Berkshire, a county adjacent to Burke's Buckinghamshire, met in the Pelican Inn in Speenhamland, and adopted a scheme to ensure laborers a living wage. A minimum wage was fixed, which varied with the price of corn; if the wages actually paid fell below that, they would be supplemented from the poor rates.

The questions arising on this scheme of arbitrary taxation are these—Whether it is better to leave all dealing, in which there is no force or fraud, collusion or combination, entirely to the persons mutually concerned in the matter contracted for; or to put the contract into the hands of those, who can have none, or a very remote interest in it, and little or no knowledge of the subject.

It might be imagined that there would be very little difficulty in solving this question; for what man, of any degree of reflection, can think, that a want of interest in any subject closely connected with a want of skill in it, qualifies a person to intermeddle in any the least affair; much less in affairs that vitally concern the agriculture of the kingdom, the first of all it's concerns, and the foundation of all it's prosperity in every other matter, by which that prosperity is produced?

The vulgar error on this subject arises from a total confusion in the very idea of things widely different in themselves; those of convention, and those of judicature. When a contract is making, it is a matter of discretion and of interest between the parties. In that intercourse, and in what is to arise from it, the parties are the masters. If they are not completely so, they are not free, and therefore their contracts are void.

But this freedom has no farther extent, when the contract is made; then their discretionary powers expire, and a new order of things takes it's origin. Then, and not till then, and on a difference between the parties, the office of the judge commences. He cannot dictate the contract. It is his business to see that it be *enforced;* provided that it is not contrary to pre-existing laws, or obtained by force or fraud. If he is in any way a maker or regulator of the contract, in so much he is disqualified from being a judge. But this sort of confused distribution of administrative and judicial characters, (of which we have already as much as is sufficient, and a little more) is not the only perplexity of notions and passions which trouble us in the present hour.

What is doing, supposes or pretends that the farmer and the labourer have opposite interests; that the farmer oppresses the labourer; and that a gentleman called a justice of peace, is the protector of the latter, and a controul and restraint on the former; and this is a point I wish to examine in a manner a good deal different from that in which gentlemen proceed, who confide more in their abilities than is fit, and suppose them capable of more than any natural abilities, fed with no other than the provender furnished by their own private speculations, can accomplish. Legislative acts, attempting to regulate this part of oeconomy, do, at least, as much as any other, require the exactest detail of circumstances, guided by the surest general principles that are necessary to direct experiment and enquiry, in order again from those details to elicit principles, firm and luminous general principles, to direct a practical legislative proceeding.

First, then, I deny that it is in this case, as in any other of necessary implication, that contracting parties should originally have had different interests. By accident it may be so undoubtedly at the outset; but then the contract is of the nature of a compromise; and compromise is founded on circumstances that suppose it the interest of the parties to be reconciled in some medium. The principle of compromise adopted, of consequence the interests cease to be different.

But in the case of the farmer and the labourer, their interests are always the same, and it is absolutely impossible that their free contracts can be onerous to either party. It is the interest of the farmer, that his work should be done with effect and celerity: and that cannot be, unless the labourer is well fed, and otherwise found with such necessaries of animal life, according to it's habitudes, as may keep the body in full force, and the mind gay and cheerful. For of all the instruments of his trade, the labour of man (what the ancient writers have called the *instrumentum vocale*) is that on which he is most to rely for the re-payment of his capital. The other two, the *semivocale* in the ancient classification, that is, the working stock of cattle, and the *instrumentum mutum,*[1] such as carts, ploughs, spades, and so forth, though not all inconsiderable in themselves, are very much inferiour in utility or in expence; and without a given portion of the first, are nothing at all. For in all things whatever, the mind is the most valuable and the most important; and in this scale the whole of agriculture is in a natural and just order; the beast is as an informing principle to the plough and cart; the labourer is as reason to the beast; and the farmer is as a thinking and presiding principle to the labourer. An attempt to break this chain of subordination in any part is equally absurd; but the absurdity is the most mischievous in practical operation, where it is the most easy, that is, where it is the most subject to an erroneous judgment.

It is plainly more the farmer's interest that his men should thrive, than that his horses should be well fed, sleek, plump, and fit for use, or than that his waggon and ploughs should be strong, in good repair, and fit for service.

On the other hand, if the farmer ceases to profit of the labourer, and that his capital is not continually manured and fructified, it is impossible that he should continue that abundant nutriment, and cloathing, and lodging, proper for the protection of the instruments he employs.

It is therefore the first and fundamental interest of the labourer, that the farmer should have a full incoming profit on the product of his labour. The proposition is self-evident, and nothing but the malignity, perverseness, and ill-governed passions of mankind, and particularly the envy they bear to each other's prosperity, could prevent their seeing and acknowledging it, with thankfulness to the benign and wise disposer of all things, who obliges men, whether they will or

1. *Instrumentum vocale,* the tool that speaks; *semivocale,* the tool that utters sounds but not words; *mutum,* the tool that is inanimate, hence mute.

not, in pursuing their own selfish interests, to connect the general good with their own individual success.

But who are to judge what that profit and advantage ought to be? certainly no authority on earth. It is a matter of convention dictated by the reciprocal conveniences of the parties, and indeed by their reciprocal necessities. But, if the farmer is excessively avaricious?—why so much the better—the more he desires to increase his gains, the more interested is he in the good condition of those, upon whose labour his gains must principally depend.

I shall be told by the zealots of the sect of regulation, that this may be true, and may be safely committed to the convention of the farmer and the labourer, when the latter is in the prime of his youth, and at the time of his health and vigour, and in ordinary times of abundance. But in calamitous seasons, under accidental illness, in declining life, and with the pressure of a numerous offspring, the future nourishers of the community but the present drains and blood-suckers of those who produce them, what is to be done? When a man cannot live and maintain his family by the natural hire of his labour, ought it not to be raised by authority?

On this head I must be allowed to submit, what my opinions have ever been; and somewhat at large.

And, first, I premise that labour is, as I have already intimated, a commodity, and as such, an article of trade. If I am right in this notion, then labour must be subject to all the laws and principles of trade, and not to regulations foreign to them, and that may be totally inconsistent with those principles and those laws. When any commodity is carried to market, it is not the necessity of the vender, but the necessity of the purchaser that raises the price. The extreme want of the seller has rather (by the nature of things with which we shall in vain contend) the direct contrary operation. If the goods at market are beyond the demand, they fall in their value; if below it, they rise. The impossibility of the subsistence of a man, who carries his labour to a market, is totally beside the question in this way of viewing it. The only question is, what is it worth to the buyer?

But if authority comes in and forces the buyer to a price, who is this in the case (say) of a farmer, who buys the labour of ten or twelve labouring men, and three or four handycrafts, what is it, but to make an arbitrary division of his property among them?

The whole of his gains, I say it with the most certain conviction, never do amount any thing like in value to what he pays to his labourers and artificers; so that a very small advance upon what *one* man pays to *many,* may absorb the whole of what he possesses, and amount to an actual partition of all his substance among them. A perfect equality will indeed be produced; that is to say, equal want, equal wretchedness, equal beggary, and on the part of the partitioners, a woeful, helpless, and desperate disappointment. Such is the event of all compulsory equalizations. They pull down what is above. They never raise what is below: and they depress high and low together beneath the level of what was originally the lowest.

If a commodity is raised by authority above what it will yield with a profit to the buyer, that commodity will be the less dealt in. If a second blundering interposition be used to correct the blunder of the first, and an attempt is made to force the purchase of the commodity (of labour for instance), the one of these two things must happen, either that the forced buyer is ruined, or the price of the product of the labour, in that proportion, is raised. Then the wheel turns round, and the evil complained of falls with aggravated weight on the complainant. The price of corn, which is the result of the expence of all the operations of husbandry, taken together, and for some time continued, will rise on the labourer, considered as a consumer. The very best will be, that he remains where he was. But if the price of the corn should not compensate the price of labour, what is far more to be feared, the most serious evil, the very destruction of agriculture itself, is to be apprehended.

Nothing is such an enemy to accuracy of judgment as a coarse discrimination; a want of such classification and distribution as the subject admits of. Encrease the rate of wages to the labourer, say the regulators—as if labour was but one thing and of one value. But this very broad generic term, *labour,* admits, at least, of two or three specific descriptions: and these will suffice, at least, to let gentlemen discern a little the necessity of proceeding with caution in their coercive guidance of those whose existence depends upon the observance of still nicer distinctions and sub-divisions, than commonly they resort to in forming their judgments on this very enlarged part of economy.

The labourers in husbandry may be divided: 1st. into those who are able to perform the full work of a man; that is, what can be done by a person from twenty-one years of age to fifty. I know no husbandry work (mowing hardly excepted) that is not equally within the power of all persons within those ages, the more advanced fully compensating by knack and habit what they lose in activity. Unquestionably, there is a good deal of difference between the value of one man's labour and that of another, from strength, dexterity, and honest application. But I am quite sure, from my best observation, that any given five men will, in their total, afford a proportion of labour equal to any other five within the periods of life I have stated; that is, that among such five men there will be one possessing all the qualifications of a good workman, one bad, and the other three middling, and approximating to the first and the last. So that in so small a platoon as that of even five, you will find the full complement of all that five men *can* earn. Taking five and five throughout the kingdom, they are equal: therefore, an error with regard to the equalization of their wages by those who employ five, as farmers do at the very least, cannot be considerable.

2dly. Those who are able to work, but not the complete task of a day-labourer. This class is infinitely diversified, but will aptly enough fall into principal divisions. *Men,* from the decline, which after fifty becomes every year more sensible, to the period of debility and decrepitude, and the maladies that precede a final dissolution. *Women,* whose employment on husbandry is but occasional, and who differ more in effective labour one from another than men do, on account of gestation, nursing, and domestic management, over and above the difference they have in common with men in advancing, in stationary, and in declining life. *Children,* who proceed on the reverse order, growing from less to greater utility, but with a still greater disproportion of nutriment to labour than is found in the second of these sub-divisions; as is visible to those who will give themselves the trouble of examining into the interior economy of a poor-house.

This inferior classification is introduced to shew, that laws prescribing, or magistrates exercising, a very stiff, and often inapplicable rule, or a blind and rash discretion, never can provide the just proportions between earning and salary on the one hand, and nutriment on the other: whereas interest, habit, and the tacit convention, that arise from a thousand nameless circumstances, produce a *tact* that regulates without difficulty, what laws and magistrates cannot regulate at all. The first class of labour wants nothing to equalize it; it equalizes itself. The second and third are not capable of any equalization.

But what if the rate of hire to the labourer comes far short of his necessary subsistence, and the calamity of the time is so great as to threaten actual famine? Is the poor labourer to be abandoned to the flinty heart and griping hand of base self-interest, supported by the sword of law, especially when there is reason to suppose that the very avarice of farmers themselves has concurred with the errors of Government to bring famine on the land.

In that case, my opinion is this. Whenever it happens that a man can claim nothing according to the rules of commerce, and the principles of justice, he passes out of that department, and comes within the jurisdiction of mercy. In that province the magistrate has nothing at all to do: his interference is a violation of the property which it is his office to protect. Without all doubt, charity to the poor is a direct and obligatory duty upon all Christians, next in order after the payment of debts, full as strong, and by nature made infinitely more delightful to us. Puffendorf,[1] and other casuists do not, I think, denominate it quite properly, when they call it a duty of imperfect obligation. But the manner, mode, time, choice of objects, and proportion, are left to private discretion; and perhaps, for that very reason it is performed with the greater satisfaction, because the discharge of it has more the appearance of freedom; recommending us besides very specially to the divine favour, as the exercise of a virtue most suitable to a being sensible of it's own infirmity.]

The cry of the people in cities and towns, though unfortunately (from a fear of their multitude and combination) the most regarded, ought, in *fact,* to be the *least* attended to upon this subject; for citizens are in a state of utter ignorance of the means by which they are to be fed, and they contribute little or nothing, except in an infinitely circuitous manner, to their own maintenance. They are truly "*Fruges consumere nati.*"[2] They are to be heard with great respect and attention upon matters within their province, that is, on trades and manufactures; but on any thing that relates to agriculture, they are to be listened to with the same *reverence* which we pay to the dogmas of other ignorant and presumptuous men.

1. Samuel Pufendorf (1632–94), whose *The Whole Duty of Man* was used as a textbook at Trinity College, Dublin, when Burke was a student there. It was a translation of Pufendorf's *De officio hominis et civis,* which in turn was an epitome, made by Pufendorf himself, of his famous *De jure gentium et naturae* (1672).

2. "Born to consume the fruits [of the earth]." Horace *Epistles* 1.2.27.

If any one were to tell them, that they were to give in an account of all the stock in their shops; that attempts would be made to limit their profits, or raise the price of the labouring manufacturers upon them, or recommend to Government, out of a capital from the publick revenues, to set up a shop of the same commodities, in order to rival them, and keep them to reasonable dealing, they would very soon see the impudence, injustice, and oppression of such a course. They would not be mistaken; but they are of opinion, that agriculture is to be subject to other laws; and to be governed by other principles.

A greater and more ruinous mistake cannot be fallen into, than that the trades of agriculture and grazing can be conducted upon any other than the common principles of commerce; namely, that the producer should be permitted, and even expected, to look to all possible profit which, without fraud or violence, he can make; to turn plenty or scarcity to the best advantage he can; to keep back or to bring forward his commodities at his pleasure; to account to no one for his stock or for his gain. On any other terms he is the slave of the consumer; and that he should be so is of no benefit to the consumer. No slave was ever so beneficial to the master as a freeman that deals with him on an equal footing by convention, formed on the rules and principles of contending interests and compromised advantages. The consumer, if he were suffered, would in the end always be the dupe of his own tyranny and injustice. The landed gentleman is never to forget, that the farmer is his representative.

[It is a perilous thing to try experiments on the farmer. The farmer's capital (except in a few persons, and in a very few places) is far more feeble than commonly is imagined. The trade is a very poor trade; it is subject to great risks and losses. The capital, such as it is, is turned but once in the year; in some branches it requires three years before the money is paid. I believe never less than three in the turnip and grassland course, which is the prevalent course on the more or less fertile, sandy and gravelly loams, and these compose the soil in the south and south-east of England, the best adapted, and perhaps the only ones that are adapted, to the turnip husbandry.

It is very rare that the most prosperous farmer, counting the value of his quick and dead stock, the interest of the money he turns, together with his own wages as a bailiff or overseer, ever does make twelve or fifteen *per centum* by the year on his capital. I speak of the prosperous. In most of the parts of England which have fallen within my observation, I have rarely known a farmer, who to his own trade has not added some other employment or traffic, that, after a course of the most unremitting parsimony and labour (such for the greater part is theirs), and persevering in his business for a long course of years, died worth more than paid his debts, leaving his posterity to continue in nearly the same equal conflict between industry and want, in which the last predecessor, and a long line of predecessors before him, lived and died.

Observe that I speak of the generality of farmers who have not more than from one hundred and fifty to three or four hundred acres. There are few in this part of the country within the former, or much beyond the latter, extent. Unquestionably in other places there are much larger. But, I am convinced, whatever part of England be the theatre of his operations, a farmer who cultivates twelve hundred acres, which I consider as a large farm, though I know there are larger, cannot proceed, with any degree of safety and effect, with a smaller capital than ten thousand pounds; and that he cannot, in the ordinary course of culture, make more upon that great capital of ten thousand pounds, than twelve hundred a year.

As to the weaker capitals, an easy judgment may be formed by what very small errors they may be farther attenuated, enervated, rendered unproductive, and perhaps totally destroyed.

This constant precariousness and ultimate moderate limits of a farmer's fortune, on the strongest capital, I press, not only on account of the hazardous speculations of the times, but because the excellent and most useful works of my friend, Mr. Arthur Young, tend to propagate that error (such I am very certain it is, of the largeness of a farmer's profits. It is not that his account of the produce does often greatly exceed, but he by no means makes the proper allowance for accidents and losses. I might enter into a convincing detail, if other more troublesome and more necessary details were not before me.

This proposed discretionary tax on labour militates with the recommendations of the Board of Agriculture: they recommend a general use of the drill culture.[1] I agree with the Board, that where the soil is not excessively heavy, or incumbered with large loose stones (which however is the case with much otherwise good land), that course is the best, and most productive, provided that the most accurate eye; the most vigilant superintendance; the most prompt activity, which has no such day as to-morrow in its calendar; the most steady foresight and pre-disposing order to have every body and every thing ready in it's place, and prepared to take advantage of the fortunate fugitive moment in this coquetting climate of ours—provided, I say, all these combine to speed the plough, I admit its superiority over the old and general methods. But under procrastinating, improvident, ordinary husbandmen, who may neglect or let slip the few opportunities of sweetening and purifying their ground with perpetually renovated toil, and undissipated attention, nothing, when tried to any extent, can be worse, or more dangerous: the farm may be ruined, instead of having the soil enriched and sweetened by it.

But the excellence of the method on a proper soil, and conducted by an husbandman, of whom there are few, being readily granted, how, and on what conditions, is this culture

1. To drill is to sow seeds or seedlings along a shallow furrow.

obtained? Why, by a very great encrease of labour; by an augmentation of the third part, at least, of the hand-labour, to say nothing of the horses and machinery employed in ordinary tillage. Now, every man must be sensible how little becoming the gravity of Legislature it is to encourage a Board, which recommends to us, and upon very weighty reasons unquestionably, an enlargement of the capital we employ in the operations of the land, and then to pass an act which taxes that manual labour, already at a very high rate; thus compelling us to diminish the quantity of labour which in the vulgar course we actually employ.]

What is true of the farmer is equally true of the middle man; whether the middle man acts as factor,[1] jobber, salesman, or speculator, in the markets of grain. These traders are to be left to their free course; and the more they make, and the richer they are, and the more largely they deal, the better both for the farmer and consumer, between whom they form a natural and most useful link of connection; though, by the machinations of the old evil counsellor, *Envy,* they are hated and maligned by both parties.

I hear that middle men are accused of monopoly. Without question, the monopoly of authority is, in every instance and in every degree, an evil; but the monopoly of capital is the contrary. It is a great benefit, and a benefit particularly to the poor. A tradesman who has but a hundred pound capital, which (say) he can turn but once a year, cannot live upon a *profit* of 10 *per cent.* because he cannot live upon ten pounds a year; but a man of ten thousand pounds capital can live and thrive upon 5 *per cent.* profit in the year, because he has five hundred pounds a year. The same proportion holds in turning it twice or thrice. These principles are plain and simple; and it is not our ignorance, so much as the levity, the envy,

1. One who acts for another as an agent, deputy, or representative; more narrowly, an agent who buys or sells for another; a commission merchant.

and the malignity of our nature, that hinders us from perceiving and yielding to them: but we are not to suffer our vices to usurp the place of our judgment.

The balance between consumption and production makes price. The market settles, and alone can settle, that price. Market is the meeting and conference of the *consumer* and *producer,* when they mutually discover each other's wants. Nobody, I believe, has observed with any reflection what market is, without being astonished at the truth, the correctness, the celerity, the general equity, with which the balance of wants is settled. They who wish the destruction of that balance, and would fain by arbitrary regulation decree, that defective production should not be compensated by encreased price, directly lay their *axe* to the root of production itself.

They may even in one year of such false policy, do mischiefs incalculable; because the trade of a farmer is, as I have before explained, one of the most precarious in its advantages, the most liable to losses, and the least profitable of any that is carried on. It requires ten times more of labour, of vigilance, of attention, of skill, and let me add, of good fortune also, to carry on the business of a farmer with success, than what belongs to any other trade. Seeing things in this light, I am far from presuming to censure the late circular instruction of Council to Lord Lieutenants[1]—but I confess I do not clearly discern its object. I am greatly afraid that the enquiry will raise some alarm as a measure, leading to the French system of putting corn into requisition. For that was preceded by an inquisition somewhat similar in it's principle, though, according to their mode, their principles are full of that violence, *which here* is not much to be feared. It goes on a principle directly opposite to mine: it presumes, that the

1. A circular letter sent by the Council through the Home Secretary to the Lords Lieutenant asking them to hold magistrates' meetings in their counties to ascertain the produce of the recent harvest. *W&S* 9:133, n. 1.

market is no fair *test* of plenty or scarcity. It raises a suspicion, which may affect the tranquillity of the public mind, "that the farmer keeps back, and takes unfair advantages by delay"; on the part of the dealer, it gives rise obviously to a thousand nefarious speculations.

In case the return should on the whole prove favourable, is it meant to ground a measure for encouraging exportation and checking the import of corn? If it is not, what end can it answer? And, I believe, it is not.

This opinion may be fortified by a report gone abroad, that intentions are entertained of erecting public granaries, and that this enquiry is to give Government an advantage in it's purchases.

I hear that such a measure has been proposed, and is under deliberation, that is, for Government to set up a granary in every market town, at the expence of the state, in order to extinguish the dealer, and to subject the farmer to the consumer, by securing corn to the latter at a certain and steady price.

If such a scheme is adopted, I should not like to answer for the safety of the granary, of the agents, or of the town itself, in which the granary was erected—the first storm of popular phrenzy would fall upon that granary.

So far in a political light.

In an economical light, I must observe, that the construction of such granaries throughout the kingdom, would be at an expence beyond all calculation. The keeping them up would be at a great charge. The management and attendance would require an army of agents, store-keepers, clerks, and servants. The capital to be employed in the purchase of grain would be enormous. The waste, decay, and corruption, would be a dreadful drawback on the whole dealing; and the dissatisfaction of the people, at having decayed, tainted, or corrupted corn sold to them, as must be the case, would be serious.

This climate (whatever others may be) is not favourable to granaries, where wheat is to be kept for any time. The best, and indeed the only good granary, is the rick-yard of the farmer, where the corn is preserved in it's own straw, sweet, clean, wholesome, free from vermin and from insects, and comparatively at a trifle of expence. This, with the barn, enjoying many of the same advantages, have been the sole granaries of England from the foundation of it's agriculture to this day. All this is done at the expence of the undertaker, and at his sole risk. He contributes to Government; he receives nothing from it but protection, and to this he has a *claim.*

The moment that Government appears at market, all the principles of market will be subverted. I don't know whether the farmer will suffer by it, as long as there is a tolerable market of competition; but I am sure that, in the first place, the trading government will speedily become a bankrupt, and the consumer in the end will suffer. If Government makes all it's purchases at once, it will instantly raise the market upon itself. If it makes them by degrees, it must follow the course of the market. If it follows the course of the market, it will produce no effect, and the consumer may as well buy as he wants—therefore all the expence is incurred gratis.

But if the object of this scheme should be, what I suspect it is, to destroy the dealer, commonly called the middle man, and by incurring a voluntary loss to carry the baker to deal with Government, I am to tell them that they must set up another trade, that of a miller or a mealman, attended with a new train of expences and risks. If in both these trades they should succeed, so as to exclude those who trade on natural and private capitals, then they will have a monopoly in their hands, which, under the appearance of a monopoly of capital, will, in reality, be a monopoly of authority, and will ruin whatever it touches. The agriculture of the kingdom cannot stand before it.

A little place like Geneva, of not more than from twenty-five to thirty thousand inhabitants, which has no territory, or next to none; which depends for it's existence on the good-will of three neighbouring powers, and is of course continually in the state of something like a *siege,* or in the speculation of it, might find some resource in state granaries, and some revenue from the monopoly of what was sold to the keepers of public-houses. This is a policy for a state too small for agriculture. It is not (for instance) fit for so great a country as the Pope possesses, where, however, it is adopted and pursued in a greater extent, and with more strictness. Certain of the Pope's territories, from whence the city of Rome is supplied, being obliged to furnish Rome and the granaries of his Holiness with corn at a certain price, that part of the papal territories is utterly ruined. That ruin may be traced with certainty to this sole cause, and it appears indubitably by a comparison of their state and condition with that of the other part of the ecclesiastical dominions not subjected to the same regulations, which are in circumstances highly flourishing.

The reformation of this evil system is in a manner impracticable; for, first, it does keep bread and all other provisions equally subject to the chamber of supply, at a pretty reasonable and regular price, in the city of Rome. This preserves quiet among the numerous poor, idle, and naturally mutinous people, of a very great capital. But the quiet of the town is purchased by the ruin of the country, and the ultimate wretchedness of both. The next cause which renders this evil incurable, is, the jobs which have grown out of it, and which, in spite of all precautions, would grow out of such things, even under governments far more potent than the feeble authority of the Pope.

This example of Rome which has been derived from the most ancient times, and the most flourishing period of the Roman empire (but not of the Roman agriculture) may serve as a great caution to all Governments, not to attempt to feed the people out of the hands of the magistrates. If once they are habituated to it, though but for one half-year, they will never be satisfied to have it otherwise. And, having looked to Government for bread, on the very first scarcity they will turn and bite the hand that fed them. To avoid that *evil,* Government will redouble the causes of it; and then it will become inveterate and incurable.

I beseech the Government (which I take in the largest sense of the word, comprehending the two Houses of Parliament) seriously to consider that years of scarcity or plenty, do not come alternately or at short intervals, but in pretty long cycles and irregularly, and consequently that we cannot assure ourselves, if we take a wrong measure, from the temporary necessities of one season; but that the next, and probably more, will drive us to the continuance of it; so that in my opinion, there is no way of preventing this evil which goes to the destruction of all our agriculture, and of that part of our internal commerce which touches our agriculture the most nearly, as well as the safety and very being of Government, but manfully to resist the very first idea, speculative or practical, that it is within the competence of Government, taken as Government, or even of the rich, as rich, to supply to the poor, those necessaries which it has pleased the Divine Providence for a while to with-hold from them. We, the people, ought to be made sensible, that it is not in breaking the laws of commerce, which are the laws of nature, and consequently the laws of God, that we are to place our hope of softening the Divine displeasure to remove any calamity under which we suffer, or which hangs over us.

So far as to the principles of general policy.

As to the state of things which is urged as a reason to deviate from them, these are the circumstances of the harvest of 1795 and 1794. With regard to the harvest of 1794, in relation to the noblest grain, wheat, it is allowed to have been somewhat short, but not excessively; and in quality, for the seven and twenty years, during which I have been a farmer,

I never remember wheat to have been so good. The world were, however, deceived in their speculations upon it—the farmer as well as the dealer. Accordingly the price fluctuated beyond any thing I can remember; for, at one time of the year, I sold my wheat at 14l. a load, (I sold off all I had, as I thought this was a reasonable price), when at the end of the season, if I had then had any to sell, I might have got thirty guineas for the same sort of grain. I sold all that I had, as I said, at a comparatively low price, because I thought it a good price, compared with what I thought the general produce of the harvest; but when I came to consider what my own *total* was, I found that the quantity had not answered my expectation. It must be remembered, that this year of produce, (the year 1794) short, but excellent, followed a year which was not extraordinary in production, nor of a superior quality, and left but little in store. At first this was not felt, because the harvest came in unusually early—earlier than common, by a full month.

The winter, at the end of 1794, and beginning of 1795, was more than usually unfavourable both to corn and grass, owing to the sudden relaxation of very rigorous frosts, followed by rains, which were again rapidly succeeded by frosts of still greater rigour than the first.

Much wheat was utterly destroyed. The clover grass suffered in many places. What I never observed before, the rye-grass, or coarse bent, suffered more than the clover. Even the meadow-grass in some places was killed to the very roots. In the spring, appearances were better than we expected. All the early sown grain recovered itself, and came up with great vigour; but that, which was late sown, was feeble, and did not promise to resist any blights, in the spring, which, however, with all its unpleasant vissicitudes passed off very well; and nothing looked better than the wheat at the time of blooming: but at that most critical time of all, a cold dry east wind, attended with very sharp frosts, longer and stronger than I recollect at that time of year, destroyed the flowers, and withered up, in an astonishing manner, the whole side of the ear next to the wind. At that time I brought to town some of the ears, for the purpose of shewing to my friends the operation of those unnatural frosts, and according to their extent I predicted a great scarcity. But such is the pleasure of agreeable prospects, that my opinion was little regarded.

On threshing, I found things as I expected—the ears not filled, some of the capsules quite empty, and several others containing only withered hungry grain, inferior to the appearance of rye. My best ears and grains were not fine; never had I grain of so low a quality—yet I sold one load for 21l. At the same time I bought my seed wheat (it was excellent) at 23l. Since then the price has risen, and I have sold about two load of the same sort at 23l. Such was the state of the market when I left home last Monday. Little remains in my barn. I hope some in the rick may be better; since it was earlier sown, as well as I can recollect. Some of my neighbours have better, some quite as bad, or even worse. I suspect it will be found, that wherever the blighting wind and those frosts at blooming time have prevailed, the produce of the wheat crop will turn out very indifferent. Those parts which have escaped, will, I can hardly doubt, have a reasonable produce.

As to the other grains, it is to be observed, as the wheat ripened very late, (on account, I conceive, of the blights) the barley got the start of it, and was ripe first. The crop was with me, and wherever my enquiry could reach, excellent; in some places far superior to mine.

The clover, which came up with the barley, was the finest I remember to have seen.

The turnips of this year are generally good.

The clover sown last year, where not totally destroyed, gave two good crops, or one crop and a plentiful feed; and, bating the loss of the rye-grass, I do not remember a better produce.

The meadow-grass yielded but a middling crop, and neither of the sown or natural grass was there in any farmer's possession any remainder from the year worth taking into account. In most places, there was none at all.

Oats with me were not in a quantity more considerable than in commonly good seasons; but I have never known them heavier, than they were in other places. The oat was not only an heavy, but an uncommonly abundant crop. My ground under pease did not exceed an acre, or thereabouts, but the crop was great indeed. I believe it is throughout the country exuberant.

It is however to be remarked, that as generally of all the grains, so particularly of the pease, there was not the smallest quantity in reserve.

The demand of the year must depend solely on it's own produce; and the price of the spring-corn is not to be expected to fall very soon, or at any time very low.

Uxbridge is a great corn market. As I came through that town, I found that at the last market-day, barley was at forty shillings a quarter; oats there were literally none; and the innkeeper was obliged to send for them to London. I forgot to ask about pease. Potatoes were 5s. the bushel.

In the debate on this subject in the House, I am told that a leading member of great ability, *little conversant in these matters,* observed, that the general uniform dearness of butcher's meat, butter, and cheese, could not be owing to a defective produce of wheat; and on this ground insinuated a suspicion of some unfair practice on the subject, that called for enquiry.

Unquestionably the mere deficiency of wheat could not cause the dearness of the other articles, which extends not only to the provisions he mentioned, but to every other without exception.

The cause is indeed so very plain and obvious, that the wonder is the other way. When a properly directed enquiry is made, the gentlemen who are amazed at the price of these commodities will find, that when hay is at six pound a load, as they must know it is, herbage, and for more than one year, must be scanty, and they will conclude, that if grass be scarce, beef, veal, mutton, butter, milk, and cheese, *must* be dear.

But to take up the matter somewhat more in detail—if the wheat harvest in 1794, excellent in quality, was defective in quantity, the barley harvest was in quality ordinary enough; and in quantity deficient. This was soon felt in the price of malt.

Another article of produce (beans) was not at all plentiful. The crop of pease was wholly destroyed, so that several farmers pretty early gave up all hopes on that head, and cut the green haulm as fodder for the cattle, then perishing for want of food in that dry and burning summer. I myself came off better than most—I had about the fourth of a crop of pease.

It will be recollected, that, in a manner, all the bacon and pork consumed in this country, (the far largest consumption of meat out of towns) is, when growing, fed on grass, and on whey, or skimmed milk; and when fatting, partly on the latter. This is the case in the dairy countries, all of them great breeders and feeders of swine; but for the much greater part, and in all the corn countries, they are fattened on beans, barley meal, and pease. When the food of the animal is scarce, his flesh must be dear. This, one would suppose, would require no great penetration to discover.

This failure of so very large a supply of flesh in one species, naturally throws the whole demand of the consumer on the diminished supply of all kinds of flesh, and, indeed, on all the matters of human sustenance. Nor, in my opinion, are we to expect a greater cheapness in that article for this year, even though corn should grow cheaper, as it is to be hoped it will. The store swine, from the failure of subsistence last year, are now at an extravagant price. Pigs, at our fairs, have sold lately for fifty shillings, which, two years ago, would not have brought more than twenty.

As to sheep, none, I thought, were strangers to the general failure of the article of turnips last year; the early having been burned as they came up, by the great drought and heat; the late, and those of the early which had escaped, were destroyed by the chilling frosts of the winter, and the wet and severe weather of the spring. In many places a full fourth of the sheep or the lambs were lost, what remained of the lambs were poor and ill-fed, the ewes having had no milk. The calves came late, and they were generally an article, the want of which was as much to be dreaded as any other. So that article of food, formerly so abundant in the early part of the summer, particularly in London, and which in a great part supplied the place of mutton for near two months, did little less than totally fail.

All the productions of the earth link in with each other. All the sources of plenty, in all and every article, were dried or frozen up. The scarcity was not as gentlemen seem to suppose, in wheat only.

Another cause, and that not of inconsiderable operation, tended to produce a scarity in flesh provision. It is one that on many accounts cannot be too much regretted, and, the rather, as it was the sole *cause* of scarcity in that article, which arose from the proceedings of men themselves. I mean the stop put to the distillery.

The hogs (and that would be sufficient) which were fed with the waste wash of that produce, did not demand the fourth part of the corn used by farmers in fattening them. The spirit was nearly so much clear gain to the nation. It is an odd way of making flesh cheap, to stop or check the distillery.

The distillery in itself produces an immense article of trade almost all over the world, to Africa, to North America, and to various parts of Europe. It is of great use, next to food itself, to our fisheries and to our whole navigation. A great part of the distillery was carried on by damaged corn, unfit for bread, and by barley and malt of the lowest quality. These things could not be more unexceptionably employed. The domestic consumption of spirits, produced, without complaints, a very great revenue, applicable, if we pleased, in bounties[1] to the bringing corn from other places, far beyond the value of that consumed in making it, or to the encouragement of it's encreased production at home.

As to what is said, in a physical and moral view, against the home consumption of spirits, experience has long since taught me very little to respect the declamations on that subject—whether the thunder of the laws, or the thunder of eloquence, "is hurled *on gin,*"[2] always I am thunder-proof. The alembic,[3] in my mind, has furnished to the world a far greater benefit and blessing, than if the *opus maximum*[4] had been really found by chemistry, and, like Midas, we could turn every thing into gold.

Undoubtedly there may be a dangerous abuse in the excess of spirits; and at one time I am ready to believe the abuse was great. When spirits are cheap, the business of drunken-

1. Bounty: a sum of money paid by government to merchants or manufacturers to encourage an industry or trade. It could be a sum paid to exporters of corn because exports produced a favorable balance of trade or, as here, to importers to encourage buying grain abroad in a time of scarcity of corn at home. Burke was obviously not opposed to all government intervention in the economy.

2. See Alexander Pope's *Epilogue to the Satires,* deploring the presumptuousness of the lower classes in imitating the vices of their social superiors:

This, this, my friend, I cannot, must not bear;
Vice thus abused demands a nation's care;
This calls the Church to deprecate our sin,
And hurls the thunder of the laws on gin.
Dialogue 1, lines 129–31.

3. An apparatus used in distilling spirits.

4. The greatest work or art, that of realizing alchemy's dream of turning base metals into gold.

ness is atchieved with little time or labour; but that evil I consider to be wholly done away. Observation for the last forty years, and very particularly for the last thirty, has furnished me with ten instances of drunkenness from other causes, for one from this. Ardent spirit is a great medicine, often to remove distempers—much more frequently to prevent them, or to chase them away in their beginnings. It is not nutritive in *any great* degree. But, if not food, it greatly alleviates the want of it. It invigorates the stomach for the digestion of poor meagre diet, not easily alliable to the human constitution. Wine the poor cannot touch. Beer, as applied to many occasions, (as among seamen and fishermen for instance) will by no means do the business. Let me add, what wits inspired with champaign and claret, will turn into ridicule—it is a medicine for the mind. Under the pressure of the cares and sorrows of our mortal condition, men have at all times, and in all countries, called in some physical aid to their moral consolations—wine, beer, opium, brandy, or tobacco.

I consider therefore the stopping of the distillery, oeconomically, financially, commercially, medicinally, and in some degree morally too, as a measure rather well meant than well considered. It is too precious a sacrifice to prejudice.

Gentlemen well know whether there be a scarcity of partridges, and whether that be an effect of hoarding and combination. All the same race of birds live and die as the wild do.

As to the lesser articles, they are like the greater. They have followed the fortune of the season. Why are fowls dear? was not this the farmer's or jobber's fault. I sold from my yard to a jobber, six young and lean fowls, for four and twenty shillings; fowls, for which, two years ago, the same man would not have given a shilling a-piece. He sold them afterwards at Uxbridge, and they were taken to London to receive the last hand.

As to the operation of the war in causing the scarcity of

provisions, I understand that Mr. Pitt has given a particular answer to it—but I do not think it worth powder and shot.

I do not wonder the papers are so full of this sort of matter, but I am a little surprised it should be mentioned in parliament. Like all great state questions, peace and war may be discussed, and different opinions fairly formed, on political grounds, but on a question of the present price of provisions, when peace with the regicides is always uppermost, I can only say, that great is the love of it.

After all, have we not reason to be thankful to the giver of all good? In our history, and when "The labourer of England is said to have been once happy," we find constantly, after certain intervals, a period of real famine; by which, a melancholy havock was made among the human race. The price of provisions fluctuated dreadfully, demonstrating a deficiency very different from the worst failures of the present moment. Never since I have known England, have I known more than a comparative scarcity. The price of wheat, taking a number of years together, has had no very considerable fluctuation, nor has it risen exceedingly until within this twelvemonth. Even now, I do not know of one man, woman, or child, that has perished from famine; fewer, if any, I believe, than in years of plenty, when such a thing may happen by accident. This is owing to a care and superintendance of the poor, far greater than any I remember.

The consideration of this ought to bind us all, rich and poor together, against those wicked writers of the newspapers, who would inflame the poor against their friends, guardians, patrons, and protectors. Not only very few (I have observed, that I know of none, though I live in a place as poor as most) have actually died of want, but we have seen no traces of those dreadful exterminating epidemics, which, in consequence of scanty and unwholesome food, in former times, not unfrequently, wasted whole nations. Let us be saved from too much wisdom of our own, and we shall do tolerably well.

[It is one of the finest problems in legislation, and what has often engaged my thoughts whilst I followed that profession, "What the State ought to take upon itself to direct by the public wisdom, and what it ought to leave, with as little interference as possible, to individual discretion." Nothing, certainly, can be laid down on the subject that will not admit of exceptions, many permanent, some occasional. But the clearest line of distinction which I could draw, whilst I had my chalk to draw any line, was this: That the State ought to confine itself to what regards the State, or the creatures of the State, namely, the exterior establishment of its religion; its magistracy; its revenue; its military force by sea and land; the corporations that owe their existence to its fiat; in a word, to every thing that is *truly and properly* public, to the public peace, to the public safety, to the public order, to the public prosperity. In it's preventive police it ought to be sparing of its efforts, and to employ means, rather few, unfrequent, and strong, than many, and frequent, and, of course, as they multiply their puny politic race, and dwindle, small and feeble. Statesmen who know themselves will, with the dignity which belongs to wisdom, proceed only in this the superior orb and first mover of their duty, steadily, vigilantly, severely, courageously: whatever remains will, in a manner, provide for itself. But as they descend from the state to a province, from a province to a parish, and from a parish to a private house, they go on accelerated in their fall. They *cannot* do the lower duty; and, in proportion as they try it, they will certainly fail in the higher. They ought to know the different departments of things; what belongs to laws, and what manners alone can regulate. To these, great politicians may give a leaning, but they cannot give a law.

Our Legislature has fallen into this fault as well as other governments; all have fallen into it more or less. The once mighty State, which was nearest to us locally, nearest to us in every way, and whose ruins threaten to fall upon our heads, is a strong instance of this error.[1] I can never quote France without a foreboding sigh—ΕΣΣΕΤΑΙ῾ΗΜΑΡ![2] Scipio said it to his recording Greek friend amidst the flames of the great rival of his country.[3] That state has fallen by the hands of the parricides of their country, called the Revolutionists, and Constitutionalists, of France, a species of traitors, of whose fury and atrocious wickedness nothing in the annals of the phrenzy and depravation of mankind had before furnished an example, and of whom I can never think or speak without a mixed sensation of disgust, of horrour, and of detestation, not easy to be expressed. These nefarious monsters destroyed their country for what was good in it: for much good there was in the constitution of that noble monarchy, which, in all kinds, formed and nourished great men, and great patterns of virtue to the world. But though it's enemies were not enemies to it's faults, it's faults furnished them with means for it's destruction. My dear departed friend,[4] whose loss is even greater to the public than to me, had often remarked, that the leading vice of the French monarchy (which he had well studied) was in good intention ill-directed, and a restless desire of governing too much. The hand of authority was seen in every thing, and in every place. All, therefore,

1. That of the fixing of prices by government.

2. The first words of a passage in Homer, in which Hector tells his wife that he knows that Troy is doomed:

The day will come when sacred Troy will perish,
And Priam and his people shall be slain.
Iliad 6.448–49.

3. The Roman general Scipio, who had finally and fully conquered Carthage, repeated Hector's words, "The day will come," when his Greek friend, the historian Polybius, asked him why he wept when he saw Carthage in flames. He feared for Rome, too, says Polybius, "when he reflected on the fate of all things human." *Histories* 38.22.1–3.

4. His son Richard, who had died the year before, on August 2, 1794.

that happened amiss in the course even of domestic affairs, was attributed to the Government; and, as it always happens in this kind of officious universal interference, what began in odious power, ended always, I may say without an exception, in contemptible imbecillity. For this reason, as far as I can approve of any novelty, I thought well of the Provincial Administrations. Those, if the superior power had been severe, and vigilant, and vigorous, might have been of much use politically in removing government from many invidious details. But as every thing is good or bad, as it is related or combined, government being relaxed above as it was relaxed below, and the brains of the people growing more and more addle with every sort of visionary speculation, the shiftings of the scene in the provincial theatres became only preparatives to a revolution in the kingdom, and the popular actings there only the rehearsals of the terrible drama of the republic.

Tyranny and cruelty may make men justly wish the downfall of abused powers, but I believe that no government ever yet perished from any other direct cause than it's own weakness. My opinion is against an over-doing of any sort of administration, and more especially against this most momentous of all meddling on the part of authority; the meddling with the subsistence of the people.]

FINIS

Speech on Fox's East India Bill

[December 1, 1783]

Between 1773 and 1783, Burke's thinking on the problem of British government in India went through a radical change. The East India Company had been chartered in 1600 as a commercial company with a monopoly of British trade with India. As such Burke and the Rockingham Whigs still regarded it in 1773. In their eyes, efforts to extend the control of government over the Company were an attack on private property and chartered rights, and a dangerous extension of the power of the Crown. They did not sufficiently attend to the fact that the Company was no longer merely a trading enterprise. By its involvement in Indian wars, it had become the ruler of extensive Indian territories, of which Bengal was the principal one, and a major military and political power that controlled a number of nominally independent states.

After 1773, Burke gradually became convinced that the Company was not only exercising political power but was abusing it badly, to the detriment of the people of India. He made himself as well versed as he could in Indian affairs, and when he was appointed in 1781 to the House of Commons Select Committee on Bengal, he had access to a steady flow of privileged information.

In April 1783, his party, the Rockingham Whigs, led since Rockingham's death by Charles James Fox, came into power in coalition with Lord North, whom they had long opposed as George III's prime minister during the greater part of the American crisis. The Coalition submitted two bills in the Commons, one of which would effectively put the political government of India under the control of a commission appointed by Parliament. The other bill would put the management of the Company's commerce under another commission. The first, and more important, of the bills was drafted and introduced by Fox but incorporated many of Burke's ideas; Burke is the acknowledged author of the second bill.

The present speech, made on a motion for the House of Commons to go into committee to consider the first bill, was Burke's major contribution to the debate on it. Burke's enlightened imperialism in regard to Britain's government of India may have been unduly idealistic in several ways. Many of his charges against the Company, and against Governor-General Warren Hastings in particular, have been controverted by historians on factual grounds. But the speech reflects his conception of the proper role of Britain in governing other countries, his sincere concern for the just treatment of the people of India, and his genuine sympathy with their sufferings.

Mr. Burke's Speech, On the 1st December 1783

[Upon the Question for the Speaker's Leaving the Chair, in Order for the House to Resolve Itself into a Committee on Mr. Fox's East India Bill]

Mr. Speaker,

I thank you for pointing to me. I really wished much to engage your attention in an early stage of the debate. I have been long very deeply, though perhaps ineffectually, engaged in the preliminary enquiries, which have continued without intermission for some years. Though I have felt, with some degree of sensibility, the natural and inevitable impressions of the several matters of fact, as they have been successively disclosed, I have not at any time attempted to trouble you on the merits of the subject; and very little on any of the points which incidentally arose in the course of our proceedings. But I should be sorry to be found totally silent upon this day. Our enquiries are now come to their final issue: It is now to be determined whether the three years of laborious parliamentary research, whether the twenty years of patient Indian suffering, are to produce a substantial reform in our Eastern administration; or whether our knowledge of the grievances has abated our zeal for the correction of them, and whether our very enquiry into the evil was only a pretext to elude the remedy which is demanded from us by humanity, by justice, and by every principle of true policy. Depend upon it, this business cannot be indifferent to our fame. It will turn out a matter of great disgrace or great glory to the whole British nation. We are on a conspicuous stage, and the world marks our demeanour.

I am therefore a little concerned to perceive the spirit and temper in which the debate has been all along pursued, upon one side of the House. The declamation of the Gentlemen who oppose the bill has been abundant and vehement, but they have been reserved and even silent about the fitness or unfitness of the plan to attain the direct object it has in view. By some gentlemen it is taken up (by way of exercise I presume) as a point of law on a question of private property, and corporate franchise;[1] by others it is regarded as the petty intrigue of a faction at court, and argued merely as it tends to set this man a little higher, or that a little lower in situation and power. All the void has been filled up with invectives against coalition; with allusions to the loss of America; with the activity and inactivity of ministers. The total silence of these gentlemen concerning the interest and well-being of the people of India, and concerning the interest which this nation has in the commerce and revenues of that country, is a strong indication of the value which they set upon these objects.

It has been a little painful to me to observe the intrusion into this important debate of such company as *Quo Warranto,* and *Mandamus,* and *Certiorari;* as if we were on a trial about mayors and aldermen, and capital burgesses; or engaged in a suit concerning the borough of Penryn, or Saltash, or St.

1. In 1773 and earlier, Burke and the Rockingham Whigs had strenuously objected on much the same grounds to bringing the East India Company under government control: it was an attack on private property and chartered rights. In later years, Burke did not disguise his earlier position but said that he had changed his mind in the light of better information.

Ives, or St. Mawes. Gentlemen have argued with as much heat and passion, as if the first things in the world were at stake; and their topics are such, as belong only to matter of the lowest and meanest litigation. It is not right, it is not worthy of us, in this manner to depreciate the value, to degrade the majesty of this grave deliberation of policy and empire.

For my part, I have thought myself bound, when a matter of this extraordinary weight came before me, not to consider (as some Gentlemen are so fond of doing) whether the bill originated from a Secretary of State for the home department, or from a Secretary for the foreign; from a minister of influence or a minister of the people; from Jacob or from Esau.[1] I asked myself, and I asked myself nothing else, what part it was fit for a member of parliament, who has supplied a mediocrity of talents by the extreme of diligence, and who has thought himself obliged, by the research of years, to wind himself into the inmost recesses and labyrinths of the Indian detail, what part, I say, it became such a member of parliament to take, when a minister of state, in conformity to a recommendation from the throne,[2] has brought before us a system for the better government of the territory and commerce of the East. In this light, and in this only, I will trouble you with my sentiments.

It is not only agreed but demanded, by the Right Honour-

1. Thomas Powys, M.P., had made this allusion, meaning that in the bill the voice was Fox's but the hand that wrote the measures it proposed expressed Lord North's view of royal prerogative.

2. The bill was only formally a recommendation from the throne. George III had only reluctantly accepted the Fox-North Coalition in April 1783 because he had no other leader who could attract the support of a majority in the Commons. He now saw the India bills as an occasion for getting rid of it. When the bills passed the Commons and were before the Lords, the king privately let his opposition to them be known, the Lords defeated them, and the king dismissed the Coalition and brought in the younger William Pitt as head of a minority government. Pitt's Tories won a resounding electoral victory in the following year, 1784.

able gentleman,[1] and by those who act with him, that a *whole* system ought to be produced; that it ought not to be an *half measure;* that it ought to be no *palliative;* but a legislative provision, vigorous, substantial, and effective. I believe that no man who understands the subject can doubt for a moment, that those must be the conditions of any thing deserving the name of a reform in the Indian government; that any thing short of them would not only be delusive, but, in this matter which admits no medium, noxious in the extreme.

To all the conditions proposed by his adversaries the mover of the bill perfectly agrees; and on his performance of them he rests his cause. On the other hand, not the least objection has been taken, with regard to the efficiency, the vigour, or the completeness of the scheme. I am therefore warranted to assume, as a thing admitted, that the bills accomplish what both sides of the House demand as essential. The end is completely answered, so far as the direct and immediate object is concerned.

But though there are no direct, yet there are various collateral objections made; objections from the effects, which this plan of reform for Indian administration may have on the privileges of great public bodies in England; from its probable influence on the constitutional rights, or on the freedom and integrity of the several branches of the legislature.

Before I answer these objections I must beg leave to observe, that if we are not able to contrive some method of governing India *well,* which will not of necessity become the means of governing Great Britain *ill,* a ground is laid for their eternal separation; but none for sacrificing the people of that country to our constitution. I am however far from being persuaded that any such incompatibility of interest does at all exist. On the contrary I am certain that every means, effectual to preserve India from oppression, is a guard to preserve

1. William Pitt the Younger (1759–1806).

the British constitution from its worst corruption. To shew this, I will consider the objections, which I think are four.

1st. That the bill is an attack on the chartered rights of men.

2dly. That it increases the influence of the crown.

3dly. That it does *not* increase, but diminishes, the influence of the crown, in order to promote the interests of certain ministers and their party.

4thly. That it deeply affects the national credit.

As to the first of these objections; I must observe that the phrase of "the chartered rights *of men,*" is full of affectation; and very unusual in the discussion of privileges conferred by charters of the present description. But it is not difficult to discover what end that ambiguous mode of expression, so often reiterated, is meant to answer.

The rights of *men,*[1] that is to say, the natural rights of mankind, are indeed sacred things; and if any public measure is proved mischievously to affect them, the objection ought to be fatal to that measure, even if no charter at all could be set up against it. If these natural rights are further affirmed and declared by express covenants, if they are clearly defined and secured against chicane, against power, and authority, by written instruments and positive engagements, they are in a still better condition:[2] they partake not only of the sanctity of the object so secured, but of that solemn public faith itself, which secures an object of such importance. Indeed this formal recognition, by the sovereign power, of an original right in the subject, can never be subverted, but by rooting

1. Burke was aware of the revolutionary theory of "the rights of men" well before the French Revolution, as his *Speech on the Reform of the Representation* in the year preceding this speech shows. But Burke's objection was not to the idea of natural rights, as he clearly states in the present passage, but to a particular radically democratic version of it.

2. Burke here denies any inherent conflict between nature and convention. Nature is the norm of convention; therefore convention is good insofar as it embodies or supports natural right and natural rights.

up the holding radical principles of government, and even of society itself. The charters, which we call by distinction *great,* are public instruments of this nature; I mean the charters of King John and King Henry the Third. The things secured by these instruments may, without any deceitful ambiguity, be very fitly called the *chartered rights of men.*

These charters have made the very name of a charter dear to the heart of every Englishman—But, Sir, there may be, and there are charters, not only different in nature, but formed on principles the *very reverse* of those of the great charter. Of this kind is the charter of the East India Company. *Magna charta* is a charter to restrain power, and to destroy monopoly. The East India charter is a charter to establish monopoly, and to create power. Political power and commercial monopoly are *not* the rights of men; and the rights to them derived from charters, it is fallacious and sophistical to call "the chartered rights of men." These chartered rights, (to speak of such charters and of their effects in terms of the greatest possible moderation) do at least suspend the natural rights of mankind at large; and in their very frame and constitution are liable to fall into a direct violation of them.

It is a charter of this latter description (that is to say a charter of power and monopoly) which is affected by the bill before you. The bill, Sir, does, without question, affect it; it does affect it essentially and substantially. But, having stated to you of what description the chartered rights are which this bill touches, I feel no difficulty at all in acknowledging the existence of those chartered rights, in their fullest extent. They belong to the Company in the surest manner; and they are secured to that body by every sort of public sanction. They are stamped by the faith of the King; they are stamped by the faith of Parliament; they have been bought for money, for money honestly and fairly paid; they have been bought for valuable consideration, over and over again.

I therefore freely admit to the East India Company their

claim to exclude their fellow-subjects from the commerce of half the globe. I admit their claim to administer an annual territorial revenue of seven millions sterling; to command an army of sixty thousand men; and to dispose, (under the control of a sovereign imperial discretion, and with the due observance of the natural and local law) of the lives and fortunes of thirty millions of their fellow-creatures. All this they possess by charter and by acts of parliament, (in my opinion) without a shadow of controversy.

Those who carry the rights and claims of the Company the furthest do not contend for more than this; and all this I freely grant. But granting all this, they must grant to me in my turn, that all political power which is set over men, and that all privilege claimed or exercised in exclusion of them, being wholly artificial, and for so much, a derogation from the natural equality of mankind at large, ought to be some way or other exercised ultimately for their benefit.[1]

If this is true with regard to every species of political dominion, and every description of commercial privilege, none of which can be original self-derived rights, or grants for the mere private benefit of the holders, then such rights, or privileges, or whatever else you choose to call them, are all in the strictest sense a *trust;* and it is of the very essence of every trust to be rendered *accountable;* and even totally to *cease,* when it substantially varies from the purposes for which alone it could have a lawful existence.

This I conceive, Sir, to be true of trusts of power vested in the highest hands, and of such as seem to hold of no human creature. But about the application of this principle to sub-

1. In Burke's political theory, all men are equal inasmuch as no men are endowed *by nature* with a right to exercise political authority over other men. Political authority in this sense is artificial and established by convention. But the convention is subject to natural law and is established to serve the natural needs and protect the natural rights of mankind. It is therefore a trust for the benefit of those who are subject to it.

ordinate *derivative* trusts, I do not see how a controversy can be maintained. To whom then would I make the East India Company accountable? Why, to Parliament[1] to be sure; to Parliament, from whom their trust was derived; to Parliament, which alone is capable of comprehending the magnitude of its object, and its abuse; and alone capable of an effectual legislative remedy. The very charter, which is held out to exclude Parliament from correcting malversation with regard to the high trust vested in the Company, is the very thing which at once gives a title and imposes a duty on us to interfere with effect, wherever power and authority originating from ourselves are perverted from their purposes, and become instruments of wrong and violence.

If Parliament, Sir, had nothing to do with this charter, we might have some sort of Epicurean[2] excuse to stand aloof, indifferent spectators of what passes in the Company's name in India and in London. But if we are the very cause of the evil, we are in a special manner engaged to the redress; and for us passively to bear with oppressions committed under the sanction of our own authority, is in truth and reason for this House to be an active accomplice in the abuse.

That the power notoriously, grossly, abused has been bought from us is very certain. But this circumstance, which is urged against the bill, becomes an additional motive for our interference; lest we should be thought to have sold the blood of millions of men, for the base consideration of money. We sold, I admit, all that we had to sell; that is our

1. Therefore not to the Crown, whose power the Rockingham Whigs had no desire to augment.

2. Epicurus (342/1–270 B.C.) was a Greek philosopher who taught a hedonistic ethic that held pleasure to be the highest good. But the greatest pleasure was health of body and tranquillity of mind, enjoyed in the company of friends. Understanding this, the wise man would not get involved in politics, which disturbs inner tranquillity.

authority, not our controul. We had not a right to make a market of our duties.

I ground myself therefore on this principle—that if the abuse is proved, the contract is broken; and we re-enter into all our rights; that is, into the exercise of all our duties. Our own authority is indeed as much a trust originally, as the Company's authority is a trust derivatively; and it is the use we make of the resumed power that must justify or condemn us in the resumption of it. When we have perfected the plan laid before us by the Right Honourable mover, the world will then see what it is we destroy, and what it is we create. By that test we stand or fall; and by that test I trust that it will be found in the issue, that we are going to supersede a charter abused to the full extent of all the powers which it could abuse, and exercised in the plenitude of despotism, tyranny, and corruption; and that, in one and the same plan, we provide a real chartered security for the *rights of men* cruelly violated under that charter.

This bill, and those connected with it, are intended to form the *Magna Charta* of Hindostan. Whatever the treaty of Westphalia[1] is to the liberty of the princes and free cities of the empire, and to the three religions there professed—Whatever the great charter,[2] the statute of tallage,[3] the peti-

1. Of 1648, which ended the Thirty Years' War in the Holy Roman Empire and legally established the three religions of Calvinism, Catholicism, and Lutheranism.

2. Magna Carta (or Charta), a charter of liberties to which the English barons forced King John to assent in 1215.

3. Tallage was a levy exacted by a lord from the boroughs in his domain, hence by a king from the boroughs in his personal domain. In 1297, in a document called by a misnomer *de tallagio non concedendo,* the king renounced for himself and his heirs the right to levy any general tax without the consent of the estates of his whole kingdom. In later centuries, this document became called a statute, and was cited as such in the Petition of Right (for which see the next note).

tion of right,[1] and the declaration of right,[2] are to Great Britain, these bills are to the people of India. Of this benefit, I am certain, their condition is capable; and when I know that they are capable of more, my vote shall most assuredly be for our giving to the full extent of their capacity of receiving; and no charter of dominion shall stand as a bar in my way to their charter of safety and protection.

The strong admission I have made of the Company's rights (I am conscious of it) binds me to do a great deal. I do not presume to condemn those who argue *a priori,* against the propriety of leaving such extensive political powers in the hands of a company of merchants. I know much is, and much more may be said against such a system. But, with my particular ideas and sentiments, I cannot go that way to work. I feel an insuperable reluctance in giving my hand to destroy any established institution of government, upon a theory, however plausible it may be. My experience in life teaches me nothing clear upon the subject. I have known merchants with the sentiments and the abilities of great statesmen; and I have seen persons in the rank of statesmen, with the conceptions and character of pedlars. Indeed, my observation has furnished me with nothing that is to be found in any habits of life or education, which tends wholly to disqualify men for the functions of government, but that, by which the power of exercising those functions is very frequently obtained, I mean, a spirit and habits of low cabal and intrigue; which I have never, in one instance, seen united with a capacity for sound and manly policy.

1. A petition of Parliament in 1628 complaining of a series of breaches of law and asserting a right not to be subjected to arbitrary taxation and imprisonment, martial law, and the billeting of soldiers on private citizens against their will, to which Charles I was forced to assent.

2. A declaration which accompanied the crown offered to William and Mary in 1689. It pledged the monarchs to observe laws passed by Parliament and provided that the monarch could not be a Catholic.

To justify us in taking the administration of their affairs out of the hands of the East India Company, on my principles, I must see several conditions. 1st. The object affected by the abuse should be great and important. 2d. The abuse affecting this great object ought to be a great abuse. 3d. It ought to be habitual, and not accidental. 4th. It ought to be utterly incurable in the body as it now stands constituted. All this ought to be made as visible to me as the light of the sun, before I should strike off an atom of their charter. A Right Honourable gentleman[1] has said, and said I think but once, and that very slightly (whatever his original demand for a plan might seem to require) that "there are abuses in the Company's government." If that were all, the scheme of the mover of this bill, the scheme of his learned friend,[2] and his own scheme of reformation (if he has any) are all equally needless. There are, and must be, abuses in all governments. It amounts to no more than a nugatory proposition. But before I consider of what nature these abuses are, of which the gentleman speaks so very lightly, permit me to recall to your recollection the map of the country which this abused chartered right affects. This I shall do, that you may judge whether in that map I can discover any thing like the first of my conditions; that is, Whether the object affected by the abuse of the East India Company's power be of importance sufficient to justify the measure and means of reform applied to it in this bill.

With very few, and those inconsiderable intervals, the British dominion, either in the Company's name, or in the

1. William Pitt, who in fact carried through his own East India Bill when he became First Lord of the Treasury after the fall of the Fox-North Coalition in the following year.

2. Henry Dundas (1742–1811), close friend and political associate of the younger Pitt, and at this time chairman of the House of Commons Secret Committee on Indian affairs. (The original purposes of the Secret and Select Committees were limited and distinct, but the scope of their investigations tended over time to merge.)

names of princes absolutely dependent upon the Company, extends from the mountains that separate India from Tartary, to Cape Comorin, that is, one-and-twenty degrees of latitude!

In the northern parts it is a solid mass of land, about eight hundred miles in length, and four or five hundred broad. As you go southward, it becomes narrower for a space. It afterwards dilates; but narrower or broader, you possess the whole eastern and north-eastern coast of that vast country, quite from the borders of Pegu. Bengal, Bahar, and Orissa, with Benares (now unfortunately in our immediate possession) measure 161,978 square English miles; a territory considerably larger than the whole kingdom of France. Oude, with its dependent provinces, is 53,286 square miles, not a great deal less than England. The Carnatic, with Tanjour and the Circars, is 65,948 square miles, very considerably larger than England; and the whole of the Company's dominion comprehending Bombay and Salsette, amounts to 281,412 square miles, which forms a territory larger than any European dominion, Russia and Turkey excepted. Through all that vast extent of country there is not a man who eats a mouthful of rice but by permission of the East India Company.

So far with regard to the extent. The population of this great empire is not easy to be calculated. When the countries, of which it is composed, came into our possession, they were all eminently peopled, and eminently productive; though at that time considerably declined from their antient prosperity. But since they are come into our hands !———! However if we take the period of our estimate immediately before the utter desolation of the Carnatic, and if we allow for the havoc which our government had even then made in these regions, we cannot, in my opinion, rate the population at much less than thirty millions of souls, more than four times the number of persons in the island of Great Britain.

My next enquiry to that of the number, is the quality and description of the inhabitants. This multitude of men does not consist of an abject and barbarous populace; much less of gangs of savages, like the Guaranies and Chiquitos, who wander on the waste borders of the river of Amazons, or the Plate; but a people for ages civilized and cultivated; cultivated by all the arts of polished life, whilst we were yet in the woods. There, have been (and still the skeletons remain) princes once of great dignity, authority, and opulence. There, are to be found the chiefs of tribes and nations. There is to be found an antient and venerable priesthood, the depository of their laws, learning, and history, the guides of the people whilst living, and their consolation in death; a nobility of great antiquity and renown; a multitude of cities, not exceeded in population and trade by those of the first class in Europe; merchants and bankers, individual houses of whom have once vied in capital with the Bank of England; whose credit had often supported a tottering state, and preserved their governments in the midst of war and desolation; millions of ingenious manufacturers and mechanicks; millions of the most diligent, and not the least intelligent, tillers of the earth. Here are to be found almost all the religions professed by men, the Bramincal, the Mussulmen, the Eastern and the Western Christians.

If I were to take the whole aggregate of our possessions there, I should compare it, as the nearest parallel I can find, with the empire of Germany. Our immediate possessions I should compare with the Austrian dominions, and they would not suffer in the comparison. The Nabob[1] of Oude might stand for the King of Prussia; the Nabob of Arcot I would compare, as superior in territory, and equal in revenue, to the Elector[2] of Saxony. Cheyt Sing, the Rajah[3] of

1. Nabob or nawab was the title (equivalent to subahdar) of Muslim officials who governed provinces or districts in the Mogul Empire. As the empire weakened they became more independent rulers.

2. A prince or prince-bishop entitled to vote in the election of an Emperor of the Holy Roman Empire.

3. A title originally given in India to a king or prince and later extended to lesser chiefs or dignitaries.

Benares, might well rank with the Prince of Hesse at least; and the Rajah of Tanjore (though hardly equal in extent of dominion, superior in revenue) to the Elector of Bavaria. The Polygars[1] and the northern Zemindars,[2] and other great chiefs, might well class with the rest of the Princes, Dukes, Counts, Marquisses, and Bishops in the empire; all of whom I mention to honour, and surely without disparagement to any or all of those most respectable princes and grandees.

All this vast mass, composed of so many orders and classes of men, is again infinitely diversified by manners, by religion, by hereditary employment, through all their possible combinations. This renders the handling of India a matter in an high degree critical and delicate. But oh! it has been handled rudely indeed. Even some of the reformers seem to have forgot that they had any thing to do but to regulate the tenants of a manor, or the shopkeepers of the next county town.

It is an empire of this extent, of this complicated nature, of this dignity and importance, that I have compared to Germany and the German government; not for an exact resemblance, but as a sort of a middle term, by which India might be approximated to our understandings, and if possible to our feelings; in order to awaken something of sympathy for the unfortunate natives, of which I am afraid we are not perfectly susceptible, whilst we look at this very remote object through a false and cloudy medium.

My second condition, necessary to justify me in touch-

1. Minor chieftains holding small territories, whom Burke mistakenly takes for "great chiefs" and "sovereign princes."

2. Persons who held the right to collect rents and dues from the cultivators of the soil, in return for which they were obliged to turn a proportion of the revenue over to the Mogul emperor. When the emperor granted the right to the revenues of Bengal to the East India Company, the zemindars owed the proportion to the Company. Depending on the amount of land and revenue they controlled, zemindars could be rich and powerful. *The Annual Register* in 1787 (vol. 24, p. 177) called them "the present great landholders of India" and "a sort of hereditary princes of the country."

ing the charter, is, Whether the Company's abuse of their trust, with regard to this great object, be an abuse of great atrocity. I shall beg your permission to consider their conduct in two lights; first the political, and then the commercial. Their political conduct (for distinctness) I divide again into two heads; the external, in which I mean to comprehend their conduct in their federal capacity, as it relates to powers and states independent, or that not long since were such; the other internal, namely their conduct to the countries either immediately subject to the Company, or to those who, under the apparent government of native sovereigns, are in a state much lower, and much more miserable, than common subjection.

The attention, Sir, which I wish to preserve to method will not be considered as unnecessary or affected. Nothing else can help me to selection out of the infinite mass of materials which have passed under my eye; or can keep my mind steady to the great leading points I have in view.

With regard therefore to the abuse of the external federal trust, I engage myself to you to make good these three positions: First, I say, that from Mount Imaus, (or whatever else you call that large range of mountains that walls the northern frontier of India) where it touches us in the latitude of twenty-nine, to Cape Comorin, in the latitude of eight, that there is not a *single* prince, state, or potentate, great or small, in India, with whom they have come into contact, whom they have not sold. I say *sold,* though sometimes they have not been able to deliver according to their bargain. Secondly, I say, that there is not a *single treaty* they have ever made, which they have not broken. Thirdly, I say, that there is not a single prince or state, who ever put any trust in the Company, who is not utterly ruined; and that none are in any degree secure or flourishing, but in the exact proportion to their settled distrust and irreconcileable enmity to this nation.

These assertions are universal. I say in the full sense *uni-*

versal. They regard the external and political trust only; but I shall produce others fully equivalent, in the internal. For the present, I shall content myself with explaining my meaning; and if I am called on for proof whilst these bills are depending (which I believe I shall not) I will put my finger on the Appendixes to the Reports, or on papers of record in the House, or the Committees, which I have distinctly present to my memory, and which I think I can lay before you at half an hour's warning.

The first potentate sold by the Company for money was the Great Mogul[1]—the descendant of Tamerlane. This high personage, as high as human veneration can look at, is by every account amiable in his manners, respectable for his piety according to his mode, and accomplished in all the Oriental literature. All this, and the title derived under his *charter,* to all that we hold in India, could not save him from the general *sale.* Money is coined in his name; In his name justice is administered; He is prayed for in every temple through the countries we possess—But he was sold.

It is impossible, Mr. Speaker, not to pause here for a moment, to reflect on the inconstancy of human greatness, and the stupendous revolutions that have happened in our age of wonders. Could it be believed, when I entered into existence, or when you, a younger man, were born, that on this day, in this House, we should be employed in discussing the conduct of those British subjects who had disposed of the power and person of the Grand Mogul? This is no idle speculation. Awful lessons are taught by it, and by other events, of which it is not yet too late to profit.

1. Title of the emperor of the Mogul Empire, held by a Muslim dynasty descended from Tamerlane and Genghis Khan. By the eighteenth century, the Company was acquiring territorial sovereignty in parts of the Empire, and particularly in Bengal, where, with the decline of the Empire, the local nabobs had become practically independent, and the Mogul was forced to ratify the Company's acquisitions.

This is hardly a digression; but I return to the sale of the Mogul. Two districts, Corah and Allahabad, out of his immense grants, were reserved as a royal demesne to the donor of a kingdom, and the rightful sovereign of so many nations. After withholding the tribute of £.260,000 a year, which the Company was, by the *charter* they had received from this prince, under the most solemn obligation to pay, these districts were sold to his chief minister Sujah ul Dowlah;[1] and, what may appear to some the worst part of the transaction, these two districts were sold for scarcely two years purchase. The descendant of Tamerlane now stands in need almost of the common necessaries of life; and in this situation we do not even allow him, as bounty, the smallest portion of what we owe him in justice.

The next sale was that of the whole nation of the Rohillas,[2] which the grand salesman, without a pretence of quarrel, and contrary to his own declared sense of duty and rectitude, sold to the same Sujah ul Dowlah. He sold the people to utter *extirpation,* for the sum of four hundred thousand pounds. Faithfully was the bargain performed upon our side. Hafiz Rhamet, the most eminent of their chiefs, one of the bravest men of his time, and as famous throughout the East for the elegance of his literature, and the spirit of his poetical compositions (by which he supported the name of Hafiz) as for his courage, was invaded with an army of an hundred thousand men, and an English brigade. This man, at the head of inferior forces, was slain valiantly fighting for his country. His head was cut off, and delivered for money to a barbarian. His wife and children, persons of that rank, were seen begging an handful of rice through the English camp. The whole nation,

1. The Nabob of Oude, who also held the title of the Great Mogul's Vizier or chief minister.

2. Afghan invaders who, earlier in the century, had seized the rulership of a fertile district populated by Hindus.

with inconsiderable exceptions, was slaughtered or banished. The country was laid waste with fire and sword; and that land distinguished above most others, by the chearful face of paternal government and protected labour, the chosen seat of cultivation and plenty, is now almost throughout a dreary desart, covered with rushes and briars, and jungles full of wild beasts.

The British officer who commanded in the delivery of the people thus sold, felt some compunction at his employment. He represented these enormous excesses to the president of Bengal, for which he received a severe reprimand from the civil governor; and I much doubt whether the breach caused by the conflict, between the compassion of the military and the firmness of the civil governor, be closed at this hour.

In Bengal, Seraja Dowla was sold to Mir Jaffier; Mir Jaffier was sold to Mir Cossim; and Mir Cossim was sold to Mir Jaffier again. The succession to Mir Jaffier was sold to his eldest son; another son of Mir Jaffier, Mobarech ul Dowla, was sold to his step-mother[1]—The Maratta empire[2] was sold to Ragoba;[3] and Ragoba was sold and delivered to the Peishwa[4] of the Marattas. Both Ragoba and the Peishwa of the Marattas were offered to sale to the Rajah of Berar. Scindia,[5] the chief of Malva, was offered to sale to the same Rajah; and the Su-

1. The names in the above lines are those of nabobs of Bengal whom the British set up and deposed in order to keep Bengal and its revenues under the Company's control.

2. A powerful confederacy of native states in west-central India.

3. Referred to later as Ragonaut Row.

4. Title of the chief minister of the Maratta princes, who became *rois fainéants,* so that in 1749 the then peishwa made himself the hereditary sovereign of the Maratta state, but without changing his title.

5. A powerful chieftain in the Maratta confederacy who, along with other chieftains, had become almost completely independent of the Confederacy's titular head and his hereditary chief minister, the peishwa.

bah[1] of the Decan was sold to the great trader Mahomet Ali, Nabob of Arcot.[2] To the same Nabob of Arcot they sold Hyder Ali[3] and the kingdom of Mysore. To Mahomet Ali they twice sold the kingdom of Tanjore. To the same Mahomet Ali they sold at least twelve sovereign princes, called the Polygars. But to keep things even, the territory of Tinnivelly, belonging to their Nabob, they would have sold to the Dutch; and to conclude the account of sales, their great customer, the Nabob of Arcot himself, and his lawful succession, has been sold to his second son, Amir ul Omrah, whose character, views, and conduct, are in the accounts upon your table. It remains with you whether they shall finally perfect this last bargain.

All these bargains and sales were regularly attended with the waste and havoc of the country, always by the buyer, and sometimes by the object of the sale. This was explained to you by the Honourable mover,[4] when he stated the mode of paying debts due from the country powers to the Company. An Honourable gentleman, who is not now in his place, objected to his jumping near two thousand miles for an example. But the southern example is perfectly applicable to the northern claim, as the northern is to the southern; for, throughout the whole space of these two thousand miles, take your stand

1. A subah was a province of the Mogul Empire or the title of the ruler thereof. On p. 158 below, Burke uses Soubah as the title of the Nabob of Bengal.

2. Arcot was a territory adjacent to the Company's presidency of Madras in South India. Its nabob was heavily in debt to both the Company and certain of its individual officials for military aid and large loans to further his own ambitions. In his great *Speech on the Nabob of Arcot's Debts* in 1785, Burke charged that these debts were a major cause of corruption in the British government both in India and in England.

3. The ruler of Mysore, a kingdom adjacent to Madras, and the most formidable foe of the British in South India.

4. Fox.

where you will, the proceeding is perfectly uniform, and what is done in one part will apply exactly to the other.

My second assertion is, that the Company never has made a treaty which they have not broken. This position is so connected with that of the sales of provinces and kingdoms, with the negotiation of universal distraction in every part of India, that a very minute detail may well be spared on this point. It has not yet been contended, by any enemy to the reform, that they have observed any public agreement. When I hear that they have done so in any one instance (which hitherto, I confess, I never heard alledged) I shall speak to the particular treaty. The governor general has even amused himself and the Court of Directors in a very singular letter to that board, in which he admits he has not been very delicate with regard to public faith; and he goes so far as to state a regular estimate of the sums which the Company would have lost, or never acquired, if the rigid ideas of public faith entertained by his colleagues had been observed. The learned gentleman over against me has indeed saved me much trouble. On a former occasion he obtained no small credit, for the clear and forcible manner in which he stated what we have not forgot, and I hope he has not forgot, that universal systematic breach of treaties which had made the British faith proverbial in the East.[1]

It only remains, Sir, for me just to recapitulate some heads. The treaty with the Mogul,[2] by which we stipulated to pay him £.260,000 annually, was broken. This treaty they have broken, and not paid him a shilling. They broke their treaty with him, in which they stipulated to pay £.400,000 a

1. A footnote in the original publication identifies "the learned gentleman" as "Mr. Dundas, Lord Advocate of Scotland," but in the speech referred to here, he had spoken from the knowledge he had gained as chairman of the Secret Committee.

2. The Treaty of Allahabad, to which the Mogul was forced to agree after his defeat at Buxar in 1764.

year to the Soubah of Bengal. They agreed with the Mogul, for services admitted to have been performed, to pay Nudjif Cawn[1] a pension. They broke this article with the rest, and stopped also this small pension. They broke their treaties with the Nizam,[2] and with Hyder Ali. As to the Marattas, they had so many cross treaties with the States General of that nation, and with each of the chiefs, that it was notorious, that no one of these agreements could be kept without grossly violating the rest. It was observed, that if the terms of these several treaties had been kept, two British armies would at one and the same time have met in the field to cut each other's throats. The wars which desolate India, originated from a most atrocious violation of public faith on our part. In the midst of profound peace, the Company's troops invaded the Maratta territories, and surprised the island and fortress of Salsette. The Marattas nevertheless yielded to a treaty of peace, by which solid advantages were procured to the Company. But this treaty, like every other treaty, was soon violated by the Company. Again the Company invaded the Maratta dominions. The disaster that ensued gave occasion to a new treaty. The whole army of the Company was obliged, in effect, to surrender to this injured, betrayed, and insulted people. Justly irritated however, as they were, the terms which they prescribed were reasonable and moderate; and their treatment of their captive invaders, of the most distinguished humanity. But the humanity of the Marattas was of no power whatsoever to prevail on the Company to attend to the observance of the terms dictated by their moderation. The war was renewed with greater vigour than ever; and such was their insatiable lust of plunder, that they never would have given ear to any terms of peace, if Hyder Ali had not broke through the Gauts, and rushing like a torrent into the

1. "A soldier of fortune who had sided with the British." *W&S* 5:395, n. 4.

2. Title of the hereditary rulers of Hyderabad.

Carnatic, swept away every thing in his career. This was in consequence of that confederacy, which by a sort of miracle united the most discordant powers[1] for our destruction, as a nation in which no other could put any trust, and who were the declared enemies of the human species.

It is very remarkable, that the late controversy between the several presidencies, and between them and the Court of Directors, with relation to these wars and treaties, has not been, which of the parties might be defended for his share in them; but on which of the parties the guilt of all this load of perfidy should be fixed. But I am content to admit all these proceedings to be perfectly regular, to be full of honour and good faith; and wish to fix your attention solely to that single transaction which the advocates of this system select for so transcendant a merit as to cancel the guilt of all the rest of their proceedings; I mean the late treaties with the Marattas.[2]

I make no observation on the total cession of territory, by which they surrendered all they had obtained by their unhappy successes in war, and almost all that they had obtained under the treaty of Poorunder.[3] The restitution was proper, if it had been voluntary and seasonable. I attach on the spirit of the treaty, the dispositions it shewed, the provisions it made for a general peace, and the faith kept with allies and confederates; in order that the House may form a judgment, from this chosen piece, of the use which has been made (and is likely to be made, if things continue in the same hands) of the trust of the federal powers of this country.

It was the wish of almost every Englishman, that the Maratta peace might lead to a general one; because the Maratta war was only a part of a general confederacy formed

1. Hyder Ali, the Nizam, and the Marattas.

2. The Peace of Salbai in 1782 and subsequent agreements in 1783.

3. In 1776, after the first and successful British invasion of the Maratta territories.

against us on account of the universal abhorrence of our conduct which prevailed in every state and almost in every house in India. Mr. Hastings[1] was obliged to pretend some sort of acquiescence in this general and rational desire. He therefore consented, in order to satisfy the point of honour of the Marattas, that an article should be inserted to admit Hyder Ali to accede to the pacification. But observe, Sir, the spirit of this man (which if it were not made manifest by a thousand things, and particularly by his proceedings with regard to Lord Macartney)[2] would be sufficiently manifest by this— What sort of article think you does he require this essential head of a solemn treaty of general pacification to be? In his instruction to Mr. Anderson,[3] he desires him to admit "a *vague* article" in favour of Hyder. Evasion and fraud were the declared basis of the treaty. These *vague* articles, intended for a more vague performance, are the things which have damned our reputation in India.

Hardly was this vague article inserted, than, without waiting for any act on the part of Hyder, Mr. Hastings enters into a negociation with the Maratta Chief, Scindia, for a partition

1. Warren Hastings (1782–1818) had been appointed Governor of Bengal by the East India Company in 1771. Parliament's Regulating Act of 1773 created a Supreme Council of Bengal with five members named in the Act itself. They were Hastings as Governor-General (with a casting vote in case of ties), General Sir John Clavering, Colonel George Monson, Richard Barwell, and Philip Francis, who was to become Hastings's bitterest enemy and Burke's closest ally in the impeachment of Hastings. Replacements and successor members to the original five were to be appointed by the Company's Court of Directors, with confirmation by the Crown.

2. George Macartney, first Earl Macartney, whom the East India Company appointed governor of the presidency of Fort St. George (Madras). He arrived there in June 1781, but after a prolonged and bitter quarrel with Warren Hastings over matters of policy, he resigned his post in 1785 and returned to England. He refused the post of Governor-General in succession to Hastings; it was ultimately given to Lord Cornwallis.

3. David Anderson, close friend and associate of Warren Hastings, with whom in later years he worked on the latter's defense in his impeachment trial.

of the territories of the prince[1] who was one of the objects to be secured by the treaty. He was to be parcelled out in three parts—one to Scindia; one to the Peishwa of the Marattas; and the third to the East India Company, or to (the old dealer and chapman) Mahomet Ali.

During the formation of this project, Hyder dies; and before his son could take any one step, either to conform to the tenour of the article, or to contravene it, the treaty of partition is renewed on the old footing, and an instruction is sent to Mr. Anderson to conclude it in form.

A circumstance intervened, during the pendency of this negociation, to set off the good faith of the Company with an additional brilliancy, and to make it sparkle and glow with a variety of splendid faces. General Matthews[2] had reduced that most valuable part of Hyder's dominions called the Country of Biddenore. When the news reached Mr. Hastings, he instructed Mr. Anderson to contend for an alteration in the treaty of partition, and to take the Biddenore country out of the common stock which was to be divided, and to keep it for the Company.

The first ground for this variation was its being a separate conquest made before the treaty had actually taken place. Here was a new proof given of the fairness, equity, and moderation, of the Company. But the second of Mr. Hastings's reasons for retaining the Biddenore as a separate portion, and his conduct on that second ground, is still more remarkable. He asserted that that country could not be put into the partition stock, because General Matthews had received it on the terms of some convention, which might be incompatible with the partition proposed. This was a reason in itself both honourable and solid; and it shewed a regard

1. Hyder Ali (who died in 1782 and was succeeded by his son, Tipu Sahib, or, as Burke called him, Tippo Saheb).

2. Richard Matthews.

to faith somewhere, and with some persons. But in order to demonstrate his utter contempt of the plighted faith which was alledged on one part as a reason for departing from it on another, and to prove his impetuous desire for sowing a new war, even in the prepared soil of a general pacification, he directs Mr. Anderson, if he should find strong difficulties impeding the partition, on the score of the subtraction of Biddenore, wholly to abandon that claim, and to conclude the treaty on the original terms. General Matthews's convention was just brought forward sufficiently to demonstrate to the Marattas the slippery hold which they had on their new confederate; on the other hand that convention being instantly abandoned, the people of India were taught, that no terms on which they can surrender to the Company are to be regarded, when farther conquests are in view.

Next, Sir, let me bring before you the pious care that was taken of our allies under that treaty which is the subject of the Company's applauses. These allies were Ragonaut Row,[1] for whom we had engaged to find a throne; the Guickwar, (one of the Guzerat princes) who was to be emancipated from the Maratta authority, and to grow great by several accessions of dominion; and lastly, the Rana of Gohud, with whom we had entered into a treaty of partition for eleven sixteenths of our joint conquests. Some of these inestimable securities, called *vague* articles, were inserted in favour of them all.

As to the first, the unhappy abdicated Peshwa, and pretender to the Maratta throne, Ragonaut Row, was delivered up to his people, with an article for safety, and some provision.[2] This man, knowing how little vague the hatred of his countrymen was towards him, and well apprised of what

1. He became Peishwa of the Marattas in 1773 but was later deposed in favor of his infant great-nephew.

2. He was to receive an allowance from the Maratta chief, Scindia, if he took up residence with him.

black crimes he stood accused (among which our invasion of his country would not appear the least) took a mortal alarm at the security we had provided for him. He was thunderstruck at the article in his favour, by which he was surrendered to his enemies. He never had the least notice of the treaty; and it was apprehended that he would fly to the protection of Hyder Ali, or some other, disposed or able to protect him. He was therefore not left without comfort; for Mr. Anderson did him the favour to send a special messenger, desiring him to be of good cheer and to fear nothing. And his old enemy, Scindia, at our request, sent him a message equally well calculated to quiet his apprehensions.

By the same treaty the Guickwar was to come again, with no better security, under the dominion of the Maratta state. As to the Rana of Gohud, a long negotiation depended for giving him up. At first this was refused by Mr. Hastings with great indignation; at another stage it was admitted as proper, because he had shewn himself a most perfidious person. But at length a method of reconciling these extremes was found out, by contriving one of the usual articles in his favour. What I believe will appear beyond all belief, Mr. Anderson exchanged the final ratifications of that treaty by which the Rana was nominally secured in his possessions, in the camp of the Maratta chief, Scindia, whilst he was (really, and not nominally) battering the castle of Gualior, which we had given, agreeably to treaty, to this deluded ally. Scindia had already reduced the town; and was at the very time, by various detachments, reducing, one after another, the fortresses of our protected ally, as well as in the act of chastising all the Rajahs who had assisted Colonel Camac in his invasion.[1] I

1. Colonel Jacob Camac had led a British expedition against Scindia and had taken the fortress of Gualior from him. It was then given to the Rana, but when Scindia switched sides and joined the British, he was allowed to retake the fortress.

have seen in a letter from Calcutta, that the Rana of Gohud's agent would have represented these hostilities (which went hand in hand with the protecting treaty) to Mr. Hastings; but he was not admitted to his presence.

In this manner the Company has acted with their allies in the Maratta war. But they did not rest here: the Marattas were fearful lest the persons delivered to them by that treaty should attempt to escape into the British territories, and thus might elude the punishment intended for them, and by reclaiming the treaty, might stir up new disturbances. To prevent this, they desired an article to be inserted in the supplemental treaty, to which they had the ready consent of Mr. Hastings and the rest of the Company's representatives in Bengal. It was this, "That the English and Maratta governments mutually agree not to afford refuge to any *chiefs, merchants, or other persons,* flying for protection to the territories of the other." This was readily assented to, and assented to without any exception whatever, in favour of our surrendered allies. On their part a reciprocity was stipulated which was not unnatural for a government like the Company's to ask; a government, conscious that many subjects had been, and would in future, be driven to fly from its jurisdiction.

To complete the system of pacific intention and public faith, which predominate in these treaties, Mr. Hastings fairly resolved to put all peace, except on the terms of absolute conquest, wholly out of his own power. For, by an article in this second treaty with Scindia, he binds the Company not to make any peace with Tippoo Saheb, without the consent of the Peishwa of the Marattas; and binds Scindia to him by a reciprocal engagement. The treaty between France and England obliges us mutually to withdraw our forces, if our allies in India do not accede to the peace within four months; Mr. Hastings's treaty obliges us to continue the war as long as the Peishwa thinks fit. We are now in that happy situation, that the breach of the treaty with France, or the violation of that with the Marattas, is inevitable; and we have only to take our choice.

My third assertion, relative to the abuse made of the right of war and peace is, that there are none who have ever confided in us who have not been utterly ruined. The examples I have given of Ragonaut Row, of Guickwar, of the Ranah of Gohud, are recent. There is proof more than enough in the condition of the Mogul; in the slavery and indigence of the Nabob of Oude; the exile of the Rajah of Benares; the beggary of the Nabob of Bengal; the undone and captive condition of the Rajah and kingdom of Tanjour; the destruction of the Polygars; and lastly, in the destruction of the Nabob of Arcot himself, who when his dominions were invaded was found entirely destitute of troops, provisions, stores, and (as he asserts) of money, being a million in debt to the Company, and four millions to others; the many millions which he had extorted from so many extirpated princes and their desolated countries having (as he has frequently hinted) been expended for the ground-rent of his mansion-house in an alley in the suburbs of Madras. Compare the condition of all these princes with the power and authority of all the Maratta states; with the independence and dignity of the Soubah of the Decan; and the mighty strength, the resources, and the manly struggle of Hyder Ali; and then the House will discover the effects, on every power in India, of an easy confidence, or of a rooted distrust in the faith of the Company.

These are some of my reasons, grounded on the abuse of the external political trust of that body, for thinking myself not only justified but bound to declare against those chartered rights which produce so many wrongs. I should deem myself the wickedest of men, if any vote of mine could contribute to the continuance of so great an evil.

Now, Sir, according to the plan I proposed, I shall take notice of the Company's internal government, as it is exercised first on the dependent provinces, and then as it affects those under the direct and immediate authority of that body. And here, Sir, before I enter into the spirit of their interior government, permit me to observe to you, upon a few of the many lines of difference which are to be found between the vices of the Company's government, and those of the conquerors who preceded us in India; that we may be enabled a little the better to see our way in an attempt to the necessary reformation.

The several irruptions of Arabs, Tartars, and Persians, into India were, for the greater part, ferocious, bloody, and wasteful in the extreme: our entrance into the dominion of that country was, as generally, with small comparative effusion of blood; being introduced by various frauds and delusions, and by taking advantage of the incurable, blind, and senseless animosity, which the several country powers bear towards each other, rather than by open force. But the difference in favour of the first conquerors is this; the Asiatic conquerors very soon abated of their ferocity, because they made the conquered country their own. They rose or fell with the rise or fall of the territory they lived in. Fathers there deposited the hopes of their posterity; and children there beheld the monuments of their fathers. Here their lot was finally cast, and it is the natural wish of all, that their lot should not be cast in a bad land. Poverty, sterility, and desolation, are not a recreating prospect to the eye of man; and there are very few who can bear to grow old among the curses of a whole people. If their passion or their avarice drove the Tartar lords to acts of rapacity or tyranny, there was time enough, even in the short life of man, to bring round the ill effects of an abuse of power upon the power itself. If hoards were made by violence and tyranny, they were still domestic hoards; and domestic profusion, or the rapine of a more powerful and prodigal hand, restored them to the people. With many disorders, and with few political checks upon power, Nature had still fair play; the sources of acquisition were not dried up; and therefore the trade, the manufactures, and the commerce of the country flourished. Even avarice and usury itself operated, both for the preservation and the employment of national wealth. The husbandman and manufacturer paid heavy interest, but then they augmented the fund from whence they were again to borrow. Their resources were dearly bought, but they were sure; and the general stock of the community grew by the general effort.

But under the English government all this order is reversed. The Tartar invasion was mischievous; but it is our protection that destroys India. It was their enmity, but it is our friendship. Our conquest there, after twenty years, is as crude as it was the first day. The natives scarcely know what it is to see the grey head of an Englishman. Young men (boys almost) govern there, without society, and without sympathy with the natives. They have no more social habits with the people, than if they still resided in England; nor indeed any species of intercourse but that which is necessary to making a sudden fortune, with a view to a remote settlement. Animated with all the avarice of age, and all the impetuosity of youth, they roll in one after another; wave after wave; and there is nothing before the eyes of the natives but an endless, hopeless prospect of new flights of birds of prey and passage, with appetites continually renewing for a food that is continually wasting. Every rupee of profit made by an Englishman is lost for ever to India. With us are no retributory superstitions, by which a foundation of charity compensates, through ages, to the poor, for the rapine and injustice of a day. With us no pride erects stately monuments which repair the mischiefs which pride had produced, and which adorn a country out of its own spoils. England has erected no churches, no hospitals,[1] no palaces, no schools; England has built no bridges,

1. A footnote in the original publication remarks, "The paltry foundation at Calcutta is scarcely worth naming as an exception."

made no high roads, cut no navigations, dug out no reservoirs. Every other conqueror of every other description has left some monument, either of state or beneficence, behind him. Were we to be driven out of India this day, nothing would remain, to tell that it had been possessed, during the inglorious period of our dominion, by any thing better than the ouran-outang or the tiger.

There is nothing in the boys we send to India worse than the boys whom we are whipping at school, or that we see trailing a pike, or bending over a desk at home. But as English youth in India drink the intoxicating draught of authority and dominion before their heads are able to bear it, and as they are full grown in fortune long before they are ripe in principle, neither nature nor reason have any opportunity to exert themselves for remedy of the excesses of their premature power. The consequences of their conduct, which in good minds, (and many of theirs are probably such) might produce penitence or amendment, are unable to pursue the rapidity of their flight. Their prey[1] is lodged in England; and the cries of India are given to seas and winds, to be blown about, in every breaking up of the monsoon, over a remote and unhearing ocean. In India all the vices operate by which sudden fortune is acquired; in England are often displayed, by the same persons,[2] the virtues which dispense hereditary wealth. Arrived in England, the destroyers of the nobility and gentry of a whole kingdom will find the best company in this nation, at a board of elegance and hospitality. Here the manufacturer and husbandman will bless the just and punctual hand, that in India has torn the cloth from the loom, or wrested the scanty portion of rice and salt from the peasant of Bengal, or wrung from him the very opium in which

1. Booty.

2. The English "nabobs," so called because of the wealth that they brought back from India.

he forgot his oppressions and his oppressor. They marry into your families; they enter into your senate; they ease your estates by loans; they raise their value by demand; they cherish and protect your relations which lie heavy on your patronage; and there is scarcely an house in the kingdom that does not feel some concern and interest that makes all reform of our eastern government appear officious and disgusting; and, on the whole, a most discouraging attempt. In such an attempt you hurt those who are able to return kindness or to resent injury. If you succeed, you save those who cannot so much as give you thanks. All these things shew the difficulty of the work we have on hand: but they shew its necessity too. Our Indian government is in its best state a grievance. It is necessary that the correctives should be uncommonly vigorous; and the work of men sanguine, warm, and even impassioned in the cause. But it is an arduous thing to plead against abuses of a power which originates from your own country, and affects those whom we are used to consider as strangers.

I shall certainly endeavour to modulate myself to this temper; though I am sensible that a cold style of describing actions which appear to me in a very affecting light, is equally contrary to the justice due to the people, and to all genuine human feelings about them. I ask pardon of truth and nature for this compliance. But I shall be very sparing of epithets either to persons or things. It has been said (and, with regard to one of them, with truth) that Tacitus and Machiavel, by their cold way of relating enormous crimes, have in some sort appeared not to disapprove them; that they seem a sort of professors of the art of tyranny, and that they corrupt the minds of their readers by not expressing the detestation and horror that naturally belong to horrible and detestable proceedings. But we are in general, Sir, so little acquainted with Indian details; the instruments of oppression under which the people suffer are so hard to be understood; and even the very names of the sufferers are so uncouth and strange to our ears, that it is very difficult for our sympathy to fix upon these objects. I am sure that some of us have come down stairs from the committee-room, with impressions on our minds, which to us were the inevitable results of our discoveries, yet if we should venture to express ourselves in the proper language of our sentiments, to other gentlemen not at all prepared to enter into the cause of them, nothing could appear more harsh and dissonant, more violent and unaccountable, than our language and behaviour. All these circumstances are not, I confess, very favourable to the idea of our attempting to govern India at all. But there we are; there we are placed by the Sovereign Disposer: and we must do the best we can in our situation. The situation of man is the preceptor of his duty.

Upon the plan which I laid down, and to which I beg leave to return, I was considering the conduct of the Company to those nations which are indirectly subject to their authority. The most considerable of the dependent princes is the Nabob of Oude. My Right Honourable friend, to whom we owe the remedial bills on your table, has already pointed out to you, in one of the Reports, the condition of that prince, and as it stood in the time he alluded to. I shall only add a few circumstances that may tend to awaken some sense of the manner in which the condition of the people is affected by that of the prince, and involved in it; and to shew you, that when we talk of the sufferings of princes, we do not lament the oppression of individuals; and that in these cases the high and the low suffer together.

In the year 1779 the Nabob of Oude represented, through the British resident at his court, that the number of Company's troops stationed in his dominions was a main cause of his distress; and that all those which he was not bound by treaty to maintain should be withdrawn, as they had greatly diminished his revenue, and impoverished his country. I will read you, if you please, a few extracts from these representations.

He states "that the country and cultivation are abandoned; and this year in particular, from the excessive drought of the season, deductions of many lacks[1] having been allowed to the farmers,[2] who are still left unsatisfied"; and then he proceeds with a long detail of his own distress, and that of his family, and all his dependants; and adds, "that the new-raised brigade is not only quite useless to my government, but is moreover the cause of much loss, both in revenues and customs. The detached body of troops under European officers bring nothing *but confusion to the affairs of my government, and are entirely their own masters.*" Mr. Middleton,[3] Mr. Hastings's confidential Resident, vouches for the truth of this representation in its fullest extent. "I am concerned to confess, that there is too good ground for this plea. *The misfortune has been general throughout the whole of the Vizier's* [the Nabob of Oude] *dominions,* obvious to every body; and so *fatal* have been its consequences, that no person, of either credit or character, would enter into engagements with government for farming the country." He then proceeds to give strong instances of the general calamity, and its effects.

It was now to be seen what steps the governor general and council took for the relief of this distressed country, long labouring under the vexations of men, and now stricken by the hand of God. The case of a general famine is known to relax the severity even of the most rigorous government. Mr. Hastings does not deny, or shew the least doubt of the fact. The representation is humble, and almost abject. On

1. One lack (lakh) = 100,000 units; thus a lack of rupees is 100,000 rupees. On p. 165 below, Burke mentions transactions in which the value of the rupee is taken as two shillings and one pence.

2. Tax farmers, to whom the collection of the revenue was sold in return for a stipulated sum to be turned over to the government. Because of the drought and the consequent drop in the revenue, the sum they owed was reduced by many lacks of rupees.

3. Nathaniel Middleton, on whom see note 2 on p. 150.

this representation from a great prince, of the distress of his subjects, Mr. Hastings falls into a violent passion; such as (it seems) would be unjustifiable in any one who speaks of any part of *his* conduct. He declares "that the *demands,* the *tone* in which they were asserted, and the *season* in which they were made, are all equally alarming, and appear to him to require an adequate degree of firmness in this board, in *opposition* to them." He proceeds to deal out very unreserved language, on the person and character of the Nabob and his ministers. He declares, that in a division between him and the Nabob, "*the strongest must decide.*" With regard to the urgent and instant necessity, from the failure of the crops, he says, "that *perhaps* expedients *may be found* for affording a *gradual* relief from the burthen of which he so heavily complains, and it shall be my endeavour to seek them out": and, lest he should be suspected of too much haste to alleviate sufferings, and to remove violence, he says, "that these must be *gradually* applied, and their complete *effect* may be *distant;* and this I conceive *is all* he can claim of right."

This complete effect of his lenity is distant indeed. Rejecting this demand (as he calls the Nabob's abject supplication) he attributes it, as he usually does all things of the kind, to the division in their government; and says, "this is a powerful motive with *me* (however inclined I might be, *upon any other occasion,* to yield to some *part* of his demand) to give them an *absolute and unconditional refusal* upon the present; and even *to bring to punishment, if my influence can produce that effect, those incendiaries who have endeavoured to make themselves the instruments of division between us.*"

Here, Sir, is much heat and passion; but no more consideration of the distress of the country, from a failure of the means of subsistence, and (if possible) the worse evil of an useless and licentious soldiery, than if they were the most contemptible of all trifles. A letter is written in consequence, in such a style of lofty despotism, as I believe has hitherto been unexampled and unheard of in the records of the East. The troops were continued. The *gradual* relief, whose effect was to be so *distant,* has *never* been substantially and beneficially applied—and the country is ruined.

Mr. Hastings, two years after, when it was too late, saw the absolute necessity of a removal of the intolerable grievance of this licentious soldiery, which, under a pretence of defending it, held the country under military execution. A new treaty and arrangement, according to the pleasure of Mr. Hastings, took place; and this new treaty was broken in the old manner, in every essential article. The soldiery were again sent, and again set loose. The effect of all his manoeuvres, from which it seems he was sanguine enough to entertain hopes, upon the state of the country, he himself informs us, "the event has proved the *reverse* of these hopes, and *accumulation of distress, debasement, and dissatisfaction* to the Nabob, and *disappointment and disgrace to me.*—Every measure [which he had himself proposed] has been *so conducted* as to give him cause of displeasure; there are no officers established by which his affairs could be regularly conducted; mean, incapable, and indigent men have been appointed. A number of the districts without authority, and without the means of personal protection; some of them have been murdered by the Zemindars, and those Zemindars, instead of punishment, have been permitted to retain their Zemindaries, with independent authority; *all* the other Zemindars suffered to rise up in rebellion, and to insult the authority of the Sircar,[1] without any attempt made to suppress them; and the Company's debt, instead of being discharged by the assignments and extraordinary sources of money provided for that *purpose, is likely to exceed even the amount at which it stood at the time in which the arrangement with his Excellency was concluded.*" The

1. A subdivision of a province for the collection of the revenue or, as here, the title of the administrator of the district.

House will smile at the resource on which the Directors take credit as such a certainty in their curious account.

This is Mr. Hastings's own narrative of the effects of his own settlement. This is the state of the country which we have been told is in perfect peace and order; and, what is curious, he informs us, that *every part of this was foretold to him in the order and manner in which it happened,* at the very time he made his arrangement of men and measures.

The invariable course of the Company's policy is this: Either they set up some prince too odious to maintain himself without the necessity of their assistance; or they soon render him odious, by making him the instrument of their government. In that case troops are bountifully sent to him to maintain his authority. That he should have no want of assistance, a civil gentleman, called a Resident, is kept at his court, who, under pretence of providing duly for the pay of these troops, gets assignments on the revenue into his hands. Under his provident management, debts soon accumulate; new assignments are made for these debts; until, step by step, the whole revenue, and with it the whole power of the country, is delivered into his hands. The military do not behold without a virtuous emulation the moderate gains of the civil department. They feel that, in a country driven to habitual rebellion by the civil government, the military is necessary; and they will not permit their services to go unrewarded. Tracts of country are delivered over to their discretion. Then it is found proper to convert their commanding officers into farmers of revenue. Thus, between the well paid civil, and well rewarded military establishment, the situation of the natives may be easily conjectured. The authority of the regular and lawful government is every where and in every point extinguished. Disorders and violences arise; they are repressed by other disorders and other violences. Wherever the collectors of the revenue, and the farming colonels and majors move, ruin is about them, rebellion before and behind them. The people in crowds fly out of the country; and the frontier is guarded by lines of troops, not to exclude an enemy, but to prevent the escape of the inhabitants.

By these means, in the course of not more than four or five years, this once opulent and flourishing country, which, by the accounts given in the Bengal consultations, yielded more than three crore of Sicca rupees, that is, above three millions sterling, annually, is reduced, as far as I can discover, in a matter purposely involved in the utmost perplexity, to less than one million three hundred thousand pounds, and that exacted by every mode of rigour that can be devised. To complete the business, most of the wretched remnants of this revenue are mortgaged, and delivered into the hands of the usurers at Benares (for there alone are to be found some lingering remains of the ancient wealth of these regions) at an interest of near *thirty per cent. per annum.*

The revenues in this manner failing, they seized upon the estates of every person of eminence in the country, and, under the name of *resumption,* confiscated their property. I wish, Sir, to be understood universally and literally, when I assert, that there is not left one man of property and substance for his rank, in the whole of these provinces, in provinces which are nearly the extent of England and Wales taken together. Not one landholder, not one banker, not one merchant, not one even of those who usually perish last, the *ultimum moriens*[1] in a ruined state, no one farmer of revenue.

One country for a while remained, which stood as an island in the midst of the grand waste of the Company's dominion. My Right Honourable friend, in his admirable speech on moving the bill, just touched the situation, the offences, and the punishment, of a native prince, called Fizulla Khân. This man, by policy and force, had protected himself from the general extirpation of the Rohilla chiefs. He was

1. The last one to die.

secured (if that were any security) by a treaty. It was stated to you, as it was stated by the enemies of that unfortunate man—"that the whole of his country *is* what the whole country of the Rohillas *was,* cultivated like a garden, without one neglected spot in it." Another accuser says, "Fyzoolah Khan though a bad soldier [that is the true source of his misfortune] has approved himself a good aumil;[1] having, it is supposed, in the course of a few years, at least *doubled* the population, and revenue of his country." In another part of the correspondence he is charged with making his country an asylum for the oppressed peasants, who fly from the territories of Oude. The improvement of his revenue, arising from this single crime, (which Mr. Hastings considers as tantamount to treason) is stated at an hundred and fifty thousand pounds a year.

Dr. Swift somewhere says,[2] that he who could make two blades of grass grow where but one grew before, was a greater benefactor to the human race than all the politicians that ever existed. This prince, who would have been deified by antiquity, who would have been ranked with Osiris, and Bacchus, and Ceres,[3] and the divinities most propitious to men, was, for those very merits, by name attacked by the Company's government, as a cheat, a robber, a traitor. In the same breath in which he was accused as a rebel, he was ordered at once to furnish 5,000 horse. On delay, or (according to the technical phrase, when any remonstrance is made to them) "*on evasion,*" he was declared a violator of treaties, and every thing he had was to be taken from him. Not one word, however, of horse in this treaty.

The territory of this Fizulla Khân, Mr. Speaker, is less than the county of Norfolk. It is an inland country, full seven hun-

1. A revenue administrator.

2. Jonathan Swift in *Gulliver's Travels,* part 2, chap. 7.

3. Egyptian god who protected the dead, Greek god of wine, Roman goddess of agriculture.

dred miles from any sea port, and not distinguished for any one considerable branch of manufacture whatsoever. From this territory a punctual payment was made to the British Resident of £.150,000 sterling a year. The demand of cavalry, without a shadow or decent pretext of right, amounted to three hundred thousand a year more, at the lowest computation; and it is stated, by the last person sent to negotiate, as a demand of little use, if it could be complied with; but that the compliance was impossible, as it amounted to more than his territories could supply, if there had been no other demand upon him—four hundred and fifty thousand pounds a year from an inland country not so large as Norfolk!

The thing most extraordinary was to hear the culprit defend himself from the imputation of his virtues, as if they had been the blackest offences. He extenuated the superior cultivation of his country. He denied its population. He endeavoured to prove that he had often sent back the poor peasant that sought shelter with him. I can make no observation on this.

After a variety of extortions and vexations, too fatiguing to you, too disgusting to me, to go through with, they found "that they ought to be in a better state to warrant forcible means"; they therefore contented themselves with a gross sum of 150,000 pounds, for their present demand. They offered him indeed an indemnity from their exactions in future, for three hundred thousand pounds more. But he refused to buy their securities; pleading (probably with truth) his poverty: but if the plea were not founded, in my opinion very wisely; not choosing to deal any more in that dangerous commodity of the Company's faith, and thinking it better to oppose distress and unarmed obstinacy to uncoloured exaction, than to subject himself to be considered as a cheat, if he should make a treaty in the least beneficial to himself. Thus they executed an exemplary punishment on Fizulla Khân for the culture of his country. But, conscious that the prevention of evils is the great object of all good regulation, they deprived him of the means of encreasing that criminal cultivation in future, by exhausting his coffers; and, that the population of his country should no more be a standing reproach and libel on the Company's government, they bound him, by a positive engagement, not to afford any shelter whatsoever to the farmers and labourers who should seek refuge in his territories, from the exactions of the British Residents in Oude. When they had done all this effectually, they gave him a full and complete acquittance from all charges of rebellion, or of any intention to rebel, or of his having originally had any interest in, or any means of rebellion.

These intended rebellions are one of the Company's standing resources. When money has been thought to be heaped up any where, its owners are universally accused of rebellion, until they are acquitted of their money and their treasons at once. The money once taken, all accusation, trial, and punishment ends. It is so settled a resource, that I rather wonder how it comes to be omitted in the Directors account; but I take it for granted this omission will be supplied in their next edition. The Company stretched this resource to the full extent, when they accused two old women, in the remotest corner of India (who could have no possible view or motive to raise disturbances) of being engaged in rebellion, with an intent to drive out the English nation in whose protection, purchased by money and secured by treaty, rested the sole hope of their existence. But the Company wanted money, and the old women *must* be guilty of a plot. They were accused of rebellion, and they were convicted of wealth. Twice had great sums been extorted from them, and as often had the British faith guaranteed the remainder. A body of British troops, with one of the military farmers general at their head, was sent to seize upon the castle in which these helpless women resided. Their chief eunuchs, who were their agents, their guardians, protectors, persons of high rank according to the Eastern manners and of great trust, were thrown into dungeons, to make them discover their hidden treasures; and there they lie at present. The lands assigned for the maintenance of the women were seized and confiscated. Their jewels and effects were taken, and set up to a pretended auction in an obscure place, and bought at such a price as the gentlemen thought proper to give. No account has ever been transmitted of the articles or produce of this sale. What money was obtained is unknown, or what terms were stipulated for the maintenance of these despoiled and forlorn creatures; for by some particulars it appears as if an engagement of the kind was made.

Let me here remark, once for all, that though the act of 1773 requires that an account of all proceedings should be diligently transmitted, that this, like all the other injunctions of the law, is totally despised; and that half at least of the most important papers are intentionally withheld.

I wish you, Sir, to advert particularly, in this transaction, to the quality and the numbers of the persons spoiled, and the instrument by whom that spoil was made. These ancient matrons called the Begums or Princesses, were of the first birth and quality in India, the one mother, the other wife, of the late Nabob of Oude, Sujah Dowlah, a prince possessed of extensive and flourishing dominions, and the second man in the Mogul empire. This prince (suspicious, and not unjustly suspicious, of his son and successor) at his death committed his treasures and his family to the British faith. That family and household, consisted of *two thousand women;* to which were added two other seraglios of near kindred, and said to be extremely numerous, and (as I am well informed) of about fourscore of the Nabob's children, with all the eunuchs, the ancient servants, and a multitude of the dependants of his splendid court. These were all to be provided, for present maintenance and future establishment, from the lands assigned as dower, and from the treasures which he left to these matrons, in trust for the whole family.

So far as to the objects of the spoil. The *instrument* chosen by Mr. Hastings to despoil the relict of Sujah Dowlah was *her own son,* the reigning Nabob of Oude. It was the pious hand of a son that was selected to tear from his mother and grandmother the provision of their age, the maintenance of his brethren, and of all the ancient household of his father. [Here a laugh from some young members]—The laugh is *seasonable,* and the occasion decent and proper.

By the last advices something of the sum extorted remained unpaid. The women in despair refuse to deliver more, unless their lands are restored and their ministers released from prison: but Mr. Hastings and his council, steady to their point, and consistent to the last in their conduct, write to the Resident to stimulate the son to accomplish the filial acts he had brought so near to their perfection. "We desire," say they in their letter to the Resident (written so late as March last) "that you will inform us if any, and what means, have been taken for recovering the balance due from the Begum [Princess] at Fizabad; and that, if necessary, you *recommend* it to the Vizier to enforce *the most effectual means* for that purpose."

What their effectual means of enforcing demands on women of high rank and condition are, I shall shew you, Sir, in a few minutes; when I represent to you another of these plots and rebellions, which *always,* in India, though so *rarely* any where else, are the offspring of an easy condition, and hoarded riches.

Benares is the capital city of the Indian religion. It is regarded as holy by a particular and distinguished sanctity; and the Gentûs[1] in general think themselves as much obliged to visit it once in their lives as the Mahometans to perform their pilgrimage to Mecca. By this means that city grew great in commerce and opulence; and so effectually was it secured by the pious veneration of that people, that in all wars and in all violences of power, there was so sure an asylum, both

1. Hindus.

for poverty and wealth, (as it were under a divine protection) that the wisest laws and best assured free constitution could not better provide for the relief of the one, or the safety of the other; and this tranquillity influenced to the greatest degree the prosperity of all the country, and the territory of which it was the capital. The interest of money there was not more than half the usual rate in which it stood in all other places. The reports have fully informed you of the means and of the terms in which this city and the territory called Gazipour, of which it was the head, came under the sovereignty of the East India Company.

If ever there was a subordinate dominion pleasantly circumstanced to the superior power, it was this; a large rent or tribute, to the amount of two hundred and sixty thousand pounds a year, was paid in monthly instalments with the punctuality of a dividend at the Bank. If ever there was a prince who could not have an interest in disturbances, it was its sovereign, the Rajah Cheit Sing. He was in possession of the capital of his religion, and a willing revenue was paid by the devout people who resorted to him from all parts. His sovereignty and his independence, except his tribute, was secured by every tie. His territory was not much less than half of Ireland, and displayed in all parts a degree of cultivation, ease, and plenty, under his frugal and paternal management, which left him nothing to desire, either for honour or satisfaction.

This was the light in which this country appeared to almost every eye. But Mr. Hastings beheld it askance. Mr. Hastings tells us that it was *reported* of this Cheit Sing, that his father left him a million sterling, and that he made annual accessions to the hoard. Nothing could be so obnoxious to indigent power. So much wealth could not be innocent. The House is fully acquainted with the unfounded and unjust requisitions which were made upon this prince. The question has been most ably and conclusively cleared up in one of the

Reports of the Select Committee, and in an answer of the Court of Directors[1] to an extraordinary publication against them by their servant, Mr. Hastings. But I mean to pass by these exactions, as if they were perfectly just and regular; and, having admitted them, I take what I shall now trouble you with, only as it serves to shew the spirit of the Company's government, the mode in which it is carried on, and the maxims on which it proceeds.

Mr. Hastings, from whom I take the doctrine, endeavours to prove that Cheit Sing was no sovereign prince; but a mere Zemindar or common subject, holding land by rent.[2] If this be granted to him, it is next to be seen under what terms he is of opinion such a land-holder, that is a British subject, holds his life and property under the Company's government. It is proper to understand well the doctrines of the person whose administration has lately received such distinguished approbation from the Company. His doctrine is—"that the Company, or the *person delegated by it,* holds *an absolute* authority over such Zemindars;—that he [such a subject] owes *an implicit* and *unreserved* obedience to its authority, at the *forfeiture* even of his *life* and *property,* at the DISCRETION of those who held *or fully represented* the sovereign authority;—and that *these* rights are *fully* delegated *to him* Mr. Hastings."

Such is a British governor's idea of the condition of a great Zemindar holding under a British authority; and this kind of authority he supposes fully delegated to *him;* though no such delegation appears in any commission, instruction, or act of parliament. At his *discretion* he may demand, of the

1. Earlier in 1783, the Court of Directors of the East India Company had censured Hastings for his treatment of the Rajah of Benares. Hastings published the letter to the Court in which he defended his conduct, and the Court published the answer to it referred to here.

2. "In this and the following paragraphs Burke made extensive use of *A Narrative of the Insurrection which happened in the Zemindary of Benaris,* which Hastings had published in Calcutta in 1782." *W&S* 5:413, n. 5.

substance of any Zemindar over and above his rent or tribute, even what he pleases, with a sovereign authority; and if he does not yield an *implicit unreserved* obedience to all his commands, he forfeits his lands, his life, and his property, at Mr. Hastings's *discretion.* But, extravagant and even frantic as these positions appear, they are less so than what I shall now read to you; for he asserts, that if any one should urge an exemption from more than a stated payment, or should consider the deeds, which passed between him and the board, "as bearing *the quality and force* of a treaty between equal states," he says, "that such an opinion is itself criminal to the state of which he is a subject; and that he was himself amenable to its justice, if he gave *countenance* to such a *belief.*" Here is a new species of crime invented, that of countenancing a belief—but a belief of what? A belief of that which the Court of Directors, Hastings's masters, and a Committee of this House, have decided as this prince's indisputable right.[1]

But supposing the Rajah of Benares to be a mere subject, and that subject a criminal of the highest form; let us see what course was taken by an upright English magistrate. Did he cite this culprit before his tribunal? Did he make a charge? Did he produce witnesses? These are not forms; they are parts of substantial and eternal justice. No, not a word of all this. Mr. Hastings concludes him, *in his own mind,* to be guilty; he makes this conclusion on reports, on hear-says, on appearances, on rumours, on conjectures, on presumptions; and even these never once hinted to the party, nor publicly to any human being, till the whole business was done.

But the governor tells you his motive for this extraordinary proceeding; so contrary to every mode of justice towards either a prince or a subject, fairly and without disguise; and

1. Hastings contested this right, asserting that when Benares came under the Company's control, the Rajah's possessions were held from the Company as the sovereign authority.

he puts into your hands the key of his whole conduct: "I will suppose, for a moment, that I have acted with unwarrantable rigour towards Cheit Sing, and even with injustice.—Let my MOTIVE be consulted. I left Calcutta, impressed with a belief that *extraordinary means* were necessary, and those exerted with a *steady hand,* to preserve the Company's *interests from sinking under the accumulated weight which oppressed them.* I saw a *political necessity* for curbing the *overgrown* power of a great member of their dominion, and for *making it contribute to the relief of their pressing exigencies.*" This is plain speaking; after this, it is no wonder that the Rajah's wealth and his offence, the necessities of the judge, and the opulence of the delinquent, are never separated, through the whole of Mr. Hastings's apology. "The justice and *policy* of exacting *a large pecuniary mulct.*" The resolution "*to draw from his guilt* the means *of relief to the Company's distresses.*" His determination "to make him *pay largely* for his pardon, or to execute a severe vengeance for past delinquency." That "as his *wealth was great,* and the *Company's exigencies* pressing, he thought it a measure of justice and policy to exact from him a large pecuniary mulct for *their relief.*" "The sum (says Mr. Wheler,[1] bearing evidence, at his desire, to his intentions) to which the governor declared his resolution to extend his fine, was forty or fifty lacks, *that is four or five hundred thousand pounds;* and that if he refused, he was to be removed from his zemindary entirely; or by taking possession of his forts, to obtain, *out of the treasure deposited in them,* the above sum for the Company."

Crimes so convenient, crimes so politic, crimes so necessary, crimes so alleviating of distress, can never be wanting to those who use no process, and who produce no proofs.

But there is another serious part (what is not so?) in this affair. Let us suppose that the power, for which Mr. Has-

1. Edward Wheler, who was sent to India (he arrived in 1777) to take Colonel Monson's place on the Supreme Council when the latter died.

tings contends, a power which no sovereign ever did, or ever can vest in any of his subjects, namely, his own sovereign authority, to be conveyed by the act of parliament to any man or body of men whatsoever; it certainly was never given to Mr. Hastings. The powers given by the act of 1773 were formal and official; they were given, not to the governor general, but to the major vote of the board, as a board, on discussion amongst themselves, in their public character and capacity; and their acts in that character and capacity were to be ascertained by records and minutes of council. The despotic acts exercised by Mr. Hastings were done merely in his *private* character; and, if they had been moderate and just, would still be the acts of an usurped authority, and without any one of the legal modes of proceeding which could give him competence for the most trivial exertion of power. There was no proposition or deliberation whatsoever in council, no minute on record, by circulation or otherwise, to authorize his proceedings. No delegation of power to impose a fine, or to take any step to deprive the Rajah of Benares of his government, his property, or his liberty. The minutes of consultation assign to his journey a totally different object, duty, and destination. Mr. Wheler, at his desire, tells us long after, that he had a confidential conversation with him on various subjects, of which this was the principal, in which Mr. Hastings notified to him his secret intentions; "and that he *bespoke* his support of the measures which he intended to pursue towards him (the Rajah.)" This confidential discourse, and *bespeaking* of support, could give him no power, in opposition to an express act of parliament, and the whole tenor of the orders of the Court of Directors.

In what manner the powers thus usurped were employed, is known to the whole world. All the House knows, that the design on the Rajah proved as unfruitful as it was violent. The unhappy prince was expelled, and his more unhappy country was enslaved and ruined; but not a rupee was acquired.

Instead of treasure to recruit the Company's finances, wasted by their wanton wars and corrupt jobbs, they were plunged into a new war, which shook their power in India to its foundation; and, to use the governor's own happy simile, might have dissolved it like a magic structure, if the talisman had been broken.

But the success is no part of my consideration, who should think just the same of this business, if the spoil of one Rajah had been fully acquired, and faithfully applied to the destruction of twenty other Rajahs. Not only the arrest of the Rajah in his palace was unnecessary and unwarrantable, and calculated to stir up any manly blood which remained in his subjects; but the despotic style, and the extreme insolence of language and demeanour, used to a person of great condition among the politest people in the world, was intolerable. Nothing aggravates tyranny so much as contumely. *Quicquid superbia in contumeliis*[1] was charged by a great man of antiquity, as a principal head of offence against the governor general of that day. The unhappy people were still more insulted. A relation, but an *enemy* to the family, a notorious robber and villain, called Ussaun Sing, kept as a hawk in a mew, to fly upon this nation, was set up to govern there, instead of a prince honoured and beloved. But when the business of insult was accomplished, the revenue was too serious a concern to be entrusted to such hands. Another was set up in his place, as guardian to an infant.

But here, Sir, mark the effect of all these *extraordinary* means, of all this policy and justice. The revenues which had been hitherto paid with such astonishing punctuality, fell into arrear. The new prince guardian was deposed without ceremony; and with as little, cast into prison. The government of that once happy country has been in the utmost confusion

1. "Arrogance in insults," with which Cicero charged Verres, the governor of Sicily, in his speech *Contra Quintum Caecilium* 3.

ever since such good order was taken about it. But, to complete the contumely offered to this undone people, and to make them feel their servitude in all its degradation, and all its bitterness, the government of their sacred city, the government of that Benares which had been so respected by Persian and Tartar conquerors, though of the Mussulman persuasion, that, even in the plenitude of their pride, power, and bigotry, no magistrate of that sect entered the place, was now delivered over by English hands to a Mahometan; and an Ali Ibrahim Khân was introduced, under the Company's authority, with power of life and death, into the sanctuary of the Gentû religion.

After this, the taking off a slight payment, chearfully made by pilgrims to a chief of their own rites, was represented as a mighty benefit. It remains only to shew, through the conduct in this business, the spirit of the Company's government, and the respect they pay towards other prejudices not less regarded in the East than those of religion; I mean the reverence paid to the female sex in general, and particularly to women of high rank and condition. During the general confusion of the country of Gazypore, Panna, the mother of Cheit Sing, was lodged with her train in a castle called Bidgé Gur, in which were likewise deposited a large portion of the treasures of her son, or more probably her own. To whomsoever they belonged was indifferent; for, though no charge of rebellion was made on this woman (which was rather singular, as it would have cost nothing) they were resolved to secure her with her fortune. The castle was besieged by Major Popham.[1]

There was no great reason to apprehend that soldiers ill paid, that soldiers who thought they had been defrauded of their plunder on former services of the same kind, would

1. William Popham.

not have been sufficiently attentive to the spoil they were expressly come for; but the gallantry and generosity of the profession was justly suspected, as being likely to set bounds to military rapaciousness. The Company's first civil magistrate discovered the greatest uneasiness left the women should have any thing preserved to them. Terms, tending to put some restraint on military violence, were granted. He writes a letter to Mr. Popham, referring to some letter written before to the same effect, which I do not remember to have seen; but it shews his anxiety on this subject. Hear himself: "I think *every* demand she has made on you, except that of safety and respect to her person, is unreasonable. If the reports brought to me are true, your rejecting her offers, or *any negotiation,* would soon obtain you the fort upon your own terms. I apprehend she will attempt to *defraud the captors of a considerable part of their booty, by being suffered to retire without examination.* But this is your concern, not mine. I should *be very sorry* that your officers and soldiers lost *any* part of the reward to which they are so well entitled; but you must be the best judge of the *promised* indulgence to the Ranny: what you have engaged for I will certainly ratify; but as to suffering the Ranny[1] to hold the purgunna of Hurlich, or any other zemindary, without being subject to the authority of the Zemindar, *or any lands whatsoever,* or indeed making *any* condition with her for a *provision,* I will *never consent.*"

Here your governor stimulates a rapacious and licentious soldiery to the personal search of women, lest these unhappy creatures should avail themselves of the protection of their sex to secure any supply for their necessities; and he positively orders that no stipulation should be made for any provision for them. The widow and mother of a prince, well

1. Ranny, roughly correspondent to "queen," used here of the Rajah's mother.

informed of her miserable situation, and the cause of it, a woman of this rank became a suppliant to the domestic servant of Mr. Hastings (they are his own words that I read); "imploring his intercession, that she may be relieved *from the hardships and dangers of her presant situation;* and offering to surrender the fort, and the *treasure and valuable effects contained* in it, provided she can be assured *of safety and protection to her person and honour,* and to that of her family and attendants." He is so good as to consent to this, "provided she surrenders every thing of value, with the reserve *only* of such articles as *you* shall think *necessary* to her condition, or as you *yourself* shall be disposed to indulge her with.—But should she refuse to execute the promise she has made, or delay it beyond the term of twenty-four hours, it is *my positive* injunction, that you immediately put a stop to any further intercourse or negociation with her, and on no pretext renew it. If she disappoints or *trifles* with me, after I have subjected *my Duan*[1] to the disgrace of returning ineffectually, and of course myself to discredit, I shall consider it as a *wanton* affront and indignity *which I can never forgive;* nor will I grant her *any* conditions whatever, but leave her exposed *to those* dangers which she has chosen to risque, rather than trust to the clemency and generosity of our government. I think she cannot be ignorant of these consequences, and will not venture to incur them; and it is for this reason I place a dependance on her offers, and have consented to send my Duan to her." The dreadful secret hinted at by the merciful governor in the latter part of the letter, is well understood in India; where those who suffer corporeal indignities, generally expiate the offences of others with their own blood. However, in spite of all these,

1. The head financial minister of a Muslim state. In Bengal, a native servant in charge of the affairs of a house of business or a large domestic establishment; a steward or master of the household.

the temper of the military did, some way or other, operate. They came to terms which have never been transmitted. It appears that a fifteenth *per cent.* of the plunder was reserved to the captives, of which the unhappy mother of the prince of Benares was to have a share. This antient matron, born to better things [a laugh from certain young gentlemen]—I see no cause for this mirth. A good author of antiquity reckons among the calamities of his time, *Nobilissimarum faeminarum exilia et fugas.*[1] I say, Sir, this antient lady was compelled to quit her house with three hundred helpless women, and a multitude of children in her train; but the lower sort in the camp it seems could not be restrained. They did not forget the good lessons of the governor general. They were unwilling "to be defrauded of a considerable part of their booty, by suffering them to pass without examination." They examined them, Sir, with a vengeance, and the sacred protection of that awful character, Mr. Hastings's maitre d'hotel, could not secure them from insult and plunder. Here is Popham's narrative of the affair: "The Ranny came out of the fort, with her family and dependants, the 10th at night, owing to which such attention was not paid to her as I wished; and I am exceedingly sorry to inform you, that the *licentiousness of our followers was beyond the bounds of controul; for, notwithstanding all I could do, her people were plundered on the road of most of the things which they brought out of the fort, by which means one of the articles of surrender has been much infringed.* The distress I have felt upon this occasion cannot be expressed, and can only be allayed by a firm performance of the other articles of the treaty, which I shall make it my business to enforce.

"The suspicions which the officers had of treachery, and the delay made to our getting possession, had enraged them,

1. "The flight and exile of so many women of the highest rank." Tacitus *Agricola* 45.

as well as the troops, so much, that the treaty was at first regarded as void, but this determination was soon succeeded by pity and compassion for the unfortunate besieged." After this comes, in his due order, Mr. Hastings; who is full of sorrow and indignation, &c. &c. &c. according to the best and most authentic precedents established upon such occasions.

The women being thus disposed of, that is, completely despoiled, and pathetically lamented, Mr. Hastings at length recollected the great object of his enterprize, which, during his zeal lest the officers and soldiers should lose any part of their reward, he seems to have forgot; that is to say, "to draw from the Rajah's guilt the means of relief to the Company's distresses." This was to be the strong hold of his defence. This compassion to the Company, he knew by experience would sanctify a great deal of rigour towards the natives. But the military had distresses of their own, which they considered first. Neither Mr. Hastings's authority, nor his supplications, could prevail on them to assign a shilling to the claim he made on the part of the Company. They divided the booty amongst themselves. Driven from his claim he was reduced to petition for the spoil as a loan. But the soldiers were too wise to venture as a loan, what the borrower claimed as a right. In defiance of all authority, they shared amongst themselves about two hundred thousand pounds sterling, besides what had been taken from the women.

In all this there is nothing wonderful. We may rest assured, that when the maxims of any government establish among its resources extraordinary means, and those exerted with a strong hand, that strong hand will provide those extraordinary means for *itself*. Whether the soldiers had reason or not (perhaps much might be said for them) certain it is, the military discipline of India was ruined from that moment; and the same rage for plunder, the same contempt of subordination, which blasted all the hopes of extraordinary means from your strong hand at Benares, have very lately lost you an army in Mysore. This is visible enough from the accounts in the last Gazette.[1]

There is no doubt but that the country and city of Benares, now brought into the same order, will very soon exhibit, if it does not already display the same appearance with those countries and cities which are under better subjection. A great master, Mr. Hastings, has himself been at the pains of drawing a picture of one of these countries, I mean the province and city of Farruckabad. There is no reason to question his knowledge of the facts; and his authority (on this point at least) is above all exception, as well for the state of the country, as for the cause. In his minute of consultation, Mr. Hastings describes forcibly the consequences which arise from the degradation into which we have sunk the native government. "The total want (says he) of all order, regularity, or authority, in his (the Nabob of Farruckabad's) government, and to which, among other obvious causes, it may no doubt be owing that the country of Farruckabad is become *almost an entire waste, without cultivation or inhabitants;* that the capital, which, but a very short time ago, was distinguished as one of the most populous and opulent commercial cities in Hindostan, at present exhibits nothing but *scenes of the most wretched poverty, desolation, and misery;* and that the *Nabob himself,* tho' in the possession of a tract of country which, with only common care, is notoriously capable of yielding an annual revenue of between thirty and forty lacks, (three or four hundred thousand pounds) with *no military establishment* to maintain, scarcely commands *the means of a bare subsistance.*"

This is a true and unexaggerated picture, not only of Farruckabad, but of at least three-fourths of the country which we possess, or rather lay waste, in India. Now, Sir, the House

1. *The London Gazette* had reported that an army of the late Hyder Ali's kingdom of Mysore had defeated a British army after a British victory had led to disputes among the troops over plunder.

will be desirous to know for what purpose this picture was drawn. It was for a purpose, I will not say laudable, but necessary, that of taking the unfortunate Prince and his country out of the hands of a sequestrator[1] sent thither by the Nabob of Oude, the mortal enemy of the Prince thus ruined, and to protect him by means of a British Resident, who might carry his complaints to the superior Resident at Oude, or transmit them to Calcutta. But mark, how the reformer persisted in his reformation. The effect of the measure was better than was probably expected. The Prince began to be at ease; the country began to recover; and the revenue began to be collected. These were alarming circumstances. Mr. Hastings not only recalled the Resident, but he entered into a formal stipulation with the Nabob of Oude, never to send an English subject again to Farruckabad; and thus the country, described as you have heard by Mr. Hastings, is given up for ever to the very persons to whom he had attributed its ruin, that is to the Sezawals or sequestrators of the Nabob of Oude.

Such was the issue of the first attempt to relieve the distresses of the dependent provinces. I shall close what I have to say on the condition of the northern dependencies, with the effect of the last of these attempts. You will recollect, Sir, the account I have not long ago stated to you as given by Mr. Hastings, of the ruined condition of the destroyer of others, the Nabob of Oude, and of the recal, in consequence, of Hannay, Middleton, and Johnson.[2] When the first little sudden gust of passion against these gentlemen was spent, the sentiments of old friendship began to revive. Some healing

1. Sequestration was the practice of diverting the income of an estate, temporarily or permanently, from its owner to other persons or institutions. A sequestrator therefore had control of property on which others, such as creditors, had claims which he was to satisfy.

2. Colonel Alexander Hannay, chief British military collector in Oude; Nathaniel Middleton, the British Resident in Oude; and Robert Johnson, his deputy Resident.

conferences were held between them and the superior government. Mr. Hannay was permitted to return to Oude; but death prevented the further advantages intended for him, and the future benefits proposed for the country by the provident care of the council general.

These three gentlemen were accused of the grossest peculations. The Court of Directors were informed, by the governor general and council, that a severe enquiry would be instituted against the two survivors; and they requested that court to suspend its judgment, and to wait the event of their proceedings. But no enquiry has been instituted, nor any steps taken towards it. By means of the bland and conciliatory dispositions of the charter governors, and proper private explanations, the public enquiry has died away, the supposed peculators and destroyers of Oude repose in all security in the bosoms of their accusers; whilst others succeed to them to be instructed by their example.

It is only to complete the view I proposed of the conduct of the Company, with regard to the dependent provinces, that I shall say *any* thing at all of the Carnatic, which is the scene, if possible, of greater disorder than the northern provinces. Perhaps it were better to say of this center and metropolis of abuse, whence all the rest in India and in England diverge; from whence they are fed and methodized, what was said of Carthage—*de Carthagine satius est silere quam parum dicere.*[1] This country, in all its denominations, is about 46,000 square miles. It may be affirmed universally, that not one person of substance or property, landed, commercial, or monied, excepting two or three bankers, who are necessary deposits and distributors of the general spoil, is left in all that region. In that country the moisture, the bounty of Heaven, is given but at a certain season. Before the aera of our in-

1. "Of Carthage it is better to say nothing than to say too little." Sallust *Jugurthine War* 19.2.

fluence, the industry of man carefully husbanded that gift of God. The Gentûs preserved, with a provident and religious care, the precious deposit of the periodical rain in reservoirs, many of them works of royal grandeur; and from these, as occasion demanded, they fructified the whole country. To maintain these reservoirs, and to keep up an annual advance to the cultivators, for feed and cattle, formed a principal object of the piety and policy of the priests and rulers of the Gentû religion.

This object required a command of money; and there was no Pollam, or castle, which in the happy days of the Carnatic was without some hoard of treasure, by which the governors were enabled to combat with the irregularity of the seasons, and to resist or to buy off the invasion of an enemy. In all the cities were multitudes of merchants and bankers, for all occasions of monied assistance; and on the other hand, the native princes were in condition to obtain credit from them. The manufacturer was paid by the return of commodities, or by imported money, and not, as at present, in the taxes that had been originally exacted from his industry. In aid of casual distress, the country was full of choultries, which were inns and hospitals, where the traveller and the poor were relieved. All ranks of people had their place in the public concern, and their share in the common stock and common prosperity; but *the chartered rights of men,* and the right which it was thought proper to set up in the Nabob of Arcot, introduced a new system. It was their policy to consider hoards of money as crimes; to regard moderate rents as frauds on the sovereign; and to view, in the lesser princes, any claim of exemption from more than settled tribute, as an act of rebellion. Accordingly all the castles were, one after the other, plundered and destroyed. The native princes were expelled; the hospitals fell to ruin; the reservoirs of water went to decay; the merchants, bankers, and manufacturers disappeared; and sterility, indigence, and depopulation, overspread the face of these once flourishing provinces.

The Company was very early sensible of these mischiefs, and of their true cause. They gave precise orders, "that the native princes, called Polygars, should *not be extirpated.*—That the rebellion [so they choose to call it] of the Polygars, may (they fear) *with too much justice,* be attributed to the maladministration of the Nabob's collectors." That "they observe with concern, that their troops have been put to *disagreeable* services." They might have used a stronger expression without impropriety. But they make amends in another place. Speaking of the Polygars, the Directors say, that "it was repugnant to humanity to *force* them to such dreadful extremities *as they underwent.*" That some examples of severity *might* be necessary, "when they fell into the Nabob's hands," *and not by the destruction of the country.* "That *they fear* his government is *none of the mildest;* and that there is *great oppression* in collecting his revenues." They state, that the wars in which he has involved the Carnatic, had been a cause of its distresses. "That these distresses have been certainly great; but those by *the Nabob's oppressions* we believe *to be greater than all.*" Pray, Sir, attend to the reason for their opinion that the government of this their instrument is more calamitous to the country than the ravages of war. Because, say they, his oppressions are "*without intermission.*—The others are temporary; by all which *oppressions* we believe the Nabob has great wealth in store." From this store neither he nor they could derive any advantage whatsoever, upon the invasion of Hyder Ali in the hour of their greatest calamity and dismay.

It is now proper to compare these declarations with the Company's conduct. The principal reason which they assigned against the *extirpation* of the Polygars was, that the *weavers* were protected in their fortresses. They might have added, that the Company itself, which stung them to death, had been warmed in the bosom of these unfortunate princes: for, on the taking of Madras by the French, it was in their hospitable Pollams, that most of the inhabitants found refuge and protection. But, notwithstanding all these orders, reasons, and declarations, they at length gave an indirect sanction, and permitted the use of a very direct and irresistible force, to measures which they had, over and over again, declared to be false policy, cruel, inhuman, and oppressive. Having, however, forgot all attention to the princes and the people, they remembered that they had some sort of interest in the trade of the country; and it is matter of curiosity to observe the protection which they afforded to this their natural object.

Full of anxious cares on this head, they direct, "that in reducing the Polygars they (their servants)[1] were to be *cautious,* not to deprive the *weavers and manufacturers* of the protection they often met with in the strong holds of the Polygar countries"; and they write to their instrument, the Nabob of Arcot, concerning these poor people in a most pathetic strain. "We *entreat* your Excellency (say they) in particular, to make the manufacturers the object of your *tenderest care;* particularly when you *root out* the Polygars, you do not deprive the *weavers of the protection they enjoyed under them.*" When they root out the protectors in favour of the oppressor, they shew themselves religiously cautious of the rights of the protected. When they extirpate the shepherd and the shepherd's dogs, they piously recommend the helpless flock to the mercy, and even to the *tenderest care,* of the wolf. This is the uniform strain of their policy, strictly forbidding, and at the same time strenuously encouraging and enforcing, every measure that can ruin and desolate the country committed to their charge. After giving the Company's idea of the government of this their instrument, it may appear singular, but it is perfectly consistent with their system, that, besides wasting for him, at two different times, the most exquisite spot upon the earth, Tanjour, and all the adjacent countries, they have even voluntarily put their own territory, that is, a large and fine coun-

1. The East India Company's officials were formally called servants.

try adjacent to Madras, called their Jaghire,[1] wholly out of their protection; and have continued to farm their subjects, and their duties towards these subjects, to that very Nabob, whom they themselves constantly represent as an habitual oppressor, and a relentless tyrant. This they have done without any pretence of ignorance of the objects of oppression for which this prince has thought fit to become their renter; for he has again and again told them, that it is for the sole purpose of exercising authority he holds the Jaghire lands; and he affirms (and I believe with truth) that he pays more for that territory than the revenues yield. This deficiency he must make up from his other territories; and thus, in order to furnish the means of oppressing one part of the Carnatic, he is led to oppress all the rest.

The House perceives that the livery of the Company's government is uniform. I have described the condition of the countries indirectly, but most substantially, under the Company's authority. And now I ask, whether, with this map of misgovernment before me, I can suppose myself bound by my vote to continue, upon any principles of pretended public faith, the management of these countries in those hands. If I kept such a faith (which in reality is no better than a *fides latronum*)[2] with what is called the Company, I must break the faith, the covenant, the solemn, original, indispensable oath, in which I am bound, by the eternal frame and constitution of things,[3] to the whole human race.

As I have dwelt so long on these who are indirectly under the Company's administration, I will endeavour to be a little shorter upon the countries immediately under this charter

1. The assignment of a government's share of the produce of a district to a person or persons for private use, or for the maintenance of a public establishment; or the district so assigned.

2. Honor among thieves.

3. The natural law.

government. These are the Bengal provinces. The condition of these provinces is pretty fully detailed in the Sixth and Ninth Reports,[1] and in their Appendixes. I will select only such principles and instances as are broad and general. To your own thoughts I shall leave it, to furnish the detail of oppressions involved in them. I shall state to you, as shortly as I am able, the conduct of the Company; 1st, towards the landed interests; next, the commercial interests; 3dly, the native government; and lastly, to their own government.

Bengal, and the provinces that are united to it, are larger than the kingdom of France; and once contained, as France does contain, a great and independent landed interest, composed of princes, of great lords, of a numerous nobility and gentry, of freeholders, of lower tenants, of religious communities, and public foundations. So early as 1769, the Company's servants perceived the decay into which these provinces had fallen under English administration, and they made a strong representation upon this decay, and what they apprehended to be the causes of it. Soon after Mr. Hastings became president of Bengal. Instead of administering a remedy, upon the heels of a dreadful famine, in the year 1772, the succour which the new president and the council lent to this afflicted nation was—shall I be believed in relating it?—the landed interest of a whole kingdom, of a kingdom to be compared to France, was set up to public auction![2] They set up (Mr. Hastings set up) the whole nobility, gentry, and freeholders, to the highest bidder. No preference was given to the ancient proprietors.[3] They must bid against every usurer,

1. Of the Select Committee.

2. Regarding the zemindars as tax farmers who worked for the government under private contracts rather than as hereditary landholders, Hastings opened up zemindaries to public bidding in order to extract more revenue for his government.

3. Burke's Whig soul, which saw old landed property as the principal bulwark of liberty against the expansive power of government, was revolted by

every temporary adventurer, every jobber and schemer, every servant of every European, or they were obliged to content themselves, in lieu of their extensive domains, with their house, and such a pension as the state auctioneers thought fit to assign. In this general calamity, several of the first nobility thought (and in all appearance justly) that they had better submit to the necessity of this pension, than continue, under the name of Zemindars, the objects and instruments of a system, by which they ruined their tenants, and were ruined themselves. Another reform has since come upon the back of the first; and a pension having been assigned to these unhappy persons, in lieu of their hereditary lands, a new scheme of oeconomy has taken place, and deprived them of that pension.

The menial servants of Englishmen, persons (to use the emphatical phrase of a ruined and patient Eastern chief) "*whose fathers they would not have set with the dogs of their flock,*"[1] entered into their patrimonial lands. Mr. Hastings's banian[2] was, after this auction, found possessed of territories yielding a rent of one hundred and forty thousand pounds a year.

Such an universal proscription, upon any pretence, has few examples. Such a proscription, without even a pretence of delinquency, has none. It stands by itself. It stands as a monument to astonish the imagination, to confound the reason of mankind. I confess to you, when I first came to know this business in its true nature and extent, my surprise did a little suspend my indignation. I was in a manner stupified by the desperate boldness of a few obscure young men, who

---

Hastings's contempt for the zemindars' hereditary right to collect the rents and dues, which, in India as in England, he regarded as private property in land.

1. Job 30:1.

2. A native broker attached to a house of business, or a person similarly employed by a private gentleman.

having obtained, by ways which they could not comprehend, a power of which they saw neither the purposes nor the limits, tossed about, subverted, and tore to pieces, as if it were in the gambols of a boyish unluckiness and malice, the most established rights, and the most ancient and most revered institutions, of ages and nations. Sir, I will not now trouble you with any detail with regard to what they have since done with these same lands and land-holders; only to inform you, that nothing has been suffered to settle for two seasons together upon any basis; and that the levity and inconstancy of these mock legislators were not the least afflicting parts of the oppressions suffered under their usurpation; nor will any thing give stability to the property of the natives, but an administration in England at once protecting and stable. The country sustains, almost every year, the miseries of a revolution. At present, all is uncertainty, misery, and confusion. There is to be found through these vast regions no longer one landed man, who is a resource for voluntary aid, or an object for particular rapine. Some of them were, not long since, great princes; they possessed treasures, they levied armies. There was a Zemindar in Bengal (I forget his name) that, on the threat of an invasion, supplied the Soubah of these provinces with the loan of a million sterling. The family this day wants credit for a breakfast at the bazar.

I shall now say a word or two on the Company's care of the commercial interest of those kingdoms. As it appears in the Reports, that persons in the highest stations in Bengal have adopted, as a fixed plan of policy, the destruction of all intermediate dealers between the Company and the manufacturer, native merchants have disappeared of course. The spoil of the revenues is the sole capital which purchases the produce and manufactures; and through three or four foreign companies transmits the official gains of individuals to Europe. No other commerce has an existence in Bengal. The transport of its plunder is the only traffic of the country. I wish to refer you to the Appendix to the Ninth Report for a full account of the manner in which the Company have protected the commercial interests of their dominions in the East.[1]

As to the native government and the administration of justice, it subsisted in a poor tottering manner for some years. In the year 1781, a total revolution took place in that establishment. In one of the usual freaks of legislation of the council of Bengal, the whole criminal jurisdiction of these courts, called the Phoujdary Judicature, exercised till then by the principal Mussulmen, was in one day, without notice, without consultation with the magistrates or the people there, and without communication with the directors or ministers here, totally subverted. A new institution took place, by which this jurisdiction was divided between certain English servants of the Company and the Gentû Zemindars of the country, the latter of whom never petitioned for it, nor, for ought that appears, ever desired this boon. But its natural use was made of it; it was made a pretence for new extortions of money.

The natives had however one consolation in the ruin of their judicature; they soon saw that it fared no better with the English government itself. That too, after destroying every other, came to its period. This revolution may well be rated for a most daring act, even among the extraordinary things that have been doing in Bengal since our unhappy acquisition of the means of so much mischief.

An establishment of English government for civil justice, and for the collection of revenue, was planned and executed by the president and council of Bengal, subject to the pleasure of the Directors, in the year 1772. According to this plan,

1. Burke was the author of the Select Committee's Ninth Report. It reflects his concern for maintaining intermediaries between governments and individuals, and expresses his severe judgment of the Company's policy of using territorial revenues instead of commercial profits as the capital with which to buy goods in India for export to Britain.

the country was divided into six great districts, or provinces. In each of these was established a provincial council, which administered the revenue; and of that council one member, by monthly rotation, presided in the courts of civil resort; with an appeal to the council of the province, and thence to Calcutta. In this system (whether, in other respects, good or evil) there were some capital advantages. There was in the very number of persons in each provincial council, authority, communication, mutual check, and controul. They were obliged, on their minutes of consultation, to enter their reasons and dissents; so that a man of diligence, of research, and tolerable sagacity, sitting in London, might, from these materials, be enabled to form some judgment of the spirit of what was going on on the furthest banks of the Ganges and Burrampûter.

The Court of Directors so far ratified this establishment, (which was consonant enough to their general plan of government) that they gave precise orders, that no alteration should be made in it, without their consent. So far from being apprised of any design against this constitution, they had reason to conceive that on trial it had been more and more approved by their council general, at least by the governor general, who had planned it. At the time of the revolution, the council general was nominally in two persons, virtually in one.[1] At that time measures of an arduous and critical nature ought to have been forborne, even if, to the fullest council,

1. At that time, in 1781, Hastings was the only one left of the five original Supreme Council members appointed in 1773. General Clavering and Colonel Monson had died, Barwell had resigned, and Philip Francis, after a duel with Hastings, was on his way back to England. General Sir Eyre Coote, who had taken Clavering's place as commander-in-chief of the Company's army and member of the Council, was off fighting a war in the South of India; John Macpherson, who was appointed to the Council in 1781, had not yet arrived; and the final replacement, John Stables, was not appointed until 1782. Hastings and Wheler were thus the only councillors on the scene in Bengal—and Hastings had a casting vote.

this specific measure had not been prohibited by the superior authority. It was in this very situation, that one man had the hardiness to conceive, and the temerity to execute, a total revolution in the form and the persons composing the government of a great kingdom. Without any previous step, at one stroke, the whole constitution of Bengal, civil and criminal, was swept away. The counsellors were recalled from their provinces. Upwards of fifty of the principal officers of government were turned out of employ, and rendered dependent on Mr. Hastings for their immediate subsistence, and for all hope of future provision. The chief of each council, and one European collector of revenue, was left in each province.

But here, Sir, you may imagine a new government, of some permanent description, was established in the place of that which had been thus suddenly overturned. No such thing. Lest these chiefs without councils should be conceived to form the ground plan of some future government, it was publicly declared, that their continuance was only temporary and permissive. The whole subordinate British administration of revenue was then vested in a committee in Calcutta, all creatures of the governor general; and the provincial management, under the permissive chief, was delivered over to native officers.

But, that the revolution, and the purposes of the revolution, might be complete, to this committee were delegated, not only the functions of all the inferior, but, what will surprize the House, those of the supreme administration of revenue also. Hitherto the governor general and council had, in their revenue department, administered the finances of those kingdoms. By the new scheme they are delegated to this committee, who are only to report their proceedings for approbation.

The key to the whole transaction is given in one of the instructions to the commitee, "that it is not necessary that they should enter dissents." By this means the ancient plan of the

Company's administration was destroyed; but the plan of concealment was perfected. To that moment the accounts of the revenues were tolerably clear; or at least means were furnished for enquiries, by which they might be rendered satisfactory. In the obscure and silent gulph of this committee every thing is now buried. The thickest shades of night surround all their transactions. No effectual means of detecting fraud, mismanagement, or misrepresentation, exist. The Directors, who have dared to talk with such confidence on their revenues, know nothing about them. What used to fill volumes is now comprised under a few dry heads on a sheet of paper. The natives, a people habitually made to concealment, are the chief managers of the revenue thoughout the provinces. I mean by natives, such wretches as your rulers select out of them as most fitted for their purposes. As a proper keystone to bind the arch, a native, one Gunga Govind Sing, a man turned out of his employment by Sir John Clavering, for malversation in office, is made the corresponding secretary; and indeed the great moving principle of their new board.

As the whole revenue and civil administration was thus subverted, and a clandestine government substituted in the place of it, the judicial institution underwent a like revolution. In 1772 there had been six courts formed out of the six provincial councils. Eighteen new ones are appointed in their place, with each a judge, taken from the *junior* servants of the Company. To maintain these eighteen courts, a tax is levied on the sums in litigation, of 2½ *per cent.* on the great, and of 5 *per cent.* on the less. This money is all drawn from the provinces to Calcutta. The chief justice (the same who stays in defiance of a vote of this House, and of His Majesty's recal) is appointed at once the treasurer and disposer of these taxes, levied, without any sort of authority, from the Company, from the Crown, or from Parliament.

In effect, Sir, every legal regular authority in matters of

revenue, of political administration, of criminal law, of civil law, in many of the most essential parts of military discipline, is laid level with the ground; and an oppressive, irregular, capricious, unsteady, rapacious, and peculating despotism, with a direct disavowal of obedience to any authority at home, and without any fixed maxim, principle, or rule of proceeding, to guide them in India, is at present the state of your charter-government over great kingdoms.

As the Company has made this use of their trust, I should ill discharge mine, if I refused to give my most chearful vote for the redress of these abuses, by putting the affairs of so large and valuable a part of the interests of this nation and of mankind, into some steady hands, possessing the confidence, and assured of the support of this House, until they can be restored to regularity, order, and consistency.

I have touched the heads of some of the grievances of the people, and the abuses of government. But I hope and trust, you will give me credit, when I faithfully assure you, that I have not mentioned one fourth part of what has come to my knowledge in your committee; and further, I have full reason to believe, that not one fourth part of the abuses are come to my knowledge, by that or by any other means. Pray consider what I have said only as an index to direct you in your enquiries.

If this then, Sir, has been the use made of the trust of political powers internal and external, given by you in the charter, the next thing to be seen is the conduct of the Company with regard to the commercial trust. And here I will make a fair offer: If it can be proved that they have acted wisely, prudently, and frugally, as merchants, I shall pass by the whole mass of their enormities as statesmen. That they have not done this their present condition is proof sufficient. Their distresses are said to be owing to their wars. This is not wholly true. But if it were, is not that readiness to engage in wars which distinguishes them, and for which the Committee of Secrecy has so branded their politics, founded on the falsest principles of mercantile speculation?

The principle of buying cheap and selling dear is the first, the great foundation of mercantile dealing. Have they ever attended to this principle? Nay, for years have they not actually authorized in their servants a total indifference as to the prices they were to pay?

A great deal of strictness in driving bargains for whatever we contract, is another of the principles of mercantile policy. Try the Company by that test! Look at the contracts that are made for them. Is the Company so much as a good commissary to their own armies? I engage to select for you, out of the innumerable mass of their dealings, all conducted very nearly alike, one contract only, the excessive profits on which during a short term would pay the whole of their year's dividend. I shall undertake to shew, that upon two others, that the inordinate profits given, with the losses incurred in order to secure those profits, would pay a year's dividend more.

It is a third property of trading men, to see that their clerks do not divert the dealings of the master to their own benefit. It was the other day only, when their governor and council taxed the Company's investment with a sum of fifty thousand pounds, as an inducement to persuade only seven members of their board of trade to give their *honour* that they would abstain from such profits upon that investment as they must have violated their *oaths* if they had made at all.

It is a fourth quality of a merchant to be exact in his accounts. What will be thought, when you have fully before you the mode of accounting made use of in the treasury of Bengal? I hope you will have it soon. With regard to one of their agencies, when it came to the material part, the prime cost of the goods on which a commission of fifteen *per cent.* was allowed, to the astonishment of the factory to whom the commodities were sent, the accountant general reports that he did not think himself authorized to call for *vouchers* relative to this and other particulars, because the agent was upon his *honour* with regard to them. A new principle of account upon honour seems to be regularly established in their dealings and their treasury, which in reality amounts to an entire annihilation of the principle of all accounts.

It is a fifth property of a merchant, who does not meditate a fraudulent bankruptcy, to calculate his probable profits upon the money he takes up to vest in business.[1] Did the Company, when they bought goods on bonds bearing 8 *per cent.* interest, at ten and even twenty *per cent.* discount, even ask themselves a question concerning the possibility of advantage from dealing on these terms?

The last quality of a merchant I shall advert to, is the taking care to be properly prepared, in cash or goods, in the ordinary course of sale, for the bills which are drawn on them.[2] Now I ask, whether they have ever calculated the clear produce of any given sales, to make them tally with the four million of bills which are come and coming upon them, so as at the proper periods to enable the one to liquidate the other? No, they have not. They are now obliged to borrow money of their own servants to purchase their investment. The servants stipulate five *per cent.* on the capital they advance, if their bills should not be paid at the time when they become due; and the value of the rupee on which they charge this interest is taken at two shillings and a penny. Has the Company ever troubled themselves to enquire whether their

1. As a purely commercial enterprise, the Company had had to calculate carefully whether the goods it bought for export would earn a profit when sold. But when the Company acquired sovereignty in Indian territories and the right to tax them, it began to use those revenues as its "investment" for the purchase of goods, and became careless about commercial considerations of profit and loss.

2. Bills payable by the Company, either for the purchase of goods not yet paid for or for money it had borrowed.

sales can bear the payment of that interest, and at that rate of exchange? Have they once considered the dilemma in which they are placed—the ruin of their credit in the East Indies, if they refuse the bills—the ruin of their credit and existence in England, if they accept them? Indeed no trace of equitable government is found in their politics; not one trace of commercial principle in their mercantile dealing; and hence is the deepest and maturest wisdom of Parliament demanded, and the best resources of this kingdom must be strained, to restore them; that is, to restore the countries destroyed by the misconduct of the Company, and to restore the Company itself, ruined by the consequences of their plans for destroying what they were bound to preserve.

I required, if you remember, at my outset a proof that these abuses were habitual. But surely this it is not necessary for me to consider as a separate head, because I trust I have made it evident beyond a doubt, in considering the abuses themselves, that they are regular, permanent, and systematical.

I am now come to my last condition, without which, for one, I will never readily lend my hand to the destruction of any established government; which is, That in its present state, the government of the East India Company is absolutely incorrigible.

Of this great truth I think there can be little doubt, after all that has appeared in this House. It is so very clear, that I must consider the leaving any power in their hands, and the determined resolution to continue and countenance every mode and every degree of peculation, oppression, and tyranny, to be one and the same thing. I look upon that body incorrigible, from the fullest consideration both of their uniform conduct, and their present real and virtual constitution.

If they had not constantly been apprized of all the enormities committed in India under their authority; if this state of things had been as much a discovery to them as it was to many of us; we might flatter ourselves that the detection of the abuses would lead to their reformation. I will go further: If the Court of Directors had not uniformly condemned every act which this House or any of its Committees had condemned; if the language in which they expressed their disapprobation against enormities and their authors had not been much more vehement and indignant than any ever used in this House, I should entertain some hopes. If they had not, on the other hand, as uniformly commended all their servants who had done their duty and obeyed their orders, as they had heavily censured those who rebelled; I might say, These people have been in an error, and when they are sensible of it they will mend. But when I reflect on the uniformity of their support to the objects of their uniform censure; and the state of insignificance and disgrace to which all of those have been reduced whom they approved; and that even utter ruin and premature death have been among the fruits of their favour; I must be convinced, that in this case, as in all others, hypocrisy is the only vice that never can be cured.

Attend, I pray you, to the situation and prosperity of Benfield,[1] Hastings, and others of that sort. The last of these has been treated by the company with an asperity of reprehension that has no parallel. They lament, "that the power of disposing of their property for perpetuity, should fall into such hands." Yet for fourteen years, with little interruption, he has governed all their affairs, of every description, with an absolute sway. He has had himself the means of heaping up immense wealth; and, during that whole period, the fortunes of hundreds have depended on his smiles and frowns.

1. Paul Benfield, who had gone to India at the age of twenty-one and had become a servant of the East India Company in 1765. He is reported to have amassed a fortune there exceeding half a million pounds, partly by lending money at high rates of interest. He made huge loans to the Nabob of Arcot, for which Burke denounced him in his *Speech on the Nabob of Arcot's Debts,* but was exonerated of wrongdoing by the Company's Court of Directors.

He himself tells you he is incumbered with two hundred and fifty young gentlemen, some of them of the best families in England, all of whom aim at returning with vast fortunes to Europe in the prime of life. He has then two hundred and fifty of your children as his hostages for your good behaviour; and loaded for years, as he has been, with the execrations of the natives, with the censures of the Court of Directors, and struck and blasted with resolutions of this House, he still maintains the most despotic power ever known in India. He domineers with an overbearing sway in the assemblies of his pretended masters; and it is thought in a degree rash to venture to name his offences in this House, even as grounds of a legislative remedy.

On the other hand, consider the fate of those who have met with the applauses of the Directors. Colonel Monson, one of the best of men, had his days shortened by the applauses, destitute of the support, of the Company. General Clavering, whose panegyric was made in every dispatch from England, whose hearse was bedewed with the tears, and hung round with eulogies of the Court of Directors, burst an honest and indignant heart at the treachery of those who ruined him by their praises. Uncommon patience and temper, supported Mr. Francis a while longer under the baneful influence of the commendation of the Court of Directors. His health however gave way at length; and, in utter despair he returned to Europe. At his return the doors of the India House were shut to this man, who had been the object of their constant admiration. He has indeed escaped with life, but he has forfeited all expectation of credit, consequence, party, and following. He may well say, *Me nemo ministro fur erit, atque ideo nulli comes exeo.*[1] This man, whose deep reach of thought, whose large legislative conceptions, and whose grand plans of policy,

1. "No one will be a thief with my help, and therefore I go abroad on no [governor's] staff." Juvenal *Satires* 3.46–47.

make the most shining part of our Reports, from whence we have all learned our lessons, if we have learned any good ones; this man, from whose materials those gentlemen who have least acknowledged it have yet spoken as from a brief; this man, driven from his employment, discountenanced by the Directors, has had no other reward, and no other distinction, but that inward "sunshine of the soul"[1] which a good conscience can always bestow upon itself. He has not yet had so much as a good word, but from a person too insignificant to make any other return for the means with which he has been furnished for performing his share of a duty which is equally urgent on us all.

Add to this, that from the highest in place to the lowest, every British subject, who, in obedience to the Company's orders, has been active in the discovery of peculations, has been ruined. They have been driven from India. When they made their appeal at home they were not heard; when they attempted to return they were stopped. No artifice of fraud, no violence of power, has been omitted, to destroy them in character as well as in fortune.

Worse, far worse, has been the fate of the poor creatures, the natives of India, whom the hypocrisy of the Company has betrayed into complaint of oppression, and discovery of peculation. The first woman in Bengal, the Ranni of Rajeshahi, the Ranni of Burdwan, the Ranni of Amboa, by their weak and thoughtless trust in the Company's honour and protection, are utterly ruined: the first of these women, a person of princely rank, and once of correspondent fortune, who paid above two hundred thousand a year quit-rent to the state, is, according to very credible information, so com-

1. Quoted from memory and inexactly by Burke from Alexander Pope's *Essay on Man,* epistle 4, sec. 6:

> What nothing earthly gives or can destroy,
> The soul's calm sunshine and the heartfelt joy,
> Is Virtue's prize. . . .

pletely beggared as to stand in need of the relief of alms. Mahomed Reza Khân, the second Mussulman in Bengal, for having been distinguished by the ill-omened honour of the countenance and protection of the Court of Directors, was, without the pretence of any enquiry whatsoever into his conduct, stripped of all his employments, and reduced to the lowest condition. His ancient rival for power, the Rajah Nundcomar,[1] was, by an insult on every thing which India holds respectable and sacred, hanged in the face of all his nation, by the judges you sent to protect that people; hanged for a pretended crime, upon an *ex post facto* British act of parliament, in the midst of his evidence against Mr. Hastings. The accuser they saw hanged. The culprit, without acquittal or enquiry, triumphs on the ground of that murder: a murder not of Nundcomar only, but of all living testimony, and even of evidence yet unborn. From that time not a complaint has been heard from the natives against their governors. All the grievances of India have found a complete remedy.

Men will not look to acts of parliament, to regulations, to declarations, to votes, and resolutions. No, they are not such fools. They will ask, what is the road to power, credit, wealth, and honours? They will ask, what conduct ends in neglect, disgrace, poverty, exile, prison, and gibbet? These will teach them the course which they are to follow. It is your distribution of these that will give the character and tone to your government. All the rest is miserable grimace.

When I accuse the Court of Directors of this habitual

1. A Brahmin and one of the wealthiest men in Bengal. He accused Hastings of having accepted bribes, and the majority of the Supreme Council, consisting of Clavering, Monson, and Francis, supported him in pressing the charge. Nundcomar was then charged with forgery and tried in the Supreme Court of Bengal, which found him guilty. Since the Court decided that he should be sentenced under English law, in which forgery was a capital offense, he was sentenced to death. When the Council majority refused to intercede on Nundcomar's behalf, he was hanged. Burke here takes his execution as a judicial murder to save Hastings.

treachery, in the use of reward and punishment, I do not mean to include all the individuals in that Court. There have been, Sir, very frequently, men of the greatest integrity and virtue amongst them; and the contrariety in the declarations and conduct of that Court has arisen, I take it, from this: That the honest Directors have, by the force of matter of fact on the records, carried the reprobation of the evil measures of the servants in India. This could not be prevented, whilst these records stared them in the face; nor were the delinquents, either here or there, very solicitous about their reputation, as long as they were able to secure their power. The agreement of their partizans to censure them, blunted for a while the edge of a severe proceeding. It obtained for them a character of impartiality, which enabled them to recommend, with some sort of grace, what will always carry a plausible appearance, those treacherous expedients, called moderate measures. Whilst these were under discussion, new matter of complaint came over, which seemed to antiquate the first. The same circle was here trod round once more; and thus through years they proceeded in a compromise of censure for punishment; until, by shame and despair, one after another, almost every man, who preferred his duty to the Company to the interests of their servants, has been driven from that Court.

This, Sir, has been their conduct; and it has been the result of the alteration which was insensibly made in their constitution. The change was made insensibly; but it is now strong and adult, and as public and declared, as it is fixed beyond all power of reformation. So that there is none who hears me, that is not as certain as I am, that the Company, in the sense in which it was formerly understood, has no existence. The question is not, what injury you may do to the proprietors of India stock; for there are no such men to be injured. If the active ruling part of the Company who form the general court, who fill the offices, and direct the measures (the rest tell for nothing) were persons who held their stock as a means of their subsistence, who in the part they took were only concerned in the government of India, for the rise or fall of their dividend, it would be indeed a defective plan of policy. The interest of the people who are governed by them would not be their primary object; perhaps a very small part of their consideration at all. But then they might well be depended on, and perhaps more than persons in other respects preferable, for preventing the peculations of their servants to their own prejudice. Such a body would not easily have left their trade as a spoil to the avarice of those who received their wages. But now things are totally reversed. The stock is of no value, whether it be the qualification of a director or proprietor; and it is impossible that it should. A director's qualification[1] may be worth about two thousand five hundred pounds —and the interest, at eight *per cent.* is about one hundred and sixty pounds a year. Of what value is that, whether it rise to ten, or fall to six, or to nothing, to him whose son, before he is in Bengal two months, and before he descends the steps of the council chamber, sells the grant of a single contract for forty thousand pounds? Accordingly the stock is bought up in qualifications. The vote is not to protect the stock, but the stock is bought to acquire the vote; and the end of the vote is to cover and support, against justice, some man of power who has made an obnoxious fortune in India; or to maintain in power those who are actually employing it in the acquisition of such a fortune; and to avail themselves in return of his patronage, that he may shower the spoils of the East, "barbaric pearl and gold,"[2] on them, their families, and dependents. So

1. The minimum qualification for a director of the Company was ownership of £2000 of East India stock.

2. In *Paradise Lost,* book 2, lines 1–4, Milton has Satan seated

High on a Throne of Royal State . . .
Where the gorgeous East with richest hand
Shows her Kings Barbaric Pearl & Gold.

that all the relations of the Company are not only changed, but inverted. The servants in India are not appointed by the Directors, but the Directors are chosen by them. The trade is carried on with their capitals. To them the revenues of the country are mortgaged. The seat of the supreme power is in Calcutta. The house in Leadenhall Street[1] is nothing more than a change for their agents, factors, and deputies to meet in, to take care of their affairs, and support their interests; and this so avowedly, that we see the known agents of the delinquent servants marshalling and disciplining their forces, and the prime spokesmen in all their assemblies.

Every thing has followed in this order, and according to the natural train of events. I will close what I have to say on the incorrigible condition of the Company, by stating to you a few facts, that will leave no doubt of the obstinacy of that corporation, and of their strength too, in resisting the reformation of their servants. By these facts you will be enabled to discover the sole grounds upon which they are tenacious of their charter. It is now more than two years that, upon account of the gross abuses and ruinous situation of the Company's affairs, (which occasioned the cry of the whole world long before it was taken up here) that we instituted two Committees[2] to enquire into the mismanagements by which the Company's affairs had been brought to the brink of ruin. These enquiries had been pursued with unremitting diligence; and a great body of facts was collected and printed for general information. In the result of those enquiries, although the Committees consisted of very different descriptions, they were unanimous. They joined in censuring the conduct of the Indian administration, and enforcing the responsibility upon two men, whom this House, in con-

1. Location of East India House, the Company's headquarters in London.

2. The Secret and Select Committees; Burke was a leading member of the latter.

sequence of these reports, declared it to be the duty of the Directors to remove from their stations, and recal to Great Britain, "*because they had acted in a manner repugnant to the honour and policy of this nation, and thereby brought great calamities on India, and enormous expences on the East India Company.*"

Here was no attempt on the charter. Here was no question of their privileges. To vindicate their own honour, to support their own interests, to enforce obedience to their own orders; these were the sole object of the monitory resolution of this House. But as soon as the general court[1] could assemble, they assembled to demonstrate who they really were. Regardless of the proceedings of this House, they ordered the Directors not to carry into effect any resolution they might come to for the removal of Mr. Hastings and Mr. Hornby.[2] The Directors, still retaining some shadow of respect to this House, instituted an enquiry themselves, which continued from June to October; and after an attentive perusal and full consideration of papers, resolved to take steps for removing the persons who had been the objects of our resolution; but not without a violent struggle against evidence. Seven Directors went so far as to enter a protest against the vote of their court. Upon this the general court takes the alarm; it re-assembles; it orders the Directors to rescind their resolution, that is, not to recal Mr. Hastings and Mr. Hornby, and to despise the resolution of the House of Commons. Without so much as the pretence of looking into a single paper, without the formality of instituting any committee of enquiry, they superseded all the labours of their own Directors, and of this House.

It will naturally occur to ask, how it was possible that they should not attempt some sort of examination into facts, as a colour for their resistance to a public authority, proceeding so very deliberately; and exerted, apparently at least, in

1. The Court of Proprietors, that is, shareholders.

2. William Hornby, Governor of Bombay.

favour of their own? The answer, and the only answer which can be given, is, that they were afraid that their true relation should be mistaken. They were afraid that their patrons and masters in India should attribute their support of them, to an opinion of their cause, and not to an attachment to their power. They were afraid it should be suspected, that they did not mean blindly to support them in the use they made of that power. They determined to shew that they at least were set against reformation; that they were firmly resolved to bring the territories, the trade, and the stock of the Company, to ruin, rather than be wanting in fidelity to their nominal servants and real masters, in the ways they took to their private fortunes.

Even since the beginning of this session, the same act of audacity was repeated, with the same circumstances of contempt of all the decorum of enquiry, on their part, and of all the proceedings of this House. They again made it a request to their favourite, and your culprit, to keep his post; and thanked and applauded him, without calling for a paper which could afford light into the merit or demerit of the transaction, and without giving themselves a moment's time to consider, or even to understand, the articles of the Maratta peace. The fact is, that for a long time there was a struggle, a faint one indeed, between the Company and their servants. But it is a struggle no longer. For some time the superiority has been decided. The interests abroad are become the settled preponderating weight both in the Court of Proprietors, and the Court of Directors. Even the attempt you have made to enquire into their practices and to reform abuses, has raised and piqued them to a far more regular and steady support. The Company has made a common cause, and identified themselves, with the destroyers of India. They have taken on themselves all that mass of enormity; they are supporting what you have reprobated; those you condemn they applaud; those you order home to answer for their conduct, they request to stay, and thereby encourage to proceed in their practices. Thus the servants of the East India Company triumph, and the representatives of the people of Great Britain are defeated.

I therefore conclude, what you all conclude, that this body, being totally perverted from the purposes of its institution, is utterly incorrigible; and because they are incorrigible, both in conduct and constitution, power ought to be taken out of their hands; just on the same principles on which have been made all the just changes and revolutions of government that have taken place since the beginning of the world.

I will now say a few words to the general principle of the plan which is set up against that of my Right Honourable friend. It is to re-commit the government of India to the Court of Directors. Those who would commit the reformation of India to the destroyers of it, are the enemies to that reformation. They would make a distinction between Directors and Proprietors, which, in the present state of things, does not, cannot exist. But a Right Honourable gentleman says he would keep the present government of India in the Court of Directors; and would, to curb them, provide salutary regulations; wonderful! That is, he would appoint the old offenders to correct the old offences; and he would render the vicious and the foolish wise and virtuous, by salutary regulations. He would appoint the wolf as guardian of the sheep; but he has invented a curious muzzle, by which this protecting wolf shall not be able to open his jaws above an inch or two at the utmost. Thus his work is finished. But I tell the Right Honourable gentleman, that controuled depravity is not innocence; and that it is not the labour of delinquency in chains, that will correct abuses. Will these gentlemen of the direction animadvert on the partners of their own guilt? Never did a serious plan of amending of any old tyrannical establishment propose the authors and abettors of the abuses as the reformers of them. If the undone people of

India see their old oppressors in confirmed power, even by the reformation, they will expect nothing but what they will certainly feel, a continuance, or rather an aggravation, of all their former sufferings. They look to the seat of power, and to the persons who fill it; and they despise those gentlemen's regulations as much as the gentlemen do who talk of them.

But there is a cure for every thing. Take away, say they, the Court of Proprietors, and the Court of Directors will do their duty. Yes; as they have done it hitherto. That the evils in India have solely arisen from the Court of Proprietors, is grossly false. In many of them, the Directors were heartily concurring; in most of them they were encouraging, and sometimes commanding; in all they were conniving.

But who are to choose this well-regulated and reforming Court of Directors? Why, the very proprietors who are excluded from all management, for the abuse of their power. They will choose undoubtedly, out of themselves, men like themselves; and those who are most forward in resisting your authority, those who are most engaged in faction or interest with the delinquents abroad, will be the objects of their selection. But Gentlemen say, that when this choice is made, the proprietors are not to interfere in the measures of the Directors, whilst those Directors are busy in the control of their common patrons and masters in India. No, indeed, I believe they will not desire to interfere. They will choose those whom they know may be trusted, safely trusted, to act in strict conformity to their common principles, manners, measures, interests, and connections. They will want neither monitor nor control. It is not easy to choose men to act in conformity to a public interest against their private: but a sure dependance may be had on those who are chosen to forward their private interest, at the expence of the public. But if the Directors should slip, and deviate into rectitude, the punishment is in the hands of the general court, and it will surely be remembered to them at their next election.

If the government of India wants no reformation; but gentlemen are amusing themselves with a theory, conceiving a more democratic or aristocratic mode of government for these dependances, or if they are in a dispute only about patronage; the dispute is with me of so little concern, that I should not take the pains to utter an affirmative or negative to any proposition in it. If it be only for a theoretical amusement that they are to propose a bill; the thing is at best frivolous and unnecessary. But if the Company's government is not only full of abuse, but is one of the most corrupt and destructive tyrannies, that probably ever existed in the world (as I am sure it is) what a cruel mockery would it be in me, and in those who think like me, to propose this kind of remedy for this kind of evil!

I now come to the third objection, That this bill will increase the influence of the Crown. An Honourable gentleman has demanded of me, whether I was in earnest when I proposed to this House a plan for the reduction of that influence.[1] Indeed, Sir, I was much, very much, in earnest. My heart was deeply concerned in it; and I hope the public has not lost the effect of it. How far my judgment was right, for what concerned personal favour and consequence to myself, I shall not presume to determine; nor is its effect upon *me* of any moment. But as to this bill, whether it encreases the influence of the Crown, or not, is a question I should be ashamed to ask. If I am not able to correct a system of oppression and tyranny, that goes to the utter ruin of thirty millions of my

1. In Burke's speech in the Commons in February 1780, he had proposed "a plan for the better security of the independence of Parliament, and the oeconomical reformation of the civil and other establishments." The purpose was to reduce the ability of the Crown to influence Parliament by patronage appointments in the royal household and to control the king's expenditure of the money voted for his civil list so that it would not be used to influence parliamentary elections. The plan failed in large measure to be adopted on that occasion.

fellow-creatures and fellow-subjects, but by some increase to the influence of the Crown, I am ready here to declare, that I, who have been active to reduce it, shall be at least as active and strenuous to restore it again. I am no lover of names; I contend for the substance of good and protecting government, let it come from what quarter it will.

But I am not obliged to have recourse to this expedient. Much, very much the contrary. I am sure that the influence of the Crown will by no means aid a reformation of this kind; which can neither be originated nor supported, but by the uncorrupt public virtue of the representatives of the people of England. Let it once get into the ordinary course of administration, and to me all hopes of reformation are gone. I am far from knowing or believing, that this bill will encrease the influence of the Crown. We all know, that the Crown has ever had some influence in the Court of Directors; and that it has been extremely increased by the acts of 1773 and 1780. The gentlemen who, as part of their reformation, propose "a more active controul on the part of the Crown," which is to put the Directors under a Secretary of State, specially named for that purpose, must know, that their project will increase it further. But that old influence has had, and the new will have, incurable inconveniences, which cannot happen under the parliamentary establishment proposed in this bill. An Honourable gentleman[1] not now in his place, but who is well acquainted with the India Company, and by no means a friend to this bill, has told you that a ministerial influence has always been predominant in that body; and that to make the Directors pliant to their purposes, Ministers generally caused persons meanly qualified to be chosen Directors. According

1. George Johnstone, commonly called Governor Johnstone because of his brief appointment in 1763 as governor of West Florida. A rather disreputable character, he served as both a naval commander and a member of Parliament.

to his idea, to secure subserviency, they submitted the Company's affairs to the direction of incapacity. This was to ruin the Company, in order to govern it. This was certainly influence in the very worst form in which it could appear. At best it was clandestine and irresponsible. Whether this was done so much upon system as that gentleman supposes, I greatly doubt. But such in effect the operation of Government on that court unquestionably was; and such under a similar constitution, it will be for ever. Ministers must be wholly removed from the management of the affairs of India, or they will have an influence in its patronage. The thing is inevitable. Their scheme of a new Secretary of State, "with a more vigorous control," is not much better than a repetition of the measure which we know by experience will not do. Since the year 1773 and the year 1780, the Company has been under the control of the Secretary of State's office, and we had then three Secretaries of State. If more than this is done, then they annihilate the direction which they pretend to support; and they augment the influence of the Crown, of whose growth they affect so great an horror. But in truth this scheme of reconciling a direction really and truly deliberative, with an office really and substantially controlling, is a sort of machinery that can be kept in order but a very short time. Either the Directors will dwindle into clerks, or the Secretary of State, as hitherto has been the course, will leave every thing to them, often through design, often through neglect. If both should affect activity, collision, procrastination, delay, and in the end, utter confusion must ensue.

But, Sir, there is one kind of influence far greater than that of the nomination to office. This gentlemen in opposition have totally overlooked, although it now exists in its full vigour; and it will do so, upon their scheme, in at least as much force as it does now. That influence this bill cuts up by the roots; I mean the *influence of protection*. I shall explain myself: The office given to a young man going to India is of trifling consequence. But he that goes out an insignificant boy, in a few years returns a great Nabob. Mr. Hastings says he has two hundred and fifty of that kind of raw materials, who expect to be speedily manufactured into the merchantable quality I mention. One of these gentlemen, suppose, returns hither, loaded with odium and with riches. When he comes to England he comes as to a prison or as to a sanctuary; and either are ready for him, according to his demeanor. What is the influence in the grant of any place in India, to that which is acquired by the protection or compromise with such guilt, and with the command of such riches, under the dominion of the hopes and fears which power is able to hold out to every man in that condition? That man's whole fortune, half a million perhaps, becomes an instrument of influence, without a shilling of charge to the Civil List; and the influx of fortunes which stand in need of this protection is continual. It works both ways; it influences the delinquent, and it may corrupt the minister. Compare the influence acquired by appointing for instance even a governor general, and that obtained by protecting him. I shall push this no further. But I wish gentlemen to roll it a little in their own minds.

The bill before you cuts off this source of influence. Its design and main scope is to regulate the administration of India upon the principles of a Court of Judicature; and to exclude, as far as human prudence can exclude, all possibility of a corrupt partiality, in appointing to office or supporting in office, or covering from enquiry and punishment, any person who has abused or shall abuse his authority. At the board, as appointed and regulated by this bill, reward and punishment cannot be shifted and reversed by a whisper.[1]

1. The commission to be established by the East India Bill was "to investigate every charge and complaint made against the Company's servants. Reasons had to be publicly stated if no action was to be taken on the complaints." *W&S* 5:444, n.1.

That commission becomes fatal to cabal, to intrigue, and to secret representation, those instruments of the ruin of India. He that cuts off the means of premature fortune, and the power of protecting it when acquired, strikes a deadly blow at the great fund, the Bank, the capital stock of Indian influence, which cannot be vested any where, or in any hands, without most dangerous consequences to the public.

The third and contradictory objection, is, That this bill does not increase the influence of the Crown. On the contrary, That the just power of the Crown will be lessened, and transferred to the use of a party, by giving the patronage of India to a commission nominated by parliament, and independent of the Crown.[1] The contradiction is glaring, and it has been too well exposed to make it necessary for me to insist upon it. But passing the contradiction, and taking it without any relation, of all objections that is the most extraordinary. Do not gentlemen know, that the Crown has not at present the grant of a single office under the Company, civil or military, at home or abroad? So far as the Crown is concerned, it is certainly rather a gainer; for the vacant offices in the new commission are to be filled up by the King.

It is argued as a part of the bill, derogatory to the prerogatives of the Crown, that the commissioners named in the bill are to continue for a short term of years (too short in my opinion) and because, during that time, they are not at the mercy of every predominant faction of the court. Does not this objection lie against the present Directors; none of whom are named by the Crown, and a proportion of whom hold for this very term of four years? Did it not lie against the governor general and council named in the act of 1773—who were invested by name, as the present commissioners are to

1. The first members of the commission were named in the Bill and were all supporters of the Fox-North Coalition. They were to serve four-year terms, but vacancies would be filled by the king, as Burke explains.

be appointed in the body of the act of parliament, who were to hold their places for a term of years, and were not removable at the discretion of the Crown? Did it not lie against the reappointment, in the year 1780, upon the very same terms? Yet at none of these times, whatever other objections the scheme might be liable to, was it supposed to be a derogation to the just prerogative of the Crown, that a commission created by act of parliament should have its members named by the authority which called it into existence? This is not the disposal by parliament of any office derived from the authority of the Crown, or now disposable by that authority. It is so far from being any thing new, violent, or alarming, that I do not recollect, in any parliamentary commission, down to the commissioners of the land tax, that it has ever been otherwise.

The objection of the tenure for four years is an objection to all places that are not held during pleasure; but in that objection I pronounce the gentlemen, from my knowledge of their complexion and of their principles, to be perfectly in earnest. The party (say these gentlemen) of the minister who proposes this scheme will be rendered powerful by it; for he will name his party friends to the commission. This objection against party is a party objection; and in this too these gentlemen are perfectly serious. They see that if, by any intrigue, they should succeed to office, they will lose the *clandestine* patronage, the true instrument of clandestine influence, enjoyed in the name of subservient Directors, and of wealthy trembling Indian delinquents. But as often as they are beaten off this ground, they return to it again. The minister will name his friends, and persons of his own party. Who should he name? Should he name his adversaries? Should he name those whom he cannot trust? Should he name those to execute his plans, who are the declared enemies to the principles of his reform? His character is here at stake. If he proposes for his own ends (but he never will propose) such names as, from their want of rank, fortune, character, ability, or knowledge, are likely to betray or to fall short of their trust, he is in an independent House of Commons; in an House of Commons which has, by its own virtue, destroyed the instruments of parliamentary subservience.[1] This House of Commons would not endure the sound of such names. He would perish by the means which he is supposed to pursue for the security of his power. The first pledge he must give of his sincerity in this great reform will be in the confidence which ought to be reposed in those names.

For my part, Sir, in this business I put all indirect considerations wholly out of my mind. My sole question, on each clause of the bill, amounts to this: Is the measure proposed required by the necessities of India? I cannot consent totally to lose sight of the real wants of the people who are the objects of it, and to hunt after every matter of party squabble that may be started on the several provisions. On the question of the duration of the commission I am clear and decided. Can I, can any one who has taken the smallest trouble to be informed concerning the affairs of India, amuse himself with so strange an imagination, as that the habitual despotism and oppression, that the monopolies, the peculations, the universal destruction of all the legal authority of this kingdom, which have been for twenty years maturing to their present enormity, combined with the distance of the scene, the boldness and artifice of delinquents, their combination, their excessive wealth, and the faction they have made in England, can be fully corrected in a shorter term than four years? None has hazarded such an assertion—None, who has a regard for his reputation, will hazard it.

1. Earlier in 1783, the Fox-North Coalition having come to power, Burke finally succeeded in getting an "economical reform" bill passed. But it was not so sweeping in its scope that it destroyed all "the instruments of parliamentary subservience," as his rhetoric here suggests.

Sir, the gentlemen, whoever they are, who shall be appointed to this commission, have an undertaking of magnitude on their hands, and their stability must not only be, but it must be thought, real; and who is it will believe, that any thing short of an establishment made, supported, and fixed in its duration, with all the authority of parliament, can be thought secure of a reasonable stability? The plan of my Honourable friend is the reverse of that of reforming by the authors of the abuse. The best we could expect from them is, that they should not continue their ancient pernicious activity. To those we could think of nothing but applying *control;* as we are sure, that even a regard to their reputation (if any such thing exists in them) would oblige them to cover, to conceal, to suppress, and consequently to prevent, all cure of the grievances of India. For what can be discovered, which is not to their disgrace? Every attempt to correct an abuse would be a satire on their former administration. Every man they should pretend to call to an account, would be found their instrument or their accomplice. They can never see a beneficial regulation, but with a view to defeat it. The shorter the tenure of such persons, the better would be the chance of some amendment.

But the system of the bill is different. It calls in persons no wise concerned with any act censured by parliament; persons generated with, and for the reform of which, they are themselves the most essential part. To these the chief regulations in the bill are helps, not fetters; they are authorities to support, not regulations to restrain them. From these we look for much more than innocence. From these we expect zeal, firmness, and unremitted activity. Their duty, their character, binds them to proceedings of vigour; and they ought to have a tenure in their office which precludes all fear, whilst they are acting up to the purposes of their trust; a tenure without which, none will undertake plans that require a series and system of acts. When they know that they cannot be whispered out of their duty, that their public conduct cannot be censured without a public discussion; that the schemes which they have begun will not be committed to those who will have an interest and credit in defeating and disgracing them; then we may entertain hopes. The tenure is for four years, or during their good behaviour. That good behaviour is as long as they are true to the principles of the bill; and the judgment is in either House of Parliament.[1] This is the tenure of your judges; and the valuable principle of the bill is, to make a judicial administration for India. It is to give confidence in the execution of a duty, which requires as much perseverance and fortitude as can fall to the lot of any that is born of woman.

As to the gain by party, from the Right Honourable gentleman's bill, let it be shewn, that this supposed party advantage is pernicious to its object, and the objection is of weight; but until this is done, and this has not been attempted, I shall consider the sole objection, from its tendency to promote the interest of a party, as altogether contemptible. The kingdom is divided into parties, and it ever has been so divided, and it ever will be so divided; and if no system for relieving the subjects of this kingdom from oppression, and snatching its affairs from ruin, can be adopted, until it is demonstrated that no party can derive an advantage from it, no good can ever be done in this country. If party is to derive an advantage from the reform of India, (which is more than I know, or believe) it ought to be that party which alone, in this kingdom, has its reputation, nay its very being, pledged to the protection and preservation of that part of the empire. Great fear is expressed, that the commissioners named in this bill will shew some regard to a minister out of place. To men made like the objectors, this

1. Either the Lords or the Commons could act to remove delinquent commissioners.

must appear criminal. Let it however be remembered by others, that if the commissioners should be his friends, they cannot be his slaves. But dependants are not in a condition to adhere to friends, nor to principles, nor to any uniform line of conduct. They may begin censors, and be obliged to end accomplices. They may be even put under the direction of those whom they were appointed to punish.

The fourth and last objection is, That the bill will hurt public credit. I do not know whether this requires an answer. But if it does, look to your foundations. The sinking fund[1] is the pillar of credit in this country; and let it not be forgot, that the distresses, owing to the mismanagement of the East India Company, have already taken a million from that fund by the non-payment of duties.[2] The bills drawn upon the Company, which are about four millions, cannot be accepted without the consent of the treasury. The treasury, acting under a parliamentary trust and authority, pledges the public for these millions. If they pledge the public, the public must have a security in its hands for the management of this interest, or the national credit is gone. For otherwise it is not only the East India Company, which is a great interest, that is undone, but, clinging to the security of all your funds, it drags down the rest, and the whole fabric perishes in one ruin. If this bill does not provide a direction of integrity and of ability competent to that trust, the objection is fatal. If it does, public credit must depend on the support of the bill.

It has been said, if you violate this charter, what security has the charter of the Bank, in which public credit is so deeply concerned, and even the charter of London, in which

1. A fund formed by periodically setting aside revenue to accumulate at interest in order to reduce the principal of a debt. The British government had established one in 1716 to reduce the national debt.

2. The government had already helped the Company in its financial difficulties by a remission of customs duties.

the rights of so many subjects are involved? I answer, In the like case they have no security at all—No—no security at all. If the Bank should, by every species of mismanagement, fall into a state similar to that of the East India Company; if it should be oppressed with demands it could not answer, engagements which it could not perform, and with bills for which it could not procure payment; no charter should protect the mismanagement from correction, and such public grievances from redress. If the city of London had the means and will of destroying an empire, and of cruelly oppressing and tyrannizing over millions of men as good as themselves, the charter of the city of London should prove no sanction to such tyranny and such oppression. Charters are kept, when their purposes are maintained: they are violated when the privilege is supported against its end and its object.

Now, Sir, I have finished all I proposed to say, as my reasons for giving my vote to this Bill. If I am wrong, it is not for want of pains to know what is right. This pledge, at least, of my rectitude I have given to my country.

And now, having done my duty to the Bill, let me say a word to the author. I should leave him to his own noble sentiments, if the unworthy and illiberal language with which he has been treated, beyond all example of parliamentary liberty, did not make a few words necessary; not so much in justice to him, as to my own feelings. I must say then, that it will be a distinction honourable to the age, that the rescue of the greatest number of the human race that ever were so grievously oppressed, from the greatest tyranny that was ever exercised, has fallen to the lot of abilities and dispositions equal to the task; that it has fallen to one who has the enlargement to comprehend, the spirit to undertake, and the eloquence to support, so great a measure of hazardous benevolence. His spirit is not owing to his ignorance of the state of men and things; he well knows what snares are spread about his path, from personal animosity, from court intrigues, and possibly from popular delusion. But he has put to hazard his ease, his security, his interest, his power, even his darling popularity, for the benefit of a people whom he has never seen. This is the road that all heroes have trod before him. He is traduced and abused for his supposed motives. He will remember, that obloquy is a necessary ingredient in the composition of all true glory: he will remember, that it was not only in the Roman customs, but it is in the nature and constitution of things, that calumny and abuse are essential parts of triumph. These thoughts will support a mind, which only exists for honour, under the burthen of temporary reproach. He is doing indeed a great good; such as rarely falls to the lot, and almost as rarely coincides with the desires, of any man. Let him use his time. Let him give the whole length of the reins to his benevolence. He is now on a great eminence, where the eyes of mankind are turned to him. He may live long, he may do much. But here is the summit. He never can exceed what he does this day.

He has faults; but they are faults that, though they may in a small degree tarnish the lustre, and sometimes impede the march of his abilities, have nothing in them to extinguish the fire of great virtues. In those faults, there is no mixture of deceit, of hypocrisy, of pride, of ferocity, of complexional despotism, or want of feeling for the distresses of mankind. His are faults which might exist in a descendant of Henry the Fourth of France,[1] as they did exist in that father of his country. Henry the Fourth wished that he might live to see a fowl in the pot of every peasant of his kingdom. That sentiment of homely benevolence was worth all the splendid sayings that are recorded of kings. But he wished perhaps for more than could be obtained, and the goodness of the man exceeded the power of the King. But this gentleman, a subject, may this day say this at least, with truth, that he secures the rice

1. Fox was a remote descendant of Henry IV of France.

in his pot to every man in India. A poet of antiquity thought it one of the first distinctions to a prince whom he meant to celebrate, that through a long succession of generations, he had been the progenitor of an able and virtuous citizen, who by force of the arts of peace, had corrected governments of oppression, and suppressed wars of rapine.

Indole proh quanta juvenis, quantumque daturus
Ausoniae populis, ventura in saecula civem.
Ille super Gangem, super exauditus et Indos,
Implebit terras voce; et furialia bella
Fulmine compescet linguae.——[1]

This was what was said of the predecessor of the only person to whose eloquence it does not wrong that of the mover of this bill to be compared. But the Ganges and the Indus are the patrimony of the fame of my Honourable friend, and not of Cicero. I confess, I anticipate with joy the reward of those, whose whole consequence, power, and authority, exist only for the benefit of mankind; and I carry my mind to all the people, and all the names and descriptions, that, relieved by this bill, will bless the labours of this Parliament, and the confidence which the best House of Commons has given to him who the best deserves it. The little cavils of party will not be heard, where freedom and happiness will be felt. There is not a tongue, a nation, or religion in India, which will not bless the presiding care and manly beneficence of this House, and of him who proposes to you this great work. Your names will never be separated before the throne of the Divine Goodness, in whatever language, or with whatever rites, pardon is asked for sin, and reward for those who imitate the Godhead

1. "How noble was his youthful promise, and how great a citizen he was to give in coming centuries to the peoples of Italy. He will be heard beyond the Ganges and the peoples of India; he will fill the earth with his voice, and with the thunder of his tongue will quell the frenzy of war." Said of Cicero in Silius Italicus *Punic Wars* 8.406–10.

in his universal bounty to his creatures. These honours you deserve, and they will surely be paid, when all the jargon, of influence, and party, and patronage, are swept into oblivion.

I have spoken what I think, and what I feel, of the mover of this Bill. An Honourable friend of mine, speaking of his merits, was charged with having made a studied panegyric. I don't know what his was. Mine, I am sure, is a studied panegyric; the fruit of much meditation; the result of the observation of near twenty years. For my own part, I am happy that I have lived to see this day; I feel myself overpaid for the labours of eighteen years, when, at this late period, I am able to take my share, by one humble vote, in destroying a tyranny that exists to the disgrace of this nation, and the destruction of so large a part of the human species.

FINIS

A Letter to Sir Hercules Langrishe on the Catholics of Ireland

[January 3, 1792]

Sir Hercules Langrishe (1731–1811) was a younger Irish contemporary of Edmund Burke and, like him, a graduate of Trinity College, Dublin. He was a member of the Irish House of Commons from 1761 to the Union with Great Britain in 1800, after which he ceased to take an active part in politics. While the Irish House lasted, however, he was one of its most independent members, as he could afford to be, since he was virtually the sole proprietor of the borough he represented.

During the American crisis he advocated a conciliatory policy toward the colonies. An early friend of Burke's, he was well aware of Burke's views on the Penal Laws against Catholics, and to some extent shared them. At the time of this letter from Burke, the Catholic Relief Acts of 1778 and 1782 had repealed certain of those laws. But in the early 1790s, the growth of sympathy with the French Revolution among the Dissenters in the North of Ireland and the cordial relations between them and some Catholics seem to have prompted Langrishe to seek Burke's views on a petition by the Irish Catholic Committee for further relaxation of the Penal Laws. Burke replied on January 3, 1792, in the letter here published. It was a veritable pamphlet, evidently designed to be passed around. After it had appeared in print in Dublin in February 1792, Burke had it published by Debrett in London as it appears here.

A Letter from the Right Hon. Edmund Burke, M.P. in the Kingdom of Great Britain, to Sir Hercules Langrishe, Bart. M.P.

[On the Subject of Roman Catholics of Ireland, and the Propriety of Admitting Them to the Elective Franchise, Consistently with the Principles of the Constitution as Established at the Revolution]

My Dear Sir,

Your remembrance of me, with sentiments of so much kindness, has given me the most sincere satisfaction. It perfectly agrees with the friendly and hospitable reception which my son and I received from you, some time since, when, after an absence of twenty-two years, I had the happiness of embracing you, among my few surviving friends.

I really imagined that I should not again interest myself in any public business. I had, to the best of my moderate faculties, paid my club to the Society, which I was born, in some way or other to serve; and I thought I had a right to put on my night-gown and slippers, and wish a cheerful evening to the good company I must leave behind. But if our resolutions of vigour and exertion are so often broken or procrastinated in the exertion; I think we may be excused, if we are not very punctual in fulfilling our engagements to indolence and inactivity. I have indeed no power of action; and am almost a cripple, even with regard to thinking: but you descend with force into the stagnant pool; and you cause such a fermentation, as to cure at least one impotent creature of his lameness, though it cannot enable him either to run or to wrestle.

You see by the paper I take[1] that I am likely to be long, with malice prepense.[2] You have brought under my view, a subject, always difficult, at present critical. It has filled my thoughts, which I wish to lay open to you with the clearness and simplicity which your friendship demands from me. I thank you for the communication of your ideas. I should be still more pleased if they had been more your own. What you hint, I believe to be the case; that if you had not deferred to the judgment of others, our opinions would not differ more materially at this day, than they did when we used to confer on the same subject, so many years ago. If I still persevere in my old opinions, it is no small comfort to me, that it is not with regard to doctrines properly yours, that I discover my indocility.

The case upon which your letter of the 10th of December turns, is hardly before me with precision enough, to enable me to form any very certain judgment upon it. It seems to be some plan of further indulgence proposed for Catholics of Ireland. You observe, "that your general principles are not changed, but *that times and circumstances are altered.*" I perfectly agree with you, that times and circumstances, considered with reference to the public, ought very much to govern our conduct; though I am far from slighting, when applied with discretion to those circumstances, general prin-

1. A footnote in the original publication explains: "The letter is written on folio sheets."

2. With premeditated malice.

ciples and maxims of policy. I cannot help observing, however, that you have said rather less upon the applicability of your own old principles to the *circumstances* that are likely to influence your conduct against these principles, than of the *general* maxims of state; which I can very readily believe not to have great weight with you personally.

In my present state of imperfect information, you will pardon the errors into which I may easily fall. The principles you lay down are, "that the Roman Catholics should enjoy every thing *under* the state, but should not be *the state itself.*" And you add, "that when you exclude them from being *a part of the state,* you rather conform to the spirit of the age, than to any abstract doctrine"; but you consider the constitution is already established—that our state is Protestant. "It was declared so at the revolution. It was so provided in the acts for settling the succession of the Crown:—the King's coronation oath was enjoined, in order to keep it so. The King, as first magistrate of the state, is obliged to take the oath of abjuration, and to subscribe the declaration; and, by laws subsequent, every other magistrate and member of the state, and legislature and executive, are bound under the same obligation."

As to the plan to which these maxims are applied, I cannot speak, as I told you, positively about it. Because, neither from your letter, nor from any information I have been able to collect, do I find any thing settled, either on the part of the Roman Catholics themselves, or on that of any persons who may wish to conduct their affairs in Parliament. But if I have leave to conjecture, something is in agitation towards admitting them, under *certain qualifications,* to have *some share* in the election of members of parliament. This I understand is the scheme of those who are intitled to come within your description of persons of consideration, property, and character: and firmly attached to the king and constitution as by "law established, with a grateful sense of your former concessions, and a patient reliance on the benignity of parliament, for the further mitigation of the laws that still affect them." As to the low, thoughtless, wild and profligate, who have joined themselves with those of other professions, but of the same character;[1] you are not to imagine, that, for a moment, I can suppose them to be met, with any thing else than the manly and enlightened energy of a firm government, supported by the united efforts of all virtuous men, if ever their proceedings should become so considerable as to demand its notice. I really think that such associations should be crushed in their very commencement.

Setting this, therefore, out of the question, it becomes an object of very serious consideration, whether, because wicked men of *various* descriptions are engaged in seditious courses, the rational, sober, and valuable part of *one* description should not be indulged their sober and rational expectations? You, who have looked deeply into the spirit of the Popery laws, must be perfectly sensible, that a great part of the present mischief, which we abhor in common, has arisen from them. Their declared object was to reduce the Catholics of Ireland to a miserable populace, without property, without estimation, without education. The professed object was to deprive the few men who, in spite of those laws, might hold or obtain any property amongst them, of all sort of influence or authority over the rest. They divided the nation into two distinct bodies, without common interest, sympathy or connexion; one of which bodies was to possess *all* the franchises, *all* the property, *all* the education: The others were to be drawers of water and cutters of turf for them. Are we to be astonished that when, by the efforts of so much violence in conquest, and so much policy in regulation, continued without intermission for near an hundred years, we had reduced

1. The reference is to Catholics who have sought relief from their oppressed state by joining with Dissenters and Deists imbued with the principles of the French Revolution.

them to a mob; that whenever they came to act at all, many of them would act exactly like a mob, without temper, measure, or foresight? Surely it might be just now a matter of temperate discussion, whether you ought not apply a remedy to the real cause of the evil—to raise an aristocratic interest; that is, an interest of property and education amongst them: And to strengthen by every prudent means, the authority and influence of men of that description. It will deserve your best thoughts, to examine whether this can be done without giving such persons the means of demonstrating to the rest, that something more is to be got by their temperate conduct, than can be expected from the wild and senseless projects[1] of those, who do not belong to their body, who have no interest in their well being, and only wish to make them the dupes of their turbulent ambition.

If the absurd persons you mention[2] find no way of providing for liberty, but by overturning this happy constitution, and introducing a frantic democracy, let us take care how we prevent better people from any rational expectations of partaking in the benefits of that constitution *as it stands.* The maxims you establish cut the matter short. They have no sort of connexion with the good or ill behaviour of the persons who seek relief, or with the proper or improper means by which they seek it. They form a perpetual bar to all pleas and to all expectations.

You begin by asserting that "they ought to enjoy all things *under* the state, but that they ought not to *be the state.*" A position which, I believe, in the latter part of it, and in the latitude

1. Of bringing the French Revolution to Ireland with the military aid of France, as happened (unsuccessfully) in 1798, the year after Burke's death.

2. Probably such Irish revolutionary leaders as Theobald Wolfe Tone (1763–98) and James Napper Tandy (1740–1803), who were among the founders of the Dublin branch of the United Irishmen, an organization that aimed to unite Irish Catholics and Dissenting Protestants for the reform and, a few years later, for the overthrow of British rule in Ireland.

there expressed, no man of common sense has ever thought proper to dispute: because the contrary implies, that the state ought to be in them *exclusively.* But before you have finished the line, you express yourself as if the other member of your proposition, namely, that "they ought not to be *a part* of the state," were necessarily included in your first—Whereas I conceive it to be as different, as a part is from the whole; that is just as different as possible. I know indeed that it is common with those who talk very different from you, that is with heat and animosity, to confound those things, and to argue the admission of the Catholics into any, however minute and subordinate parts of the state, as a surrender into their hands of the whole government of the kingdom. To them I have nothing at all to say.

Wishing to proceed with a deliberative spirit and temper in so very serious a question, I shall attempt to analyze, as well as I can, the principles you lay down, in order to fit them for the grasp of an understanding so little comprehensive as mine—"State"—"Protestant"—"Revolution"—These are terms, which if not well explained, may lead us into many errors. In the word *State,* I conceive there is much ambiguity. The state is sometimes used to signify *the whole common-wealth,* comprehending all its orders, with the several privileges belonging to each. Sometimes it signifies only *the higher and ruling part* of the common-wealth; which we commonly call *the Government.* In the first sense, to be under the state, but not the state itself, *nor any part of it,* is a situation perfectly intelligible: but to those who fill that situation, not very pleasant, when it is understood. It is a state of *civil servitude* by the very force of the definition. *Servorum non est respublica,*[1] is a very old and a very true maxim. This servitude, which makes men *subject* to a state without being *citizens,* may be more or less tolerable from many circumstances: but these circum-

1. "Slaves are not members of the commonwealth."

stances, more or less favourable, do not alter the nature of the thing. The mildness by which absolute masters exercise their dominion, leaves them masters still. We may talk a little presently of the manner in which the majority of the people of Ireland (the Catholics) are affected by this situation; which at present undoubtedly is theirs, and which you are of opinion, ought to continue for ever.

In the other sense of the word *State,* by which is understood the *Supreme Government* only, I must observe this upon the question: that to exclude whole classes of men entirely from this *part* of government, cannot be considered as *absolute slavery.* It only implies a lower and degraded state of citizenship; such is (with more or less strictness) the condition of all countries, in which an hereditary nobility possess the exclusive rule. This may be no bad mode of government; provided that the personal authority of individual nobles be kept in due bounds, that their cabals and factions are guarded against with a severe vigilance: and that the people, (who have no share in granting their own money) are subjected to but light impositions, and are otherwise treated with attention, and with indulgence to their humours and prejudices.

The republic of Venice is one of those which strictly confines all the great functions and offices, such as are truly *state* functions and *state-offices,* to those who, by hereditary right or admission, are noble Venetians. But there are many offices, and some of them not mean nor unprofitable, which are reserved for the *Citadini.*[1] Of these all citizens of Venice are capable. The inhabitants of the *Terra firma,*[2] who are mere subjects of conquest, that is, as you express it, under the state, but "not a part of it," are not, however, subjects in so very rigorous a sense as not to be capable of numberless sub-

1. Citizens.

2. The solid ground; that is, that part of the mainland owned by the island republic.

ordinate employments. It is indeed one of the advantages attending the narrow bottom of their aristocracy (narrow as compared with their acquired dominions, otherwise broad enough) that an exclusion from such employments cannot possibly be made amongst their subjects. There are, besides, advantages in states so constituted, by which those who are considered as of an inferior race, are indemnified for their exclusion from the government and from noble employments. In all these countries, either by express laws, or by usage more operative, the noble casts are almost universally, in their turn, excluded from commerce, manufacture, farming of land, and in general from all lucrative civil professions. The nobles have the monopoly of honour. The plebeians a monopoly of all the means of acquiring wealth. Thus some sort of a balance is formed among conditions; a sort of compensation is furnished to those, who, in a *limited sense,* are excluded from the government of the state.

Between the extreme of *a total exclusion,* to which your maxim goes, and *an universal unmodified capacity,* to which the fanatics pretend, there are many different degrees and stages, and a great variety of temperaments, upon which prudence may give full scope to its exertions. For you know that the decisions of prudence (contrary to the system of the insane reasoners) differ from those of judicature: and that almost all the former are determined on the more or the less, the earlier or the later, and on a balance of advantage and inconvenience, of good and evil.

In all considerations which turn upon the question of vesting or continuing the state solely and exclusively in some one description of citizens; prudent legislators will consider, how far *the general form and principles of their commonwealth render it fit to be cast into an oligarchical shape, or to remain always in it.* We know that the government of Ireland (the same as the British) is not in its constitution *wholly* Aristocratical; and as it is not such in its form, so neither is it in its spirit. If it had been inveterately aristocratical, exclusions might be more patiently submitted to. The lot of one plebeian would be the lot of all; and an habitual reverence and admiration of certain families, might make the people content to see government wholly in hands to whom it seemed naturally to belong. But our constitution has *a plebeian member,* which forms an essential integrant part of it. A plebeian oligarchy is a monster in itself: and no people, not absolutely domestic or predial slaves,[1] will long endure it. The Protestants of Ireland are not *alone* sufficiently the people to form a democracy; and they are *too numerous* to answer the ends and purposes of *an aristocracy.* Admiration, that first source of obedience, can be only the claim or the imposture of the few. I hold it to be absolutely impossible for two millions of plebeians, composing certainly a very clear and decided majority in that class, to become so far in love with six or seven hundred thousand of their fellow-citizens (to all outward appearance plebeians like themselves, and many of them tradesmen, servants, and otherwise inferior to them) as to see with satisfaction, or even with patience, an exclusive power vested in them, by which constitutionally they become their absolute masters; and by the manners derived from their circumstances, must be capable of exercising upon them, daily and hourly, an insulting and vexatious superiority; nor are they indemnified (as in some aristocracies) for this state of humiliating vassalage (often inverting the nature of things and relations) by having the lower walks of industry wholly abandoned to them. They are rivalled, to say the least of the matter, in every laborious and lucrative course of life: while every franchise, every honour, every trust, every place down to the very lowest and least confidential (besides whole professions), is reserved for the master cast.

1. Predial slaves are those who work on the land, as distinguished from those who work in the house.

Our constitution is not made for great, general, and proscriptive exclusions; sooner or later, it will destroy them, or they will destroy the constitution. In our constitution there has always been a difference made between *a franchise* and *an office,* and between the capacity for the one and for the other. Franchises were supposed to belong to the *subject,* as *a subject,* and not *as a member of the governing part of the state.* The policy of Government has considered them as things very different: for whilst Parliament excluded by the test acts (and for a while these test acts[1] were not a dead letter, as now they are in England) Protestant dissenters from all civil and military employments, they *never touched their right of voting for members of Parliament, or sitting in either House;* a point I state, not as approving or condemning the measure of exclusion from employments, but to prove that the distinction has been admitted in legislature, as, in truth, it is founded in reason.

I will not here examine, whether the principles of the British [the Irish] constitution, be wise or not. I must assume that they are; and that those who partake the franchises which make it, partake of a benefit. They who are excluded from votes (under proper qualifications inherent in the constitution that gives them) are excluded, not from the *state,* but from *the British constitution.* They cannot by any possibility, whilst they hear its praises continually rung in their ears, and are present at the declaration which is so generally and so bravely made by those who possess the privilege—that the best blood in their veins ought to be shed, to preserve their share in it; they cannot, I say, think themselves in an *happy* state, to be utterly excluded from all its direct and all its con-

1. Test Acts were those designed to keep all but members of the Established Church from being eligible for public office, proscribing both Catholics and Dissenters. In England and Ireland, the tests included such requirements as receiving the sacrament of the Lord's Supper according to the rite of the Church of England and subscribing to a declaration against the Catholic doctrine of transubstantiation.

sequential advantages. The popular part of the constitution must be to them, by far the most odious part of it. To them it is not *an actual,* and, if possible, still less a *virtual* representation.[1] It is indeed the direct contrary. It is power unlimited, placed in the hands of *an adverse* description, *because it is an adverse description.* And if they who compose the privileged body have not an interest, they must but too frequently have motives of pride, passion, petulance, peevish jealousy, or tyrannic suspicion, to urge them to treat the people with contempt and rigour.

This is not a mere theory; though whilst men are men, it is a theory that cannot be false. I do not wish to revive all the particulars in my memory; I wish them to sleep for ever; but it is impossible I should wholly forget, what happened in some parts of Ireland, with very few and short intermissions, from the year 1761 to the year 1766, both inclusive. In a country of miserable police, passing from the extremes of laxity to the extremes of rigour, among a neglected, and therefore disorderly populace—if any disturbance or sedition, from any grievance real or imaginary happened to arise, it was presently perverted from its true nature (often criminal enough in itself to draw upon it a severe appropriate punishment), it was metamorphosed into a conspiracy against the state, and prosecuted as such. The object was, that those persons in the obnoxious description (in which all offenders will be most commonly found, because the most numerous and the most wretched) who could not easily, from their character and property, be suspected of the crimes of the lowest people, might be involved in the odium, in the suspicion, and sometimes in the punishment, of a higher and far more criminal species of offence. This did not arise from any one of the Popery laws since repealed, but from this circumstance, that the people of that description had no hold on the

1. For the meaning of virtual representation, see p. 240 below.

gentlemen who aspired to be popular representatives; and that the candidates neither loved, nor respected, nor feared them individually or collectively. I do not think this evil (an evil amongst a thousand others) at this day entirely over; for I conceive I have lately seen some indication of a disposition perfectly similar to the old ones; that is, a disposition to carry the imputation of crimes from persons to descriptions, and wholly to alter the character and quality of the offences themselves.

This universal exclusion seems to me a serious evil—because many collateral oppressions, besides what I have just now stated, have arisen from it. In things of this nature, it would not be either easy or proper to quote chapter and verse: but I have great reason to believe, particularly since the octenial act,[1] that several have refused at all to let their lands to Roman Catholics; because it would so far disable them from promoting such interests in counties as they were inclined to favour.[2] They who consider also the state of all sorts of tradesmen, shopkeepers, and particularly publicans in towns, must soon discern the disadvantages under which those labour who have no votes. It cannot be otherwise, whilst the spirit of elections, and the tendencies of human nature continue as they are. If property be artificially separated from franchise, the franchise must in some way or other, and in some proportion, naturally attract property to it. Many are the collateral disadvantages, amongst a *privileged* people, which must attend those who have *no* privileges. Among the rich, each individual is of importance; the poor and the middling are no otherwise so, than as they obtain some collective capacity, and can be aggregated to some corps. If

1. An Act of 1768 that provided for a general election every eight years.

2. The greater frequency of parliamentary elections was an incentive for Protestant landlords not to rent land to Catholics, because by making Protestant tenants freeholders with the right to vote, the lords could promote their political interests in elections.

legal ways are not found, illegal will be resorted to; and seditious clubs and confederacies, such as no man living holds in greater horror than I do, will grow and flourish, in spite, I am afraid, of any thing which can be done to prevent the evil. Lawful enjoyment is the surest method to prevent unlawful gratification. Where there is property, there will be less theft; where there is marriage, there will always be less fornication.

I have said enough of the question of state, *as it affects the people, merely as such.* But it is complicated with a political question relative to religion, to which it is very necessary I should say something; because the term *Protestant,* which you apply, is too general for the conclusions which one of your accurate understanding would wish to draw from it; and because a great deal of argument will depend on the use that is made of that term.

It is *not* a fundamental part of the settlement at the revolution, that the state should be protestant without *any qualification of the term.* With a qualification it is unquestionably true; not in all its latitude. With the qualification, it was true before the revolution. Our predecessors in legislation were not so irrational (not to say impious) as to form an operose ecclesiastical establishment, and even to render the state itself in some degree subservient to it, when their religion (if such it might be called) was nothing but a mere *negation* of some other—without any positive idea either of doctrine, discipline, worship, or morals, which they professed themselves, and which they imposed upon others, even under penalties and incapacities—No! No! This never could have been done even by reasonable Atheists. They who think religion of no importance to the state have abandoned it to the conscience, or caprice of the individual; they make no provision for it whatsoever, but leave every club to make, or not, a voluntary contribution according to their fancies. This would be consistent. The other always appeared to me to be a monster of contradiction and absurdity. It was for that reason, that some years ago I strenuously opposed the clergy who petitioned, to the number of about three hundred, to be freed from the subscription to the 39 Articles, without proposing to substitute any other in their place. There never has been a religion of the state (the few years of the Parliament only excepted) but that of *the church of England;* the church of England, before the reformation, connected with the See of Rome, since then, disconnected and protesting against some of her doctrines, and the whole of her authority, as binding in our national church: nor did the fundamental laws of this kingdom (in Ireland it has been the same) ever know, at any period, any other church *as an object of establishment;* or in that light, any other Protestant religion. Nay our Protestant *toleration* itself at the revolution, and until within a few years, required a signature of thirty-six, and a part of a thirty-seventh, out of the thirty-nine Articles. So little idea had they at the revolution of *establishing* Protestantism indefinitely, that they did not indefinitely *tolerate* it under that name. I do not mean to praise that strictness, where nothing more than merely religious toleration is concerned. Toleration being a part of moral and political prudence, ought to be tender and large, and not too scrupulous in its investigations; but may bear without blame, not only very ill-grounded doctrines, but even many things that are positively vices, where they are *adulta et praevalida.*[1] The good of the common-wealth is the rule which rides over the rest; and to this every other must completely submit.

The church of Scotland knows as little of Protestantism *undefined,* as the church of England and Ireland do. She has by the articles of union[2] secured to herself the perpetual establishment of *the Confession of Faith,* and the *Presbyterian*

1. Burke has reversed the order of Tacitus's words, which should be *praevalida et adulta vitia,* "prevalent and full-blown vices." *Annales* 1.3.53.

2. The articles concerning religion in the Act of Union of 1707, which merged England and Scotland into one kingdom with one Parliament.

church government. In England, even during the troubled interregnum, it was not thought fit to establish a *negative* religion; but the Parliament settled the *Presbyterian,* as the church *discipline;* the directory, as the rule of public *worship;* and the *Westminster catechism,* as the institute of *faith.* This is to shew, that at no time was the Protestant religion *undefined,* established here, or any where else, as I believe. I am sure that when the three religions were established in Germany, they were expressly characterized and declared to be the *Evangelic* and *Reformed,* and the *Catholic;* each of which has its confession of faith, and its settled discipline; so that you always may know the best and the worst of them, to enable you to make the most of what is good, and to correct or qualify, or guard against whatever may seem evil or dangerous.

As to the coronation oath, to which you allude as opposite to admitting a Roman Catholic to the use of any franchise whatsoever, I cannot think that the king would be perjured if he gave his assent to any regulation which Parliament might think fit to make, with regard to that affair. The king is bound by law, as clearly specified in several acts of Parliament, to be in communion with the church of England. It is a part of the tenure by which he holds his crown; and though no provision was made till the revolution, which could be called positive and valid in law, to ascertain this great principle; I have always considered it as in fact fundamental, that the king of England should be of the Christian religion, according to the national legal church for the time being. I conceive it was so before the reformation, and that since the reformation it became doubly necessary; because the king is the head of that church; in some sort an ecclesiastical person; and it would be incongruous and absurd, to have the head of the church of one faith, and the members of another. The king may *inherit* the crown as a *Protestant,* but he cannot *hold it* according to law, without being a Protestant *of the church of England.*

Before we take it for granted, that the king is bound by

his coronation oath, not to admit any of his Catholic subjects to the rights and liberties, which ought to belong to them as Englishmen (not as religionists) or to settle the conditions or proportions of such admission by an act of Parliament; I wish you to place before your eyes that oath itself, as it is settled in the act of William and Mary.

"Will you to the utmost of your power maintain—[1] The laws of God—[2] the true Profession of [3] the gospel—and [4] The protestant reformed religion *as it is established by law.*—And [5] will you preserve unto *bishops* and clergy, and the churches committed to *their* charge, all such rights and privileges as by law do, or shall appertain to them, or any of them.—All this I promise to do."

Here are the coronation engagements of the King. In them I do not find one word to preclude his Majesty from consenting to any arrangement which Parliament may make with regard to the civil privileges of any part of his subjects.

It may not be amiss, on account of the light which it may throw on this discussion, to look a little more narrowly into the matter of that oath—in order to discover how far it has hitherto operated as a bar to any proceedings of the Crown and Parliament, in favour of those against whom it may be supposed that the king has engaged to support the Protestant church of England in the two kingdoms, in which it is established by law. First, the king swears he will maintain to the utmost of his power, "the laws of God." I suppose it means the natural moral laws. Secondly, he swears to maintain "the true profession of the Gospel." By which I suppose is understood *affirmatively* the Christian religion. Thirdly, that he will maintain "the Protestant reformed religion." This leaves me no power of supposition or conjecture; for it is defined and described by the subsequent words, "established by law," and in this instance to define it beyond all possibility of doubt, he "swears to maintain the bishops and clergy, and the churches committed to their charge," in their rights, present and future.

This oath as effectually prevents the King from doing any thing to the prejudice of the church in favour of Sectaries, Jews, Mahometans, or plain avowed Infidels; just as if he should do the same thing in favour of the Catholics. You will see, that it is the same Protestant Church, so described, which the King is to maintain and communicate with, according to the act of settlement of the 12th and 13th of William III. The act of the 5th of Anne, made in prospect of the union, is entitled "An act for securing the Church of England as by law established." It meant to guard the church implicitly against any other mode of Protestant religion which might creep in by means of the union. It proves beyond all doubt, that the legislature did not mean to guard the church on one part only, and to leave it defenceless and exposed upon every other. This church, in that act, is declared to be "fundamental and essential" for ever, in the constitution of the united kingdom, so far as England is concerned; and I suppose as the law stands, even since the independence,[1] it is so in Ireland.

All this shews, that the religion which the King is bound to maintain, has a positive part in it as well as a negative; and that the positive part of it (in which we are in perfect agreement[2] with the Catholics and with the Church of Scotland) is infinitely the most valuable and essential. Such an agreement we had with Protestant Dissenters in England, of those descriptions who came under the toleration act of King

1. The independence of the Irish Parliament since 1783, when the British Parliament acknowledged the right of the people of Ireland "to be bound only by laws enacted by his Majesty and the Parliament of that kingdom, in all cases whatever."

2. Burke always assumed that there were fundamental doctrines on which all the principal religions of Christendom agreed, but he never stated what they were.

William and Queen Mary; an act coeval with the revolution; and which ought, on the principles of the gentlemen who oppose the relief to the Catholics, to have been held sacred and unalterable. Whether we agree with the present Protestant Dissenters in the points at the revolution held essential and fundamental among Christians, or in any other fundamental, at present it is impossible for us to know; because, at their own very earnest desire, we have repealed the toleration act of William and Mary, and discharged them from the signature required by that act; and because we know that, for the far greater part, they publicly declare against all manner of confessions of faith, even the *consensus.*

I dwell a little the longer upon this matter, and take the more pains, to put us both in mind that it was not settled at the revolution, that the state should be protestant, in the latitude of the term, but in a defined and limited sense only, and that, in that sense only, the King is sworn to maintain it, for reasons forcible enough at all times, but at this time peculiarly so. To suppose that the King has sworn with his utmost power to maintain what it is wholly out of his power to discover, or which, if he could discover, he might discover to consist of things directly contradictory to each other, some of them perhaps, impious, blasphemous, and seditious upon principle, would be not only a gross, but a most mischievous absurdity. It would make a merit of dissenting from the church of England, because the man happens to dissent from the church of Rome also; for a man is certainly the most perfect Protestant, and the most perfect Dissenter, who protests against, and dissents from the whole Christian Religion. Whether a person's having no Christian Religion, be a title to favour in exclusion to the largest description of Christians who hold all the doctrines of Christianity, though holding along with them some errors and some superfluities, is rather more than any man who has not become recreant and apostate from his baptism, will, I believe, choose to affirm. The countenance given from a spirit of controversy to that negative religion, may, by degrees, encourage light and unthinking people to a total indifference to every thing positive in matters of doctrine; and, in the end, of practice too. If continued, it would play the game of that sort of active, proselytizing, and persecuting atheism, which is the disgrace and calamity of our time, and which we see to be as capable of subverting a government, as any mode of misguided zeal for better things.

Now let us fairly see what course has been taken relative to those, against whom, in part at least, the King has sworn to maintain a church, *positive in its doctrine and its discipline.* The first thing done, even when the oath was fresh in the mouth of the sovereigns, was to give a toleration to Protestant Dissenters, *whose doctrines they ascertained.* As to the mere civil privileges which the Dissenters held as subjects before the revolution, these were not touched at all. The laws have fully permitted, in a qualification for all offices, to such Dissenters, *an occasional conformity;* a thing I believe singular, where tests are admitted. The act called the Test Act itself, is, with regard to them, grown to be hardly any thing more than a dead letter. Whenever the Dissenters cease by their conduct to give any alarm to the government, in church and state, I think it very probable that even this matter, rather disgustful than inconvenient to them, may be removed, or at least so modified as to distinguish the qualification to those offices which really *guide the state,* from those which are *merely instrumental;* or that some other and better tests may be put in their place.

So far as to England. In Ireland you have outran us. Without waiting for an English example, you have totally, and without any modification whatsoever, repealed the test as to Protestant Dissenters. Not having the repealing act by me, I ought not to say positively that there is no exception in it; but if it be, what I suppose you know very well, that a Jew in religion, or a Mahometan, or even *a public, declared Athiest,* and blasphemer, is perfectly qualified to be lord lieutenant, a lord justice, or even keeper of the king's conscience; and by virtue of his office (if with you it be as it is with us) administrator to a great part of the ecclesiastical patronage of the crown.

Now let us deal a little fairly. We must admit, that Protestant dissent was one of the quarters from which danger was apprehended at the revolution, and against which a part of the coronation oath was peculiarly directed. By this unqualified repeal, you certainly did not mean to deny that it was the duty of the crown to preserve the church against Protestant Dissenters; or taking this to be the true sense of the two revolution acts of King William, and of the previous and subsequent union acts of Queen Anne, you did not declare by this most unqualified repeal, by which you broke down all the barriers, not invented, indeed, but carefully preserved at the revolution; you did not then and by that proceeding declare, that you had advised the king to perjury towards God, and perfidy towards the church. No! far, very far from it! you never would have done it, if you did not think it could be done with perfect repose to the royal conscience, and perfect safety to the national established religion. You did this upon a full consideration of the circumstances of your country. Now if circumstances required it, why should it be contrary to the king's oath, his parliament judging on those circumstances, to restore to his Catholic people, in such measure, and with such modifications as the public wisdom shall think proper to add, *some part* in these franchises which they formerly had held without any limitation at all, and which, upon no sort of urgent reason at the time, they were deprived of? If such means can with any probability be shewn, from circumstances, rather to add strength to our mixed ecclesiastical and secular constitution, than to weaken it; surely they are means infinitely to be preferred to penalties, incapacities and proscriptions continued from generation to generation. They are perfectly consistent with the other parts of the Coronation Oath, in which the king swears to maintain "the laws of God and the true profession of the gospel, and to govern the people according to the statutes in Parliament agreed upon, and the laws and customs of the realm." In consenting to such a statute, the Crown would act at least as agreeable to the laws of God, and to the true profession of the gospel, and to the laws and customs of the kingdom, as George I. did when he passed the statute which took from the body of the people, every thing which, to that hour, and even after the monstrous acts of the 2d and 8th of Anne, (the objects of common hatred) they still enjoyed inviolate.[1]

It is hard to distinguish with the last degree of accuracy, what laws are fundamental, and what not. However there is a distinction authorized by the writers on jurisprudence, and recognized in some of our statutes. I admit the acts of King William and Queen Anne to be fundamental, but they are not the *only* fundamental laws. The law called *Magna Charta,* by which it is provided that, "no man shall be disseized of his liberties and free customs but by the judgment of his peers, or the laws of the land" (meaning clearly for some proved crime tried and adjudged), I take to be a *fundamental law.* Now, although this Magna Charta, or some of the statutes establishing it, provide that that law shall be perpetual, and all statutes contrary to it shall be void: yet I cannot go so far as to deny the authority of statutes made in defiance of Magna Charta and all its principles. This however I will say, that it is a very venerable law, made by very wise and learned men, and that the legislature in their attempt to perpetuate it, even against the authority of future parliaments, have shewn their judgment that it is *fundamental,* on the same grounds, and in the same manner that the act of the fifth of

1. It was, in fact, an Act of George II in 1728 that provided that "no papist . . . shall be intitled or admitted to vote at the election of any member to serve in Parliament." *W&S* 9:570, n. 1; 610, n. 1.

Anne has considered, and declared the establishment of the church of England to be fundamental. Magna Charta, which secured these franchises to the subjects, regarded the rights of freeholders in counties to be as much a fundamental part of the constitution, as the establishment of the church of England was thought either at that time, or in the act of King William, or in the act of Queen Anne.

The churchmen, who led in that transaction, certainly took care of the material interest of which they were the natural guardians. It is the first article of Magna Charta, "that the church of England shall be free," &c. &c. But churchmen, and barons, and knights, took care of the franchises and free customs of the people too. Those franchises are part of the constitution itself, and inseparable from it. It would be a very strange thing if there should not only exist, anomalies in our laws, a thing not easy to prevent, but, that the fundamental parts of the constitution should be perpetually and irreconcilably at variance. I cannot persuade myself that the lovers of our church are not as able to find effectual ways of reconciling its safety with the franchises of the people, as the ecclesiastics of the thirteenth century were able to do; I cannot conceive how any thing worse can be said of the Protestant religion of the church of England than this, that wherever it is judged proper to give it a legal establishment, it becomes necessary to deprive the body of the people, if they adhere to their old opinions, of "their liberties and of all their free customs," and to reduce them to a state of *civil* servitude.

There is no man on earth, I believe, more willing than I am to lay it down as a fundamental of the constitution, that the church of England should be united and even identified with it: but allowing this, I cannot allow that all *laws of regulation,* made from time to time, in support of that fundamental law, are, of course, equally fundamental and equally unchangeable. This would be to confound all the branches of legislation and of jurisprudence. The *Crown* and the personal safety of the monarch are *fundamentals* in our constitution: Yet, I hope that no man regrets, that the rabble of statutes got together during the reign of Henry the Eighth, by which treasons are multiplied with so prolific an energy, have been all repealed in a body; although they were all, or most of them, made in support of things truly fundamental in our constitution. So were several of the acts by which the crown exercised its supremacy; such as the act of Elizabeth, for making the *high commission courts,*[1] and the like; as well as things made treason in the time of Charles II. None of this species of *secondary and subsidiary laws* have been held fundamental. They have yielded to circumstances: particularly where they were thought, even in their consequences, or obliquely, to affect other fundamentals. How much more, certainly, ought they to give way, when, as in our case, they effect, not here and there, in some particular point, or in their consequence, but universally, collectively, and directly, the fundamental franchises of a people, equal to the whole inhabitants of several respectable kingdoms and states; equal to the subjects of the kings of Sardinia or Denmark; equal to those of the United Netherlands; and more than are to be found in all the states of Switzerland. This way of proscribing men by whole nations, as it were, from all the benefits of the constitution to which they were born, I never can believe to be politic or expedient, much less necessary for the existence of any state or church in the world. Whenever I shall be convinced, which will be late and reluctantly, that the safety of the church is utterly inconsistent with all the civil rights whatsoever of the far larger part of the inhabitants of our country, I shall be extremely sorry for it; because I shall think the church to be truly in danger. It is putting things into the position of an ugly alternative, into which, I hope in God, they never will be put.

I have said most of what occurs to me on the topics you

1. Courts created to exercise the Crown's ecclesiastical jurisdiction.

touch upon, relative to the religion of the king, and his coronation oath. I shall conclude the observations which I wished to submit to you on this point, by assuring you, that I think you the most remote that can be conceived from the metaphysicians of our times, who are the most foolish of men, and who, dealing in universals and essences, see no difference between more and less; and who of course would think that the reason of the law which obliged the king to be a communicant of the church of England, would be as valid to exclude a Catholic from being an exciseman, or to deprive a man who has five hundred a year, under that description, from voting on a par with a factitious Protestant Dissenting freeholder of forty shillings.

Recollect, my dear friend, that it was a fundamental principle in the French monarchy, whilst it stood, that the state should be Catholic; yet the edict of Nantz gave, not a full ecclesiastical, but a complete civil *establishment,* with places of which only they were capable, to the Calvinists of France; and there were very few employments indeed of which they were not capable. The world praised the Cardinal de Richlieu, who took the first opportunity to strip them of their fortified places and cautionary towns.[1] The same world held and does hold in execration (so far as that business is concerned) the memory of Louis the Fourteenth, for the total repeal of that favourable edict; though the talk of "fundamental laws, established religion, religion of the prince, safety to the state," *&c. &c.* was then as largely held, and with as bitter a revival of the animosities of the civil confusions during the struggles between the parties, as now they can be in Ireland.

Perhaps there are those who think that the same reason does not hold when the religious relation of the sovereign and subject is changed; but they who have their shop full of

1. *Places de sûreté:* towns held by French Protestants for their security and garrisoned at the king's expense.

false weights and measures, and who think that the adding or taking away the name of Protestant or Papist, Guelph or Ghibelline,[1] alters all the principles of equity, policy, and prudence, leave us no common data upon which we can reason. I therefore pass by all this, which on you will make no impression, to come to what seems to be a serious consideration in your mind; I mean the dread you express of "reviewing, for the purpose of altering, the *principles of the Revolution.*" This is an interesting topic; on which I will, as fully as your leisure and mine permits, lay before you the ideas I have formed.

First, I cannot possibly confound in my mind all the things which were done at the Revolution, with the *principles* of the Revolution. As in most great changes many things were done from the necessities of the time, well or ill understood, from passion or from vengeance, which were not only, not perfectly agreeable to its principles, but in the most direct contradiction to them. I shall not think that the *deprivation of some millions of people of all the rights of citizens, and all interest in the constitution, in and to which they were born,* was a thing conformable to the *declared principles* of the Revolution. This I am sure is true relatively to England (where the operation of these *anti-principles* comparatively were of little extent), and some of our late laws on that subject admit it. But the Revolution operated differently in England and Ireland, in many, and these essential particulars. Supposing the principles to have been altogether the same in both kingdoms, by the application of those principles to very different objects, the whole spirit of the system was changed, not to say reversed. In England it was the struggle of the *great body* of the people for the establishment of their liberties, against the efforts of a very *small faction,* who would have oppressed them. In Ireland it was the establishment of the power of the smaller number,

1. Partisans respectively of the Pope or of the Holy Roman Emperor in the struggles between the two potentates in medieval Italy.

at the expence of the civil liberties and properties of the far greater part; and at the expence of the political liberties of the whole. It was, to say the truth, not a revolution, but a conquest; which is not to say a great deal in its favour. To insist on every thing done in Ireland at the Revolution, would be to insist on the severe and jealous policy of a conqueror, in the crude settlement of his new acquisition, as a *permanent* rule for its future government. This, no power, in no country that ever I heard of, has done or professed to do—except in Ireland; where it is done, and possibly by some people will be professed. Time has, by degrees, in all other places and periods, blended and coalited the conquered with the conquerors. So, after some time, and after one of the most rigid conquests that we read of in history, the Normans softened into the English. I wish you to turn your recollection to the fine speech of Cerealis[1] to the Gauls, to dissuade them from revolt. Speaking of the Romans, "*Nos* quamvis toties lacessiti, jure victoriae id solum vobis addidimus, quo pacem tueremur; nam neque quies gentium sine armis; neque arma sine stipendiis; neque stipendia sine tributis, haberi queant. *Caetera in communi sita sunt:* ipsi plerumque nostris exercitibus *praesidetis:* ipsi has aliasque provincias, *regitis: nil seperatum clausumve*—Proinde Pacem et urbem, quam *victores victique eodem jure obtinemus,* amate, colite."[2] You will consider, whether the arguments used by that Roman to these Gauls, would apply to the case in Ireland; and whether you could

1. The Roman general Cerialis Petilius.

2. "Although often provoked, the only use we have made of our right of conquest has been to impose on you the necessary costs of maintaining peace; for tranquillity among nations cannot be had without arms, nor arms without soldiers' pay, nor pay without taxes. Everything else we have in common. You often command our armies, you rule these and other provinces; no privileges are set aside for us or closed to you. . . . Therefore love and cherish peace and the city wherein we, conquerors and conquered alike, enjoy an equal right." Tacitus *Histories* 4:74.

use so plausible a preamble to any severe warning you might think it proper to hold out to those who should resort to sedition instead of supplication, to obtain any object that they may pursue with the governing power.

For a much longer period than that which had sufficed to blend the Romans with the nation to which of all others they were the most adverse, the Protestants settled in Ireland, considered themselves in no other light than that of a sort of a colonial garrison, to keep the natives in subjection to the other state of Great Britain. The whole spirit of the revolution in Ireland, was that of not the mildest conqueror. In truth, the spirit of those proceedings did not commence at that aera, nor was religion of any kind their primary object. What was done, was not in the spirit of a contest between two religious factions; but between two adverse nations. The statutes of Kilkenny[1] shew, that the spirit of the popery laws, and some even of their actual provisions, as applied between Englishry and Irishry, had existed in that harassed country before the words Protestant and Papist were heard of in the world. If we read Baron Finglas, Spenser, and Sir John Davis,[2] we cannot miss the true genius and policy of the English government there before the revolution, as well as during the whole reign of Queen Elizabeth. Sir John Davis boasts of the benefits received by the natives, by extending to them the English law, and turning the whole kingdom into shire ground.

1. A Parliament held in Kilkenny in 1366 attempted to cut English losses and keep as much of Ireland as possible under English control. It decreed that, within the pale of English law, the English and the Irish who lived among them must use English surnames, speak English, and follow English customs. They were forbidden to marry "the Irish enemies" who remained outside the pale or to follow Irish law or customs. The Irish from beyond the pale were to be unable to plead in the courts or to purchase or inherit land among the English.

2. Patrick Finglas and Sir John Davies held high offices in Ireland in the reigns of Henry VIII and James I, respectively. Edmund Spenser, the poet, held minor offices there in the reign of Elizabeth I. All of them wrote at some length about conditions in Ireland under English rule.

But the appearance of things alone was changed. The original scheme was never deviated from for a single hour. Unheard of confiscations were made in the northern parts, upon grounds of plots and conspiracies, never proved upon their supposed authors. The war of chicane succeeded to the war of arms and of hostile statutes; and a regular series of operations were carried on, particularly from Chichester's[1] time, in the ordinary courts of justice, and by special commissions and inquisitions; first, under pretence of tenures, and then of titles in the crown, for the purpose of the total extirpation of the interest of the natives in their own soil—until this species of subtile ravage, being carried to the last excess of oppression and insolence under Lord Stafford,[2] it kindled at length the flames of that rebellion which broke out in 1641. By the issue of that war, by the turn which the Earl of Clarendon[3] gave to things at the restoration, and by the total reduction of the kingdom of Ireland in 1691; the ruin of the native Irish, and in a great measure too, of the first races of the English, was completely accomplished. The new English interest was settled with as solid a stability as any thing in human affairs can look for. All the penal laws of that unparalleled code of oppression, which were made after the last event, were manifestly the effects of national hatred and scorn towards a conquered people; whom the victors delighted to trample upon, and were not at all afraid to provoke. They were not the effect

1. Sir Arthur Chichester, Lord Deputy of Ireland from 1604 to 1616, carried out a policy of coercing Catholics into conforming to the religion by law established.

2. Sir Thomas Wentworth, created Lord Deputy of Ireland in 1632 and Lord Lieutenant and Earl of Stafford in 1639. He was zealous in raising revenue for the Stuart monarchy.

3. Edward Hyde, first Earl of Clarendon, as Charles II's Lord Chancellor of England, presided over the Restoration settlement. Although Clarendon was eager to restore and support the Anglican establishment, certain harsh measures adopted by Parliament, which became known as the Clarendon Code, did not reflect the conciliatory spirit he favored in England and Ireland.

of their fears but of their security. They who carried on this system, looked to the irresistible force of Great Britain for their support in their acts of power. They were quite certain that no complaints of the natives would be heard on this side of the water, with any other sentiments than those of contempt and indignation. Their cries served only to augment their torture. Machines which could answer their purposes so well, must be of an excellent contrivance. Indeed at that time in England, the double name of the complainants, Irish and Papists (it would be hard to say, singly, which was the most odious) shut up the hearts of every one against them. Whilst that temper prevailed, and it prevailed in all its force to a time within our memory, every measure was pleasing and popular, just in proportion as it tended to harass and ruin a set of people, who were looked upon as enemies to God and man; and indeed as a race of bigotted savages who were a disgrace to human nature itself.

However, as the English in Ireland began to be domiciliated, they began also to recollect that they had a country. The *English interest* at first by faint and almost insensible degrees, but at length openly and avowedly, became an *independent Irish interest;* full as independent as it could ever have been, if it had continued in the persons of the native Irish; and it was maintained with more skill, and more consistency than probably it would have been in theirs. With their views, they changed their maxims—it was necessary to demonstrate to the whole people, that there was something at least, of a common interest, combined with the independency, which was to become the object of common exertions. The mildness of government produced the first relaxation towards the Irish; the necessities, and, in part too, the temper that predominated at this great change, produced the second and the most important of these relaxations. English government, and Irish legislature felt jointly the propriety of this measure. The Irish parliament and nation became independent.

The true revolution to you, that which most intrinsically and substantially resembled the English revolution of 1688, was the Irish revolution of 1782. The Irish Parliament of 1782, bore little resemblance to that which sat in that kingdom, after the period of the first revolution;[1] it bore a much nearer resemblance (though not at all in its temper) to that which sat under King James.[2] The change of the Parliament in 1782 from the character of the Parliament which, as a token of its indignation, had burned all the journals indiscriminately of the former Parliament in the council chamber,[3] was very visible. The address of King William's Parliament, the Parliament which assembled after the Revolution, amongst other causes of complaint (many of them sufficiently just), complains of the repeal by their predecessors of Poyning's law;[4] no absolute idol with the Parliament of 1782.

1. The Irish Parliament in 1782 had taken the initial step toward legislative independence; the one that met in 1695 after the defeat of James II was entirely Protestant in membership, frankly subordinate to England, and determined to crush any possibility of another Irish Catholic uprising.

2. When James II fled to Ireland, he called a Parliament in Dublin in 1689. The great majority of its members were Anglo-Irish Catholics who attempted to reverse many of the results of the English and Protestant conquest of Ireland.

3. The Irish Parliament of 1695 declared the acts of the Parliament held under James II in 1689 null and void, and had all of its records burned.

4. In 1468, the Irish Parliament had asserted that acts of the English Parliament were not valid in Ireland unless ratified by the Irish Parliament. In 1494, Henry VII sent Sir Edward Poynings to Ireland as Lord Deputy with orders to reduce the country to "whole and perfect obedience" to the English Crown. Poynings pushed through a Parliament held in Drogheda a series of statutes for that purpose, the most famous of which became known as Poynings' Law.

This law provided that the Irish Parliament could not meet unless it was so authorized by the English lord chancellor, could act only on topics approved beforehand by the king and his English council, could enact legislation only after it had been sent to the king and council, and could not amend the legislation from the form in which it was sent back to Ireland.

Burke erred regarding the Address presented to William and Mary in

Great Britain finding the Anglo-Irish highly animated with a spirit, which had indeed shewn itself before, though with little energy, and many interruptions, and therefore suffered a multitude of uniform precedents to be established against it, acted in my opinion, with the greatest temperance and wisdom. She saw, that the disposition of the *leading part* of the nation, would not permit them to act any longer the part of a *garrison.* She saw, that true policy did not require that they ever should have appeared in that character; or if it had done so formerly, the reasons had now ceased to operate. She saw that the Irish of her race, were resolved, to build their constitution and their politics, upon another bottom. With those things under her view, she instantly complied with the whole of your demands, without any reservation whatsoever. She surrendered that boundless superiority, for the preservation of which, and the acquisition, she had supported the English colonies in Ireland for so long a time, and at so vast an expence (according to the standard of those ages) of her blood and treasure.

When we bring before us the matter which history affords for our selection, it is not improper to examine the spirit of the several precedents, which are candidates for our choice. Might it not be as well for your statesmen, on the other side of the water, to take an example from this latter, and surely more conciliatory revolution, as a pattern for your conduct towards your own fellow-citizens, than from that of 1688, when a paramount sovereignty over both you and them, was more loftily claimed, and more sternly exerted, than at any former, or at any subsequent period? Great Britain in 1782, rose above the vulgar ideas of policy, the ordinary jealousies of state, and all the sentiments of national pride and national ambition. If she had been more disposed than, I thank God

1692. It did not mention Poynings' Law, and the Parliament held by James II in 1689 had not repealed it. *W&S* 9:617, n. 3.

for it, she was, to listen to the suggestions of passion, than to the dictates of prudence; she might have urged the principles, the maxims, the policy, the practice of the revolution, against the demands of the leading description in Ireland, with full as much plausibility, and full as good a grace, as any amongst them can possibly do, against the supplications of so vast and extensive a description of their own people. A good deal too, if the spirit of domination and exclusion had prevailed in England, might be excepted against some of the means then employed in Ireland, whilst her claims were in agitation; they were, at least, as much out of ordinary course, as those which are now objected against admitting your people to any of the benefits of an English constitution.

Most certainly, neither with you, nor here, was any one ignorant of what was at that time said, written, and done. But on all sides we separated the means from the end: and we separated the cause of the moderate and rational, from the ill-intentioned and seditious; which on such occasions are so frequently apt to march together. At that time, on your part, you were not afraid to review what was done at the revolution of 1688; and what had been continued during the subsequent flourishing period of the British empire. The change then made was a great and fundamental alteration. In the execution, it was an operose business on both sides of the water. It required the repeal of several laws, the modification of many, and a new course to be given to an infinite number of legislative, judicial, and official practices and usages in both kingdoms. This did not frighten any of us. You are now asked to give, in some moderate measure, to your fellow-citizens, what Great Britain gave to you, without any measure at all. Yet, notwithstanding all the difficulties at the time, and the apprehensions which some very well-meaning people entertained, through the admirable temper in which this revolution (or restoration in the nature of a revolution) was conducted in both kingdoms; it has hitherto produced no inconvenience to either; and I trust, with the continuance of the same temper, that it never will. I think that this small inconsiderable change relative to an exclusion statute (not made at the revolution) for restoring the people to the benefits, from which the green soreness of a civil war had not excluded them, will be productive of no sort of mischief whatsoever. Compare what was done in 1782, with what is wished in 1792; consider the spirit of what has been done at the several periods of reformation; and weigh maturely, whether it be exactly true, that conciliatory concessions, are of good policy only in discussions between nations; but that among descriptions in the same nation, they must always be irrational and dangerous. What have you suffered in your peace, your prosperity, or, in what ought ever to be dear to a nation, your glory, by the last act by which you took the property of that people under the protection of the *laws?* What reason have you to dread the consequences of admitting the people possessing that property to some share in the protection of the *constitution?*

I do not mean to trouble you with any thing to remove the objections, I will not call them arguments, against this measure, taken from a ferocious hatred to all that numerous description of Christians. It would be to pay a poor compliment to your understanding or your heart. Neither *your* religion, nor *your* politics consist "in odd perverse antipathies." You are not resolved to persevere in proscribing from the constitution, so many millions of your countrymen, because, in contradiction to experience and to common sense, you think proper to imagine, that their principles are subversive of common human society. To that I shall only say, that whoever has a temper, which can be gratified by indulging himself in these good-natured fancies, ought to do a great deal more. For an exclusion from the privileges of British subjects, is not a cure for so terrible a distemper of the human mind, as they are pleased to suppose in their countrymen. I rather conceive those privileges to be itself a remedy for some mental disorders.

As little shall I detain you with matters that can as little obtain admission into a mind like yours; such as the fear, or pretence of fear, that in spite of your own power, and the trifling power of Great Britain, you may be conquered by the Pope; or that this commodious bugbear (who is of infinitely more use to those who pretend to fear, than to those who love him) will absolve his Majesty's subjects from their allegiance, and send over the cardinal of York to rule you as his viceroy; or that, by the plenitude of his power, he will take that fierce tyrant, the king of the French, out of his jail, and arm that nation (which on all occasions treats his Holiness so very politely) with his bulls and pardons, to invade poor old Ireland, to reduce you to popery and slavery, and to force the free-born, naked feet of your people into the wooden shoes of that arbitrary monarch. I do not believe that discourses of this kind are held, or that any thing like them will be held, by any who walk about without a keeper. Yet, I confess, that on occasions of this nature, I am the most afraid of the weakest reasonings; because they discover the strongest passions. These things will never be brought out in definite propositions; they would not prevent pity towards any persons; they would only cause it for those who were capable of talking in such a strain. But I know, and am sure, that such ideas as no man will distinctly produce to another, or hardly venture to bring in any plain shape to his own mind—he will utter in obscure, ill explained doubts, jealousies, surmises, fears, and apprehensions; and that in such a fog, they will appear to have a good deal of size, and will make an impression; when, if they were clearly brought forth and defined, they would meet with nothing but scorn and derision.

There is another way of taking an objection to this concession, which I admit to be something more plausible, and worthy of a more attentive examination. It is, that this numerous class of people is mutinous, disorderly, prone to sedition, and easy to be wrought upon by the insidious arts of wicked and designing men; that conscious of this, the sober, rational, and wealthy part of that body, who are totally of another character, do by no means desire any participation for themselves, or for any one else of their description, in the franchises of the British constitution.

I have great doubt of the exactness of any part of this observation. But let us admit that the body of the Catholics are prone to sedition (of which, as I have said, I entertain much doubt), is it possible, that any fair observer or fair reasoner, can think of confining this description to them only? I believe it to be possible for men to be mutinous and seditious who feel no grievance: but I believe no man will assert seriously, that when people are of a turbulent spirit, the best way to keep them in order, is to furnish them with something substantial to complain of.

You separate very properly the sober, rational, and substantial part of their description from the rest. You give, as you ought to do, weight only to the former. What I have always thought of the matter is this—that the most poor, illiterate, and uninformed creatures upon earth, are judges of a *practical* oppression. It is a matter of feeling; and as such persons generally have felt most of it, and are not of an overlively sensibility, they are the best judges of it. But for the *real cause,* or the *appropriate remedy,* they ought never to be called into council about the one or the other. They ought to be totally shut out; because their reason is weak; because when once roused, their passions are ungoverned; because they want information; because the smallness of the property which individually they possess, renders them less attentive to the consequence of the measures they adopt in affairs of moment. When I find a great cry amongst the people, who speculate little, I think myself called seriously to examine into it, and to separate the real cause from the ill effects of the passion it may excite; and the bad use which artful men may make of an irritation of the popular mind. Here we must be aided by persons of a contrary character; we must not listen to the desperate or the furious; but it is therefore necessary for us to distinguish who are the *really* indigent, and the *really* intemperate. As to the persons who desire this part in the constitution, I have no reason to imagine that they are persons who have nothing to lose and much to look for in public confusion. The popular meeting from which apprehensions have been entertained, has assembled.[1] I have accidentally had conversation with two friends of mine, who knew something of the gentleman who was put into the chair upon that occasion; one of them has had money transactions with him; the other, from curiosity, has been to see his concerns: they both tell me he is a man of some property; but you must be the best judge of this, who by your office, are likely to know his transactions. Many of the others are certainly persons of fortune; and all, or most, fathers of families, men in respectable ways of life; and some of them far from contemptible; either for their information, or for the abilities which they have shewn in the discussion of their interests. What such men think it for their advantage to acquire, ought not, *prima facia,* to be considered as rash or heady, or incompatible with the public safety or welfare.

I admit, that men of the best fortunes and reputations, and of the best talents and education too, may, by accident, shew themselves furious and intemperate in their desires. This is a great misfortune when it happens; for the first presumptions are undoubtedly in their favour. We have two standards of judging in this case of the sanity and sobriety of any

1. A meeting of the Catholic Committee of Ireland. The Committee had been led by Thomas Browne, Lord Kenmare (1726–95), one of those few who remained of the old Catholic aristocracy and gentry of Ireland. When he was defeated in a vote on policy by a majority led by John Keogh, a wealthy Dublin silk merchant, Kenmare and his followers seceded from the Committee. The majority then restructured it on a wider and more popular basis by adding two members elected from each county and borough of Ireland. But, as Burke points out, the "popular" members were respectable, and many of them were well-to-do.

proceedings of the subject proceeding; of unequal certainty indeed, but neither of them to be neglected: the first is by the value of the object sought, the next is by the means through which it is pursued.

The object pursued, I understand, and have all along reasoned as if it were so, is in some degree or measure to be admitted to the franchises of the constitution. Men are considered as under some derangement of their intellects, when they see good and evil in a different light from other men; when they choose nauseous and unwholesome food; and reject such as to the rest of the world seems pleasant, and is known to be nutritive. I have always considered the British constitution, not to be a thing in itself so vitious, as that none but men of deranged understanding, and turbulent tempers could desire a share in it: on the contrary, I should think very indifferently of the understanding and temper of any body of men, who did not wish to partake of this great and acknowledged benefit. I cannot think quite so favourably either of the sense or temper of those, if any such there are, who would voluntarily persuade their brethren that the object is not fit for them, or they for the object. Whatever may be my thoughts, I am quite sure, that they who hold such language, must forfeit all credit with the rest. This is infallible—If they conceive any opinion of their judgment, they cannot possibly think them their friends. There is, indeed, one supposition, which would reconcile the conduct of such gentlemen to sound reason, and to the purest affection towards their fellow-sufferers; that is, that they act under the impression of a well-grounded fear for the general interest. If they should be told, and should believe the story, that if they dare attempt to make their condition better, they will infallibly make it worse—that if they aim at obtaining liberty, they will have their slavery doubled—that their endeavour to put themselves upon any thing which approaches towards an equitable footing with their fellow-subjects, will be considered as an indication of a seditious and rebellious disposition—such a view of things ought perfectly to restore the gentlemen, who so anxiously dissuade their countrymen from wishing a participation with the privileged part of the people,[1] to the good opinion of their fellows. But what is to *them* a very full justification, is not quite so honourable to that power from whose maxims and temper so good a ground of rational terror is furnished. I think arguments of this kind will never be used by the friends of a government which I greatly respect; or by any of the leaders of an opposition whom I have the honour to know, and the sense to admire. I remember Polybius tells us,[2] that during his captivity in Italy as a Peloponesian hostage—he solicited old Cato to intercede with the senate for his release, and that of his countrymen: this old politician told him that he had better continue in his present condition, however irksome, than apply again to that formidable authority for their relief; that he ought to imitate the wisdom of his countryman Ulysses, who, when he was once out of the den of the Cyclops, had too much sense to venture again into the same cavern. But I conceive too high an opinion of the Irish Legislature[3] to think that they are to their fellow citizen, what the grand oppressors of mankind were to a people whom the fortune of war had subjected to their power. For though Cato could do so with regard to his senate, I should really think it nothing short of impious, to compare an Irish Parliament to a den of Cyclops.

1. Lord Kenmare and his followers, who were more eager to be accepted by the Protestant ruling class than desirous of winning Catholic representation in Parliament.

2. *Histories* 35.6. Burke's memory of this passage is faulty, but his recollection of Cato's remark about entering the den of the Cyclops again is reasonably accurate.

3. In fact, Burke had a very low opinion of the Irish Legislature, which, in the same year, 1792, he described in a private letter as "the curse, scourge, and bane of the Irish nation." *Corr. 1844* 4:66.

I hope the people, both here and with you, will always apply to their representatives with becoming modesty; but at the same time with minds unembarrassed with any sort of terror.

As to the means which they employ to obtain this object, so worthy of the sober and rational minds; I do admit that such means may be used in the pursuit of it, as may make it proper for legislature, in this case, to defer their compliance until the demandants are brought to a proper sense of their duty. A concession in which the governing power of our country loses its dignity, is dearly bought even by him who obtains his object. All the people have a deep interest in the dignity of Parliament. But, as the refusal of franchises which are drawn out of the first vital stamina of the British constitution, is a very serious thing, we ought to be very sure, that the manner and spirit of the application is offensive and dangerous indeed, before we ultimately reject all applications of this nature. The mode of application, I hear, is by petition. It is the manner in which all the sovereign powers of the world are approached, and I never heard (except in the case of James the second) that any prince considered this manner of supplication to be contrary to the humility of a subject, or to the respect due to the person or authority of the sovereign. This rule, and a correspondent practice, are observed, from the Grand Seignior, down to the most petty Prince, or Republic in Europe.

You have sent me several papers, some in print, some in manuscript. I think I had seen all of them, except the formula of association. I confess they appear to me to contain matter mischievous, and capable of giving alarm, if the spirit in which they are written should be found to make any considerable progress. But I am at a loss to know how to apply them, as objections to the case now before us. When I find that *the general committee* which acts for the Roman Catholics in Dublin, prefers the association proposed in the written draft you have sent me,[1] to a respectful application in Parliament, I shall think the persons who sign such a paper, to be unworthy of any privilege which may be thought fit to be granted; and that such men ought, *by name,* to be excepted from any benefit under the constitution to which they offer this violence. But I do not find that this form of a seditious league has been signed by any person whatsoever, either on the part of the supposed projectors, or on the part of those whom it is calculated to seduce. I do not find, on enquiry, that such a thing was mentioned, or even remotely alluded to, in the general meeting of the Catholics, from which so much violence was apprehended. I have considered the other publications, signed by individuals, on the part of certain societies—I may mistake, for I have not the honour of knowing them personally, but I take Mr. Butler and Mr. Tandy not to be Catholics, but members of the established church.[2] Not *one* that I recollect of these publications, which you and I equally dislike, appears to be written by persons of that persuasion. Now, if, whilst a man is dutifully soliciting a favour from Parliament, any person should chuse, in an improper manner, to shew his inclination towards the cause depending; and if that *must* destroy the cause of the petitioner; then, not only the petitioner, but the legislature itself is in the power of any weak friend or artful enemy, that the supplicant, or that the Parliament may have. A man must be judged by his own actions only. Certain Protestant Dissenters make seditious propositions to the Catholics, which it does not appear that they have yet accepted. It would be strange that the tempter should escape all punishment, and that he who, under circumstances

1. Burke may refer here to the *Declaration of the Catholic Society of Dublin,* issued toward the end of 1791, in which the Society asserted that its members were justified in associating with the aim of attaining the repeal of the Catholic disabilities by all the constitutional means at their disposal. *W&S* 9:624, n. 2.

2. Simon Butler (1757–97) and James Napper Tandy were both members of the United Irishmen and, at least nominally, Anglicans.

full of seduction and full of provocation, has resisted the temptation, should incur the penalty. You know, that, with regard to the Dissenters, who are *stated* to be the chief movers in this vile scheme of altering the principles of election to a right of voting by the head, you are not able (if you ought even to wish such a thing) to deprive them of any part of the franchises and privileges which they hold on a footing of perfect equality with yourselves. *They* may do what they please with constitutional impunity; but the others cannot even listen with civility to an invitation from them to an ill-judged scheme of liberty, without forfeiting, for ever, all hopes of any of those liberties which we admit to be sober and rational.

It is known, I believe, that the greater, as well as the sounder part of our excluded countrymen, have not adopted the wild ideas, and wilder engagement, which have been held out to them; but have rather chosen to hope small and safe concessions from the legal power, than boundless objects from trouble and confusion. This mode of action seems to me to mark men of sobriety, and to distinguish them from those who are intemperate, from circumstance or from nature. But why do they not instantly disclaim and disavow those who make such advances to them? In this too, in my opinion, they shew themselves no less sober and circumspect. In the present moment, nothing short of insanity could induce them to take such a step. Pray consider the circumstances. Disclaim, says somebody, all union with the Dissenters;—right—But, when this your injunction is obeyed, shall I obtain the object which I solicit from you?—Oh, no—nothing at all like it!—But, in punishing us by an exclusion from the constitution, for having been invited to enter into it by a postern, will you punish by deprivation of their privileges; or mulct in any other way, those who have tempted us?—Far from it—we mean to preserve all *their* liberties and immunities, as *our* life blood. We mean to cultivate *them,* as brethren whom we love and respect—with *you,* we have no fellowship. We can bear, with patience, their enmity to ourselves; but their friendship with you, we will not endure. But mark it well! All our quarrels with *them,* are always to be revenged upon you. Formerly, it is notorious, that we should have resented with the highest indignation, your presuming to shew any ill-will to them. You must not suffer them, now, to shew any good-will to you. Know—and take it once for all—that it is, and ever has been, and ever will be, a fundamental maxim in our politics, that you are not to have any part, or shadow, or name of interest whatever, in our state.[1] That we look upon you, as under an irreversible outlawry from our constitution—as perpetual and unalliable aliens.

Such, my dear Sir, is the plain nature of the argument drawn from the revolution maxims, enforced by a supposed disposition in the Catholics to unite with the Dissenters. Such it is, though it were clothed in never such bland and civil forms, and wrapped up, as a poet says, in a thousand "artful folds of sacred lawn."[2] For my own part, I do not know in what manner to shape such arguments, so as to obtain admission for them into a rational understanding. Every thing of this kind is to be reduced, at last, to threats of power. I cannot say *vae victis,*[3] and then throw the sword into the scale. I have no sword; and if I had, in this case most certainly I would not use it as a make-weight, in politic reasoning.

Observe, on these principles, the difference between the procedure of the Parliament and the Dissenters, towards the people in question. One employs courtship, the other force. The Dissenters offer bribes, the Parliament nothing but the *front negative* of a stern and forbidding authority. A man may

1. After the Battle of the Boyne, a Test Act of 1691 excluded Catholics from membership in the Irish Parliament, and an Act of 1728 deprived them of the franchise.

2. Sacred lawn: a bishop's linen.

3. Woe to the conquered. Livy 5.48.9.

be very wrong in his ideas of what is good for him. But no man affronts me, nor can therefore justify my affronting him, by offering to make me as happy as himself, according to his own ideas of happiness. This the Dissenters do to the Catholics. You are on the different extremes. The Dissenters offer, with regard to constitutional rights and civil advantages of all sorts, *every thing*—you refuse *every thing*. With them, there is boundless, tho' not very assured hope; with you, a very sure and very unqualified despair. The terms of alliance, from the Dissenters, offer a representation of the Commons, chosen out of the people by the head. This is absurdly and dangerously large, in my opinion; and that scheme of election is known to have been, at all times, perfectly odious to me. But I cannot think it right of course, to punish the Irish Roman Catholics by an universal exclusion, because others, whom you would not punish at all, propose an universal admission. I cannot dissemble to myself, that, in this very kingdom, many persons who are not in the situation of the Irish Catholics, but who, on the contrary, enjoy the full benefit of the constitution as it stands, and some of whom, from the effect of their fortunes, enjoy it in a large measure, had some years ago associated to procure great and undefined changes (they considered them as reforms) in the popular part of the constitution. Our friend, the late Mr. Flood[1] (no slight man) proposed in his place, and in my hearing, a representation not much less extensive than this, for England; in which every house was to be inhabited by a voter—*in addition* to all the actual votes by other titles—all those (some of the corporate) which we know do not require a house, or a shed. Can I forget that a person of the very highest rank, of very large fortune, and

1. Henry Flood (1732–91), Irish M.P. from 1759 to 1783, in which year he bought a seat in the British House of Commons. An accomplished orator and leader of the opposition in the Irish House, he advocated parliamentary reform there. In the British Commons, on March 4, 1790, he introduced (unsuccessfully) the bill for parliamentary reform that Burke describes here.

of the first class of ability,[1] brought a bill into the House of Lords, in the head-quarters of aristocracy, containing identically the same project, for the supposed adoption of which by a club or two, it is thought right to extinguish all hopes in the Roman Catholics of Ireland? I cannot say it was very eagerly embraced or very warmly pursued. But the Lords neither did disavow the bill, nor treat it with any disregard, nor express any sort of disapprobation of its noble author, who has never lost, with king or people, the least degree of the respect and consideration which so justly belongs to him.

I am not at all enamoured, as I have told you, with this plan of representation; as little do I relish any bandings or associations for procuring it. But if the question was to be put to you and me—*universal* popular representation, or *none at all for us and ours*—we should find ourselves in a very awkward position. I don't like this kind of dilemmas, especially when they are practical.

Then, since our oldest fundamental laws follow, or rather couple, freehold with franchise; since no principle of the Revolution shakes these liberties; since the oldest and one of the best monuments of the constitution, demands for the Irish the privilege which they supplicate; since the principles of the Revolution coincide with the declarations of the Great Charter; since the practice of the Revolution, in this point, did not contradict its principles; since, from that event, twenty-five years had elapsed, before a domineering party, on a party principle, had ventured to disfranchise, without any proof whatsoever of abuse, the greater part of the community; since the King's coronation oath does not

1. Charles Lennox, third Duke of Richmond (1735–1806), brought in the bill described here on June 3, 1780. As a leading member of the Rockingham Whigs, he was a close political associate of Burke, who nonetheless once remarked of him in a private letter, "The Duke of Richmond, with the best parts, as well as the best intentions in the world, has some singular opinions, of which he is extremely tenacious." *Corr.* 2:544.

stand in his way to the performance of his duty to all his subjects; since you have given to all other Dissenters these privileges without limit, which are hitherto withheld, without any limitation whatsoever, from the Catholics; since no nation in the world has ever been known to exclude so great a body of men (not born slaves) from the civil state, and all the benefits of its constitution; the whole question comes before Parliament, as a matter for its prudence. I do not put the thing on a question of right. That discretion which in judicature is well said by Lord Coke[1] to be a crooked cord, in legislature is a golden rule.[2] Supplicants ought not to appear too much in the character of litigants. If the subject thinks so highly and reverently of the sovereign authority, as not to claim any thing of right, that it may seem to be independent of its power and its free choice: and the sovereign, on his part, considers the advantages of the subjects as their right, and all their reasonable wishes as so many claims; in the fortunate conjunction of these mutual dispositions are laid the foundations of a happy and prosperous commonwealth. For my own part, desiring of all things that the authority of the legislature under which I was born, and which I cherish, not only with a dutiful awe, but with a partial and cordial affection, to be maintained in the utmost possible respect, I never will suffer myself to suppose, that, at bottom, their discretion will be found to be at variance with their justice.

The whole being at discretion, I beg leave just to suggest some matters for your consideration—Whether the government in church or state is likely to be more secure by continuing causes of grounded discontent, to a very great number (say two millions) of the subjects? or, Whether the constitu-

1. Sir Edward Coke (1552–1634), commonly called Lord Coke, Chief Justice of the King's Bench (1613–16) and a leading authority on English law.

2. Burke insisted that the exercise of prudence and discretion in applying the norms of justice or natural law is a legislative, not a judicial, function.

tion, combined and balanced as it is, will be rendered more solid, by depriving so large a part of the people of all concern, or interest, or share, in its representation, actual or *virtual?* I here mean to lay an emphasis on the word *virtual.* Virtual representation is that in which there is a communion of interests, and a sympathy in feelings and desires between those who act in the name of any description of people, and the people in whose name they act, though the trustees are not actually chosen by them. This is virtual representation.[1] Such a representation I think to be, in many cases, even better than the actual. It possesses most of its advantages, and is free from many of its inconveniences: it corrects the irregularities in the literal representation, when the shifting current of human affairs, or the acting of public interests in different ways, carry it obliquely from its first line of direction. The people may err in their choice; but common interest and common sentiment are rarely mistaken. But this sort of virtual representation cannot have a long or sure existence, if it has not a substratum in the actual. The member must have some relation to the constituent. As things stands, the Catholic, as a Catholic and belonging to a description, has no *virtual* relation to the representative; but the *contrary.* There is a relation in mutual obligation. Gratitude may not always have a very lasting power; but the frequent recurrency for favours will revive and refresh it, and will necessarily produce some degree of mutual attention. It will produce, at least, acquaintance; the several descriptions of people will not be kept so much apart, as if they were not only separate nations, but separate species. The stigma and reproach, the hideous mask will be taken off, and men will see each other as they are. Sure I am,

1. It often happens, even in present-day democracies, that a particular legislator represents the views and interests of people in constituencies other than his own better than the elected representatives of those constituencies do.

that there have been thousands in Ireland, who have never conversed with a Roman Catholic in their whole lives, unless they happened to talk to their gardiner's workmen, or to ask their way, when they had lost it, in their sports; or, at best, who had known them only as footmen, or other domestics of the second and third order: and so averse were they, some time ago, to have them near their persons, that they would not employ even those who could never find their way beyond the stable. I well remember a great, and, in many respects, a good man, who advertised for a blacksmith; but, at the same time, added, he must be a Protestant. It is impossible that such a state of things, though natural goodness in many persons would undoubtedly make exceptions, must not produce alienation on one side, and pride and insolence on the other.

Reduced to a question of discretion, and that discretion exercised solely upon what will appear best for the conservation of the state on its present basis, I should recommend it to your serious thoughts, whether the narrowing of the foundation is always the best way to secure the building? The body of disfranchised men will not be perfectly satisfied to remain always in that state. If they are not satisfied, you have two millions of subjects in your bosom, full of uneasiness; not that they cannot overturn the act of settlement, and put themselves and you under an arbitrary master; or, that they are not permitted to spawn an hydra of wild republics, on principles of a pretended natural equality in man; but, because you will not suffer them to enjoy the ancient, fundamental, tried advantages of a British constitution: that you will not permit them to profit of the protection of a common father, or the freedom of common citizens: and that the only reason which can be assigned for this disfranchisement, has a tendency more deeply to ulcerate their minds than the act of exclusion itself. What the consequence of such feelings must be, it is for you to look to. To warn, is not to menace.

I am far from asserting, that men will not excite disturbances without just cause. I know that such an assertion is not true. But, neither is it true that disturbances have never just complaints for their origin. I am sure that it is hardly prudent to furnish them with such causes of complaint, as every man who thinks the British constitution a benefit, may think; at least, colourable and plausible.

Several are in dread of the manoeuvres of certain persons among the Dissenters, who turn this ill humour to their own ill purposes. You know, better than I can, how much these proceedings of certain among the Dissenters are to be feared. You are to weigh, with the temper which is natural to you, whether it may be for the safety of our establishment, that the Catholics should be ultimately persuaded that they have no hope to enter into the constitution, but through the Dissenters.

Think, whether this be the way to prevent, or dissolve factious combinations against the church, or the state. Reflect seriously on the possible consequences of keeping, in the heart of your country, a bank of discontent, every hour accumulating, upon which every description of seditious men may draw at pleasure. They, whose principles of faction would dispose them to the establishment of an arbitrary monarchy, will find a nation of men who have no sort of interest in freedom; but who will have an interest in that equality of justice or favour, with which a wise despot must view all his subjects who do not attack the foundations of his power. Love of liberty itself may, in such men, become the means of establishing an arbitrary domination. On the other hand, they who wish for a democratic republic, will find a set of men who have no choice between civil servitude, and the entire ruin of a mixed constitution.

Suppose the people of Ireland divided into three parts; of these (I speak within compass) two are Catholic. Of the remaining third, one half is composed of Dissenters. There is no natural union between those descriptions. It may be produced. If the two parts Catholic be driven into a close confederacy with half the third part of Protestants, with a view to a change in the constitution in church or state, or both; and you rest the whole of their security on a handful of gentlemen, clergy, and their dependants; compute the strength *you have in Ireland,* to oppose to grounded discontent; to capricious innovation; to blind popular fury, and to ambitious turbulent intrigue. You mention that the minds of some gentlemen are a good deal heated: and that it is often said, that, rather than submit to such persons having a share in their franchises, they would throw up their independence, and precipitate an union with Great Britain.[1]

I have heard a discussion concerning such an union amongst all sorts of men, ever since I remember any thing. For my own part, I have never been able to bring my mind to any thing clear and decisive upon the subject. There cannot be a more arduous question. As far as I can form an opinion, it would not be for the mutual advantage of the two kingdoms; but persons more able than I am, think otherwise. But, whatever the merits of this union may be, to make it a *menace,* it must be shewn to be an *evil;* and an evil more particularly to those who are threatened with it, than to those who hold it out as a terror. I really do not see how this threat of an union can operate, or that the Catholics are more likely to be losers by that measure than the churchmen.

The humours of the people, and of politicians too, are so variable in themselves and are so much under the occasional influence of some leading men, that it is impossible to know what turn the public mind here would take in such

1. An Act of Union, which merged the kingdoms of Great Britain and Ireland into one and absorbed the Irish Parliament into the British one, was carried through in 1800, after Burke's death and after the unsuccessful Irish uprising of 1798. Ironically, one of Prime Minister William Pitt's motives for promoting that Act was that only by means of it could Catholics safely be given the right to vote for members of Parliament.

an event. There is but one thing certain concerning it: that this union would excite a strong ferment on both sides of the water, with strong animosities and violent passions, whilst the arrangement continued in agitation. Great divisions and vehement passions would precede this union, both on the measure itself and on its terms; and particularly, this very question of a share in the representation for the Catholics, from whence the project of an union originated, would form a principal part in the discussion; and in the temper in which some gentlemen seem inclined to throw themselves, by a sort of high indignant passion, into the scheme, those points would not be deliberated with all possible calmness.

From my best observation, I should greatly doubt, whether, in the end, these gentlemen would obtain their object, so as to make the exclusion of two millions of their countrymen a fundamental article in the union. The demand would be of a nature quite unprecedented. You might obtain the union: and yet, a gentleman who, under the new union establishment, would aspire to the honour of representing his county, might possibly be as much obliged, as he may fear to be, under the old separate establishment, to the unsupportable mortification of asking his neighbours, who have a different opinion concerning the elements in the sacrament, for their votes.

I believe, nay, I am sure, that the people of Great Britain, with or without an union, might be depended upon, in cases of any real danger, to aid the government of Ireland with the same cordiality as they would support their own against any wicked attempts to shake the security of the happy constitution in church and state. But, before Great Britain engages in any quarrel, the *cause of the dispute* would certainly be a part of her consideration. If confusions should arise in that kingdom, from too steady an attachment to a proscriptive monopolizing system, and from the resolution of regarding the franchise, and, in it the security of the subject, as belonging rather to religious opinions than to civil qualification and civil conduct, I doubt whether you might quite certainly reckon on obtaining an aid of force from hence, for the support of that system. We might extend your distractions to this country, by taking part in them. England will be indisposed, I suspect, to send an army for the conquest of Ireland. What was done in 1782 is a decisive proof of her sentiments of justice and moderation. She will not be fond of making another American war in Ireland. The principles of such a war would but too much resemble the former one. The well-disposed and the ill-disposed in England, would (for different reasons perhaps) be equally averse to such an enterprize. The confiscations, the public auctions, the private grants, the plantations, the transplantations, which formerly animated so many adventurers, even among sober citizens, to such Irish expeditions, and which possibly might have animated some of them to the American, can have no existence in the case that we suppose.

Let us form a supposition (no foolish or ungrounded supposition) that in an age, when men are infinitely more disposed to heat themselves with political than religious controversies, the former should entirely prevail, as we see that in some places they have prevailed, over the latter: and that the Catholics of Ireland, from the courtship paid them on the one hand, and the high tone of refusal on the other, should, in order to enter into all the rights of subjects, all become Protestant Dissenters; and as the others do, take all your oaths. They would all obtain their civil objects, and the change; for any thing I know to the contrary, (in the dark as I am about the Protestant Dissenting tenets) might be of use to the health of their souls. But, what security our constitution, in church or state, could derive from that event, I cannot possibly discern. Depend upon it, it is as true as nature is true, that if you force them out of the religion of habit, education or opinion, it is not to yours they will ever go. Shaken in their minds, they will go to that where the dogmas are fewest; where they are the most uncertain; where they lead them the least to a consideration of what they have abandoned. They will go to that uniformly democratic system, to whose first movements they owed their emancipation. I recommend you seriously to turn this in your mind. Believe that it requires your best and maturest thoughts. Take what course you please—union or no union; whether the people remain Catholics, or become Protestant Dissenters, sure it is, that the present state of monopoly, *cannot* continue.

If England were animated, as I think she is not, with her former spirit of domination, and with the strong theological hatred which she once cherished for that description of her fellow-christians and fellow-subjects; I am yet convinced, that, after the fullest success in a ruinous struggle, you would be obliged finally to abandon that monopoly. We were obliged to do this, even when every thing promised success in the American business. If you should make this experiment at last, under the pressure of any necessity, you never can do it well. But if, instead of falling into a passion, the leading gentlemen of the country themselves should undertake the business cheerfully, and with hearty affection towards it, great advantages would follow. What is forced, cannot be modified; but here, you may measure your concessions.

It is a consideration of great moment, that you may make the desired admission, without altering the system of your representation in the smallest degree, or in any part. You may leave that deliberation of a parliamentary change or reform, if ever you should think fit to engage in it, uncomplicated and unembarrassed with the other question. Whereas, if they are mixed and confounded, as some people attempt to mix and confound them, no one can answer for the effects on the constitution itself.

There is another advantage in taking up this business, singly and by an arrangement for the single object. It is, that you may proceed by *degrees.* We must all obey the great law of change, it is the most powerful law of nature, and the means perhaps of its conservation. All we can do, and that human wisdom can do, is to provide that the change shall proceed by insensible degrees. This has all the benefits which may be in change, without any of the inconveniences of mutation. Every thing is provided for as it arrives. This mode will, on the one hand, prevent the *unfixing old interests at once;* a thing which is apt to breed a black and sullen discontent, in those who are at once dispossessed of all their influence and consideration. This gradual course, on the other side, will prevent men, long under depression, from being intoxicated with a large draught of new power, which they always abuse with a licentious insolence. But, wishing, as I do, the change to be gradual and cautious, I would, in my first steps, lean rather to the side of enlargement than restriction.

It is one excellence of our constitution, that all our rights of election regard rather property than person. The standard may be so low, or not so judiciously chosen, as in some degree to frustrate the end. But all this is for your prudence in the case before you, You may rise, a step or two, the qualification of the Catholic voters. But if you were, to-morrow, to put the Catholic freeholder on the footing of the most favoured forty-shilling[1] Protestant Dissenter, you know that, such is the actual state of Ireland, this would not make a sensible alteration in almost any *one* election in the kingdom. The effect in their favour, even defensively, would be infinitely slow. But it would be healing; it would be satisfactory and protecting. The stigma would be removed. By admitting settled permanent substance in lieu of the numbers, you would avoid the great danger of our time, that of setting up number against

1. A freehold could be a lifelong or even a heritable tenancy, or an estate held in fee simple. A freehold worth forty shillings a year carried with it the right to vote for members of Parliament.

property. The numbers ought never to be neglected; because, (besides what is due to them as men) collectively, though not individually, they have great property: they ought to have therefore protection: they ought to have security: they ought to have even consideration: but they ought not to predominate.

My dear Sir, I have nearly done; I meant to write you a long letter; I have written a long dissertation. I might have done it early and better. I might have been more forcible and more clear, if I had not been interrupted as I have been; and this obliges me not to write to you in my own hand. Though my hand but signs it, my heart goes with what I have written. Since I could think at all, those have been my thoughts. You know that thirty-two years ago they were as fully matured in my mind as they are now. A letter of mine to Lord Kenmare, though not by my desire, and full of lesser mistakes, has been printed in Dublin. It was written ten or twelve years ago, at the time when I began the employment, which I have not yet finished, in favour of another distressed people, injured by those who have vanquished them, or stolen a dominion over them.[1] It contained my sentiments then; you will see how far they accord with my sentiments now. Time has more and more confirmed me in them all. The present circumstances fix them deeper in my mind.

I voted last session, if a particular vote could be distinguished, in unanimity, for an establishment of the Church of England *conjointly* with the establishment which was made some years before by act of parliament, of the Roman Catholic, in the French conquered country of Canada.[2] At the time

1. The people of India who were under British rule.

2. The Quebec Act of 1774 allowed the exercise of the Roman Catholic religion and authorized the Catholic Church in Quebec to continue to collect the tithe. By waiving the Test Acts and substituting an oath of allegiance, it allowed Catholics to hold public office. The Canada Act of 1791 provided for the establishment of the Church of England in Canada.

of making this English ecclesiastical establishment, we did not think it necessary for its safety, to destroy the former Gallican church settlement. In our first act we settled a government altogether monarchical, or nearly so. In that system, the Canadian Catholics were far from being deprived of the advantages or distinctions, of any kind, which they enjoyed under their former monarchy. It is true, that some people, and amongst them one eminent divine, predicted at that time, that by this step we should lose our dominions in America. He foretold that the Pope would send his indulgences thither; that the Canadians would fall in with France; declare their independence, and draw or force our colonies into the same design. The independence happened according to his prediction; but in directly the reverse order. All our English Protestant colonies revolted. They joined themselves to France; and it so happened that Popish Canada was the only place which preserved its fidelity; the only place in which France got no footing; the only peopled colony which now remains to Great Britain. Vain are all the prognostics taken from ideas and passions, which survive the state of things which give rise to them. When last year we gave a popular representation to the same Canada, by the choice of the landholders, and an aristocratic representation, at the choice of the crown, neither was the choice of the crown, nor the election of the landholders, limited by a consideration of religion. We had no dread for the Protestant church, which we settled there, because we permitted the French Catholics, in the utmost latitude of the description, to be free subjects. They are good subjects, I have no doubt; but I will not allow that any French Canadian Catholics are better men or better citizens than the Irish of the same communion. Passing from the extremity of the west, to the extremity almost of the east; I have been many years (now entering into the twelfth) employed in supporting the rights, privileges, laws and immunities of a very remote people. I have not as yet been able to finish my task. I have struggled through much discouragement and much opposition; much obloquy; much calumny, for a people with whom I have no tie, but the common bond of mankind. In this I have not been left alone. We did not fly from our undertaking, because the people were Mahometans or Pagans, and that a great majority of the Christians amongst them were Papists. Some gentlemen in Ireland, I dare say, have good reasons for what they may do, which do not occur to me. I do not presume to condemn them; but, thinking and acting, as I have done, towards these remote nations, I should not know how to shew my face, here or in Ireland, if I should say that all the Pagans, all the Mussulmen, and even Papists (since they must form the highest stage in the climax of evil) are worthy of a liberal and honourable condition, except those of one of the descriptions, which forms the majority of the inhabitants of the country in which you and I were born. If such are the Catholics of Ireland; ill-natured and unjust people, from our own data, may be inclined not to think better of the Protestants of a soil, which is supposed to infuse into its sects a kind of venom unknown in other places.

You hated the old system as early as I did. Your first juvenile lance[1] was broken against that giant. I think you were even the first who attacked the grim phantom. You have an exceeding good understanding, very good humour, and the best heart in the world. The dictates of that temper and that heart, as well as the policy pointed out by that understanding, led you to abhor the old code.[2] You abhorred it, as I did, for its vicious perfection. For I must do it justice: it was a

1. This may refer to a speech that Langrishe gave in 1772 in favor of a bill to enable papists to take building leases.

2. The Penal Laws against Catholics that Burke described in his never-completed *Tracts, relative to the Laws against Popery in Ireland.* Most of them had been repealed by the Catholic Relief Acts of 1778 and 1782. The franchise was conceded to a very limited number of Catholics in 1793, the year after this letter was written, but they were not made eligible to sit in Parliament.

complete system, full of coherence and consistency; well digested and well composed in all its parts. It was a machine of wise and elaborate contrivance; and as well fitted for the oppression, impoverishment and degradation of a people, and the debasement, in them, of human nature itself, as ever proceeded from the perverted ingenuity of man. It is a thing humiliating enough, that we are doubtful of the effect of the medicines we compound. We are sure of our poisons. My opinion ever was (in which I heartily agreed with those that admired the old code) that it was so constructed, that if there was once a breach in any essential part of it; the ruin of the whole, or nearly of the whole, was, at some time or other, a certainty. For that reason I honour, and shall for ever honour and love you, and those who first caused it to stagger, crack, and gape. Others may finish; the beginners have the glory; and, take what part you please at this hour, (I think you will take the best) your first services will never be forgotten by a grateful country. Adieu! Present my best regards to those I know, and as many as I know in our country, I honour. There never was so much ability, or, I believe, virtue, in it. They have a task worthy of both. I doubt not they will perform it, for the stability of the church and state, and for the union and the separation of the people: for the union of the honest and peaceable of all sects; for their separation from all that is ill-intentioned and seditious in any of them.

Beaconsfield,
January 3, 1792

FINIS

Sketch of the Negro Code

[1780]

Burke's covering letter to Henry Dundas, dated April 9, 1792, explains that he had written his sketch of a code for the regulation and eventual suppression of both the slave trade and slavery itself in the British West Indian colonies "near twelve years ago," in the first half of 1780. When he wrote the sketch, Burke was ahead of his times, since organized efforts to abolish the slave trade did not begin until the second half of that decade, when William Wilberforce and Thomas Clarkson founded the Abolition Society in 1787, and the Crown in 1788 appointed a committee of the Privy Council to inquire into the trade.

Henry Dundas (1742–1811) was Home Secretary in William Pitt the Younger's government when he asked Burke for a copy of the sketch, with a view to introducing legislation to regulate and ameliorate the harsh conditions of the slave trade. Partial abolition of the trade in the British dominions did not begin, however, until 1806, and complete abolition was enacted only in 1811. Partial abolition of slavery itself began in 1823; complete abolition was enacted in 1833, but was intended to be achieved gradually through a period of apprenticeship for the slaves, not all of whom were set free until 1838.

This gradualist approach to freeing the slaves was much in Burke's way of thinking. Carl Cone remarks in his Burke and the Nature of Politics: The French Revolution *(p. 388): "On July 9, 1823, Lord Bathurst, as Colonial Secretary, transmitted instructions for the more humane treatment of slaves. His dispatch reads like an expansion of Burke's 'Sketch.'" It was typical of Burke that he would not change even so evil an institution as slavery suddenly and dras-*

tically, but only prudently and through planned stages. But it was also typical of him that he recognized the evil as such and proposed to rid the British Empire of it. It should also be noted that he did not regard the long continuance and legal acceptance of the institution as having created a prescriptive right to it on the part of slave-owners.

It may be that the end of slavery in the United States could have been achieved only through a long and bloody war, as great historical changes so often have been, and that Burke's program of gradual and progressive abolition was unduly idealistic in American circumstances. Yet emancipation à la Burke surely would have been a better way of doing it, if it were possible. In any case, this Sketch of the Negro Code *once again demonstrates Burke's sincere concern for the downtrodden and oppressed.*

A Letter to the Right Hon. Henry Dundas, One of His Majesty's Principal Secretaries of State

[With the Sketch of a Negro Code]

Dear Sir,

I should have been punctual in sending you the Sketch I promised of my old African Code, if some friends from London had not come in upon me last Saturday, and engaged me till noon this day; I send this pacquet by one of them, who is still here. If what I send be, as under present circumstances it must be, imperfect, you will excuse it, as being done near twelve years ago. About four years since I made an abstract of it; upon which I cannot at present lay my hands; but I hope the marginal heads will in some measure supply it.

If the African Trade could be considered with regard to itself only, and as a single object, I should think the utter abolition to be, on the whole, more advisable, than any scheme of regulation and reform. Rather than suffer it to continue as it is, I heartily wish it at an end. What has been lately done, has been done by a popular spirit, which seldom calls for, and indeed very rarely relishes, a system made up of a great variety of parts, and which is to operate its effect in a great length of time. The people like short methods; the consequences of which they sometimes have reason to repent of. Abolition is but a single act. To prove the nature of the trade, and to expose it properly, required, indeed, a vast collection of materials, which have been laboriously collected, and compiled with great judgment. It required also much perseverance and address to excite the spirit, which has been excited without doors, and which has carried it through. The greatest eloquence ever displayed in the House has been employed to second the efforts, which have been made abroad. All this, however, leads but to one single resolve. When this was done, all was done. I speak of absolute and immediate abolition, the point, which the first motions went to, and which is in effect still pressed; though in this Session, according to order, it cannot take effect. A *remote,* and a *gradual* abolition, though they may be connected, are not the same thing. The idea of the House seems to me, if I rightly comprehend it, that the two things are to be combined; that is to say, that the trade is gradually to decline, and to cease entirely at a determinate period. To make the abolition gradual, the regulations must operate as a strong discouragement. But it is much to be feared, that a trade continued and discouraged, and with a sentence of death passed upon it, will perpetuate much ill blood between those, who struggle for the abolition, and those, who contend for an effectual continuance.

At the time when I formed the plan, which I have the honour to transmit to you, an abolition of the Slave Trade would have appeared a very chimerical project. My plan, therefore, supposes the continued existence of that commerce. Taking for my basis that I had an incurable evil to deal with, I cast about how I should make it as small an evil as possible, and draw out of it some collateral good.

In turning the matter over in my mind, at that time, and since, I never was able to consider the African Trade upon a ground disconnected with the employment of Negroes in the

West Indies, and distinct from their condition in the plantations, whereon they serve. I conceived, that the true origin of the trade was not in the place it was begun at, but at the place of its final destination. I therefore was, and I still am, of opinion, that the whole work ought to be taken up together; and that a gradual abolition of Slavery in the West Indies ought to go hand in hand with any thing, which should be done with regard to its supply from the Coast of Africa. I could not trust a cessation of the demand for this supply to the mere operation of any abstract principle, (such as, that if their supply was cut off the Planters would encourage and produce an effectual population,) knowing that nothing can be more uncertain than the operation of general principles, if they are not embodied in specifick regulations. I am very apprehensive, that so long as the Slavery continues some means for its supply will be found. If so, I am persuaded that it is better to allow the evil, in order to correct it, than by endeavouring to forbid, what we cannot be able wholly to prevent, to leave it under an illegal, and therefore an unreformed, existence. It is not that my plan does not lead to the extinction of the Slave Trade; but it is through a very slow progress, the chief effect of which is to be operated in our own plantations; by rendering, in a length of time, all foreign supply unnecessary. It was my wish, whilst the Slavery continued, and the consequent commerce, to take such measures as to civilize the Coast of Africa by the trade, which now renders it more barbarous; and to lead, by degrees, to a more reputable, and, possibly, a more profitable, connection with it, than we maintain at present.

I am sure that you will consider, as a mark of my confidence in yours and Mr Pitt's honour and generosity, that I venture to put into your hands a scheme composed of many and intricate combinations, without a full explanatory preface, or any attendant notes, to point out the principles, upon which I proceeded, in every regulation, which I have proposed towards the civilization and gradual manumission of Negroes in the two hemispheres. I confess, I trust infinitely more (according to the sound principles of those, who ever have at any time meliorated the state of mankind) to the effect and influence of religion, than to all the rest of the regulations put together.

Whenever, in my proposed reformation, we take our *point of departure* from a state of Slavery, we must precede the donation of freedom by disposing the minds of the objects to a disposition to receive it without danger to themselves or to us. The process of bringing *free* Savages to order and civilization is very different. When a state of Slavery is that, upon which we are to work, the very means, which lead to liberty, must partake of compulsion. The minds of men being crippled with that restraint can do nothing for themselves; every thing must be done for them. The regulations can owe little to consent. Every thing must be the creature of power. Hence it is, that regulations must be multiplied; particularly as you have two parties to deal with. The Planter you must at once restrain and support; and you must control, at the same time that you ease, the servant. This necessarily makes the work a matter of care, labour, and expense. It becomes in its nature complex. But I think neither the object impracticable, nor the expense intolerable; and I am fully convinced, that the cause of humanity would be far more benefited by the continuance of the trade and servitude, regulated and reformed, than by the total destruction of both or either. What I propose, however, is but a beginning of a course of measures, which an experience of the effects of the evil and the reform will enable the Legislature hereafter to supply and correct.

I need not observe to you, that the forms are often neglected, penalties not provided, &c. &c. &c. But all this is merely mechanical, and what a couple of days application would set to rights.

I have seen what has been done by the West Indian Assemblies.[1] It is arrant trifling. They have done little; and what they have done is good for nothing; for it is totally destitute of an *executory* principle. This is the point, to which I have applied my whole diligence. It is easy enough to say what shall be done: to cause it to be done, *Hic labor, hoc opus.*[2]

I ought not to apologize for letting this scheme lie beyond the period of the *Horatian* keeping— [3] I ought much more to entreat an excuse for producing it now. Its whole value (if it has any) is the coherence and mutual dependency of parts in the scheme; separately they can be of little or no use.

I have the honour to be, with very great respect and regard,

Dear Sir,
Your most faithful, and
obedient humble Servant,

Edmund Burke
Beaconsfield,
Easter-Monday Night, 1792

1. The West Indian sugar plantations were so dependent on a steady supply of slaves from Africa that little support for limiting the slave trade could be expected of them.

2. Burke quotes from memory the words of the Sybil to Aeneas before he goes down into Hades. *Facilis descensus Averni,* she tells him—the way down is easy, but the way back is hard: *Hoc opus, hic labor est* (as it is in the original)— "This is the task, this the toil." Virgil *Aeneid* 7.129.

3. Horace advised a writer to leave nine years between the completion of a composition and its publication, in order to allow time for further thought and revision. *Ars Poetica* 388–90.

Sketch of the Negro Code

This Constitution consists of four principal members.

I. The rules for qualifying a ship for the African Trade.

II. The mode of carrying on the Trade upon the Coast of Africa, which includes a plan for introducing civilization in that part of the world.

III. What is to be observed from the time of shipping Negroes to the sale in the West India Islands.

IV. The regulations relative to the state and condition of Slaves in the West Indies, their manumission, &c.

Whereas it is expedient, and conformable to the principles of true religion and morality, and to the rules of sound policy, to put an end to all traffick in the persons of men, and to the detention of their said persons in a state of slavery, as soon as the same may be effected without producing great inconveniences in the sudden change of practices of such long standing; and, during the time of the continuance of the said practices, it is desirable and expedient, by proper regulations, to lessen the inconveniences and evils attendant on the said traffick and state of servitude, until both shall be gradually done away:

And whereas the objects of the said trade, and consequential servitude, and the grievances resulting therefrom, come under the principal heads following, the regulations ought thereto to be severally applied; that is to say, that provision should be made by the said regulations,

1st. For duly qualifying ships for the said traffick;

2d. For the mode and conditions of permitting the said trade to be carried on upon the Coast of Africa;

3d. For the treatment of the Negroes in their passage to the West India Islands;

4th. For the government of the Negroes, which are or shall be employed in His Majesty's Colonies and Plantations in the West Indies:

Be it therefore enacted, that every ship or trading vessel, which is intended for the Negro Trade, with the name of the owner or owners thereof, shall be entered and registered as ships trading to the West Indies are by law to be registered, with the further provisions following:

1. The said entry and register shall contain an account of the greatest number of Negroes, of all descriptions, which are proposed to be taken into the said ship or trading vessel; and the said ship, before she is permitted to be entered outwards, shall be surveyed by a Ship-Carpenter to be appointed by the Collector of the Port, from which the said vessel is to depart, and by a Surgeon, also appointed by the Collector, who hath been conversant in the service of the said trade, but not at the time actually engaged or covenanted therein; and the said Carpenter and Surgeon shall report to the Collector, or, in his absence, to the next principal Officer of the Port, upon oath (which oath the said Collector or principal Officer is hereby empowered to administer) her measurement, and what she contains in builder's tonnage, and that she has feet of grated port-holes between the decks, and that she is otherwise fitly found as a good transport-vessel.

2. And be it enacted, that no ship employed in the said trade shall upon any pretence take in more Negroes than one grown man or woman for one ton and half of builder's tonnage, nor more than one boy or girl for one ton.

3. That the said ship or other vessel shall lay in, in propor-

tion to the ship's company of the said vessel, and the number of Negroes registered, a full and sufficient store of sound provision, so as to be secure against all probable delays and accidents; namely, salted beef, pork, salt-fish, butter, cheese, biscuit, flour, rice, oatmeal, and white peas; but no horse-beans, or other inferiour provisions; and the said ship shall be properly provided with water-casks or jars, in proportion to the intended number of the said Negroes; and the said ship shall be also provided with a proper and sufficient stock of coals or fire-wood.

4. And every ship, entered as aforesaid, shall take out a coarse shirt, and a pair of trowsers, or petticoat, for each Negro intended to be taken aboard; as also a mat, or coarse mattress, or hammock, for the use of the said Negroes.

The proportions of provision, fuel and clothing, to be regulated by the Table annexed to this Act.

5. And be it enacted, that no ship shall be permitted to proceed on the said voyage or adventure, until the Searcher of the Port, from whence the said vessel shall sail, or such person as he shall appoint to act for him, shall report to the Collector, that he hath inspected the said stores, and that the ship is accommodated and provided in the manner hereby directed.

6. And be it enacted, that no guns be exported to the Coast of Africa, in the said or any other trade, unless the same be duly marked with the maker's name on the barrels before they are put into the stocks, and vouched by an Inspector in the place where the same are made, to be without fraud, and sufficient and merchantable arms.

7. And be it enacted, that before any ship as aforesaid shall proceed on her voyage, the owner or owners, or an Attorney by them named, if the owners are more than two, and the master, shall severally give bond, the owners by themselves, the master for himself, that the said master shall duly conform himself in all things to the regulations in this Act

contained, so far as the same regards his part in executing and conforming to the same.

II. And whereas in providing for the second object of this Act, that is to say, for the trade on the Coast of Africa, it is first prudent not only to provide against the manifold abuses, to which a trade of that nature is liable, but that the same may be accompanied, as far as it is possible, with such advantages to the Natives as may tend to the civilizing them, and enabling them to enrich themselves by means more desirable, and to carry on hereafter a trade more advantageous and honourable to all parties:

And whereas religion, order, morality and virtue, are the elemental principles, and the knowledge of letters, arts and handicraft trades, the chief means of such civilization and improvement; for the better attainment of the said good purposes,

1. Be it hereby enacted, that the Coast of Africa, on which the said trade for Negroes may be carried on, shall be and is hereby divided into Marts or Staples[1] as hereafter follows [here name the Marts.] And be it enacted, that it shall not be lawful for the master of any ship to purchase any Negro or Negroes, but at one of the said Marts or Staples.

2. That the Directors of the African Company[2] shall appoint, where not already appointed, a Governour, with three Counsellors, at each of the said Marts, with a salary of to the Governour, and of to each of the said Counsellors. The said Governour, or in his absence or illness, the

1. Towns or places which were principal markets for some particular class of merchandise; more narrowly, places in which a body of merchants was granted by the Crown the exclusive right of purchasing certain classes of goods destined for export.

2. The African Company was formed in 1671 to buy out and succeed the Company of Royal Adventurers trading to Africa. It was given a monopoly of the African trade, consisting largely, though not exclusively, in the slave trade.

senior Counsellor, shall and is hereby empowered to act as a Justice of the Peace, and they or either of them are authorized, ordered and directed, to provide for the peace of the Settlement, and the good regulation of their station and stations severally, according to the rules of justice, to the directions of this Act, and the instructions they shall receive from time to time from the said African Company: and the said African Company is hereby authorized to prepare instructions, with the assent of the Lords of His Majesty's Privy Council, which shall be binding in all things not contrary to this Act, or to the Laws of England, on the said Governours and Counsellors, and every of them, and on all persons acting in commission with them under this Act, and on all persons residing within the jurisdiction of the Magistrates of the said Mart.

3. And be it enacted, that the Lord High Admiral, or Commissioners for executing his office, shall appoint one or more, as they shall see convenient, of his Majesty's ships or sloops of war, under the command severally of a Post Captain, or Master and Commander, to each Mart, as a naval station.

4. And be it enacted, that the Lord High Treasurer, or the Commissioners for executing his office, shall name two Inspectors of the said trade at every Mart, who shall provide for the execution of this Act, according to the directions thereof, so far as shall relate to them; and it is hereby provided and enacted, that as cases of sudden emergency may arise, the said Governour or first Counsellor and the first Commander of his Majesty's ship or ships on the said station, and the said Inspectors, or the majority of them, the Governour having a double or casting vote, shall have power and authority to make such occasional rules and orders relating to the said trade, as shall not be contrary to the instructions of the African Company, and which shall be valid until the same are revoked by the said African Company.

5. That the said African Company is hereby authorized

to purchase, if the same may conveniently be done, with the consent of the Privy Council, any lands adjoining to the Fort or principal Mart aforesaid, not exceeding acres, and to make allotments of the same. No allotment to one person to exceed (on pain of forfeiture) acres.

6. That the African Company shall, at each Fort or Mart, cause to be erected, in a convenient place, and at a moderate cost, the estimate of which shall be approved by the Treasury, one church, and one school-house, and one hospital; and shall appoint one principal Chaplain, with a Curate or Assistant in holy orders, both of whom shall be recommended by the Lord Bishop of London; and the said Chaplain, or his Assistant, shall perform Divine Service, and administer the Sacraments, according to the usage of the Church of England, or to such mode, not contrary thereto, as to the said Bishop shall seem more suitable to the circumstances of the people. And the said principal Chaplain shall be the third Member in the Council, and shall be entitled to receive from the Directors of the said African Company a salary of and his Assistant a salary of and he shall have power to appoint one sober and discreet person, white or black, to be his Clerk and Catechist, at a salary of

7. And be it enacted, that the African Company shall appoint one sufficient schoolmaster, who shall be approved by the Bishop of London, and who shall be capable of teaching writing, arithmetick, surveying, and mensuration, at a salary of and the said African Company is hereby authorized to provide, for each Settlement, a Carpenter and Blacksmith, with such encouragement as to them shall seem expedient; who shall take each two apprentices from amongst the Natives, to instruct them in the several trades, the African Company allowing them, as a fee for each apprentice, And the said African Company shall appoint one Surgeon, and one Surgeon's Mate, who are to be approved on examination at Surgeon's Hall, to each Fort or Mart, with a salary

of   for the Surgeon, and for his Mate   and the said Surgeon shall take one native apprentice, at a fee to be settled by the African Company.

8. And be it enacted, that the said Catechist, Schoolmaster, Surgeon, and Surgeon's Mate, as well as the tradesmen in the Company's Service, shall be obedient to the orders they shall from time to time receive from the Governour and Council of each Fort; and if they, or any of them, or any other person, in whatever station, shall appear, on complaint and proof to the majority of the Commissioners, to lead a disorderly and debauched life, or use any profane or impious discourses, to the danger of defeating the purposes of this institution, and to the scandal of the Natives, who are to be led, by all due means, into a respect for our holy religion, and a desire of partaking of the benefits thereof, they are authorized and directed to suspend the said person from his office, or the exercise of his trade, and to send him to England (but without any hard confinement, except in case of resistance) with a complaint, with inquiry and proofs adjoined, to the African Company.

9. And be it enacted, that the Bishop of London for the time being shall have full authority to remove the said Chaplain, for such causes as to him shall seem reasonable.

10. That no Governour, Counsellor, Inspector, Chaplain, Surgeon, or Schoolmaster, shall be concerned, or have any share, directly or indirectly, in the Negro Trade, on pain of

11. Be it enacted, that the said Governour and Council shall keep a journal of all their proceedings, and a book, in which copies of all their correspondence shall be entered, and they shall transmit copies of the said journals and letter-book, and their books of accounts, to the African Company, who, within   of their receipt thereof, shall communicate the same to one of His Majesty's principal Secretaries of State.

12. And be it enacted, that the said Chaplain, or princi-

pal Minister, shall correspond with the Bishop of London, and faithfully and diligently transmit to him an account of whatever hath been done for the advancement of religion, morality and learning, amongst the Natives.

13. And be it enacted, that no Negro shall be conclusively sold until he shall be attested by the two Inspectors and Chaplain; or in case of the illness of any of them, by one Inspector, and the Governour, or one of the Council; who are hereby authorized and directed, by the best means in their power, to examine into the circumstances and condition of the persons exposed to sale.

14. And, for the better direction of the said Inspectors, no persons are to be sold, who, to the best judgment of the said Inspectors, shall be above thirty-five years of age, or who shall appear, on examination, stolen or carried away, by the dealers, by surprise; nor any person, who is able to read in the Arabian or any other book; nor any woman, who shall appear to be advanced three months in pregnancy; nor any person distorted or feeble, unless the said persons are consenting to such sale; or any person afflicted with a grievous or contagious distemper. But if any person so offered is only lightly disordered, the said person may be sold; but must be kept in the Hospital of the Mart, and shall not be shipped until completely cured.

15. Be it enacted, that no Black or European Factor or Trader into the interiour country, or on the coast, (the Masters of English ships only excepted, for whose good conduct provision is otherwise herein made) shall be permitted to buy or sell in any of the said Marts, unless he be approved by the Governour of the Mart, in which he is to deal, or, in his absence or disability, by the senior Counsellor for the time being, and obtaining a license from such Governour or Counsellor: and the said Traders and Factors shall, severally or jointly, as they shall be concerned, before they shall obtain the said license, be bound in a recognizance, with such

Surety for his or their good behaviour, as to the said Governour shall seem the best, that can be obtained.

16. Be it enacted, that the said Governour, or other authority aforesaid, shall examine, as by duty of office, into the conduct of all such Traders and Factors, and shall receive and publickly hear (with the assistance of the Council and Inspectors aforesaid, and of the Commodore, Captain, or other principal Commander of one of His Majesty's ships on the said station, or as many of the same as can be assembled, two whereof, with the Governour, are hereby enabled to act) all complaints against them, or any of them; and if any black or white Trader or Factor, (other than in this Act excepted) either on inquisition of office, or on complaint, shall be convicted by a majority of the said Commissioners present of stealing or taking by surprise any person or persons whatsoever, whether free, or the Slaves of others, without the consent of their masters; or of wilfully and maliciously killing or maiming any person; or of any cruelty, (necessary restraint only excepted) or of firing houses, or destroying goods, the said Trader or Factor shall be deemed to have forfeited his recognizance, and his Surety to have forfeited his; and the said Trader or Factor, so convicted, shall be for ever disabled from dealing in any of the said Marts, unless the offence shall not be that of murder, maiming, arson, or stealing or surprising the person, and shall appear to the Commissioners aforesaid to merit only, besides the penalty of his bond, a suspension for one year: and the said Trader or Factor, so convicted of murder, maiming, arson, stealing or surprising the person, shall, if a Native, be delivered over to the Prince, to whom he belongs, to execute further justice on him. But it is hereby provided and enacted, that if any European shall be convicted of any of the said offences, he shall be sent to Europe, together with the evidence against him; and on the warrant of the said Commissioners the Keeper of any of His Majesty's Jails in London, Bristol, Liverpool, or Glasgow, shall receive

him, until he be delivered according to due course of law, as if the said offences had been committed within the cities and towns aforesaid.

17. Be it further enacted, that if the said Governour, &c. shall be satisfied that any person or persons are exposed to sale, who have been stolen or surprised as aforesaid, or are not within the qualifications of sale in this Act described, they are hereby authorized and required, if it can be done, to send the persons so exposed to sale to their original habitation or settlement, in the manner they shall deem best for their security (the reasonable charges whereof shall be allowed to the said Governour by the African Company) unless the said persons choose to sell themselves; and then, and in that case, their value in money and goods, at their pleasure, shall be secured to them, and be applicable to their use, without any dominion over the same of any purchaser, or of any master, to whom they may in any Colony or Plantation be sold, and which shall always be in some of his Master's Colonies and Plantations only. And the Master of the ship, in which such person shall embark, shall give bond for the faithful execution of his part of the trust at the Island where he shall break bulk.

18. Be it further enacted, that besides the hospitals on shore, one or more hospital-ships shall be employed at each of the said chief Marts, wherein Slaves taken ill in the trading ships shall be accommodated until they shall be cured; and then the owner may reclaim, and shall receive them, paying the charges, which shall be settled by regulation to be made by the authority in this Act enabled to provide such regulations.

III. And whereas it is necessary that regulations be made to prevent abuses in the passage from Africa to the West Indies;

1. Be it further enacted, that the Commander or Lieuten-

ant of the King's ship on each station shall have authority, as often as he shall see occasion, attended with one other of his Officers, and his Surgeon or Mate, to enter into and inspect every trading ship, in order to provide for the due execution of this Act, and of any ordinances made in virtue thereof and conformable thereto, by the authorities herein constituted and appointed: and the said Officer and Officers are hereby required to examine every trading ship before she sails, and to stop the sailing of the said ship, for the breach of the said rules and ordinances, until the Governour in Council shall order and direct otherwise; and the Master of the said ship shall not presume, under the penalty of ——— to be recovered in the Courts of the West Indies, to sail without a certificate from the Commander aforesaid, and one of the Inspectors in this Act appointed, that the vessel is provided with stores and other accommodation sufficient for her voyage, and has not a greater number of Slaves on board than by the provisions of this Act is allowed.

2. And be it enacted, that the Governour and Council, with the assistance of the said Naval Commander, shall have power to give such special written instructions, for the health, discipline, and care of the said Slaves, during their passage, as to them shall seem good.

3. And be it further enacted, that each Slave, at entering the said ship, is to receive some present, not exceeding in value ———, to be provided according to the instructions aforesaid, and musical instruments, according to the fashion of the country, are to be provided.

4. And be it further enacted, that the Negroes on board the transports, and the seamen, who navigate the same, are to receive their daily allowance, according to the Table hereunto annexed, together with a certain quantity of spirits to be mixed with their water. And it is enacted, that the Table is to be fixed, and continue for one week after sailing, in some conspicuous part of the said ship, for the seamen's inspection of the same.

5. And be it enacted, that the Captain of each trading vessel shall be enabled, and is required, to divide the Slaves in his ship into crews of not less than ten, nor more than twenty persons each, and to appoint one Negro man to have such authority severally over each crew, as according to his judgment, with the advice of the Mate and Surgeon, he and they shall see good to commit to them, and to allow to each of them some compensation, in extraordinary diet and presents, not exceeding [ten shillings.]

6. And be it enacted, that any European Officer or seaman, having unlawful communication with any woman Slave, shall, if an Officer, pay five pounds to the use of the said woman, on landing her from the said ship, to be stopped out of his wages; or if a seaman, forty shillings; the said penalties to be recovered on the testimony of the woman so abused, and one other.

7. And be it enacted, that all and every Commander of a vessel or vessels employed in slave trade, having received certificates from the port of the outfit, and from the proper Officers in Africa and the West Indies of their having conformed to the regulations of this Act, and of their not having lost more than one in thirty of their Slaves by death, shall be entitled to a bounty or premium of [ten pounds.]

IV. And whereas the condition of persons in a state of slavery is such that they are utterly unable to take advantage of any remedy, which the laws may provide for their protection, and the amendment of their condition, and have not the proper means of pursuing any process for the same, but are and must be under guardianship; and whereas it is not fitting that they should be under the sole guardianship of their Masters, or their Attornies and Overseers, to whom their grievances, whenever they suffer any, must ordinarily be owing;

1. Be it therefore enacted, that His Majesty's Attorney General for the time being successively shall, by his office, exercise the trust and employment of Protector of Negroes

within the island, in which he is or shall be Attorney General to His Majesty, His Heirs and Successors: and that the said Attorney General, Protector of Negroes, is hereby authorized to hear any complaint on the part of any Negro or Negroes, and inquire into the same, or to institute an inquiry *ex officio* into any abuses, and to call before him, and examine, witnesses upon oath, relative to the subject matter of the said official inquiry or complaint; and it is hereby enacted and declared, that the said Attorney General, Protector of Negroes, is hereby authorized and empowered, at his discretion, to file an information *ex officio* for any offences committed against the provisions of this Act, or for any misdemeanors or wrongs against the said Negroes, or any of them.

2. And it is further enacted, that in all trials of such informations, the said Protector of Negroes may and is hereby authorized to challenge, peremptorily, a number not exceeding ——— of the Jury, who shall be impannelled to try the charge in the said information contained.

3. And be it enacted, that the said Attorney General, Protector of Negroes, shall appoint Inspectors, not exceeding the number of ———, at his discretion; and the said Inspectors shall be placed in convenient districts in each island severally, or shall twice in the year make a circuit in the same, according to the direction, which they shall receive from the Protector of Negroes aforesaid; and the Inspectors shall, and they are hereby required, twice in the year, to report in writing to the Protector aforesaid the state and condition of the Negroes in their districts, or on their circuit severally, the number, sex, age, and occupation of the said Negroes on each plantation; and the Overseer, or chief manager on each plantation, is hereby required to furnish an account thereof, within [ten days] after the demand of the said Inspectors, and to permit the Inspector or Inspectors aforesaid to examine into the same; and the said Inspectors shall set forth, in the said report, the distempers, to which the Negroes are most liable, in the several parts of the island.

4. And be it enacted, that the said Protector of Negroes, by and with the consent of the Governour and Chief Judge of each Island, shall form instructions, by which the said Inspectors shall discharge their trust in the manner the least capable of exciting any unreasonable hopes in the said Negroes, or of weakening the proper authority of the Overseer, and shall transmit them to one of His Majesty's Principal Secretaries of State; and when sent back with his approbation, the same shall become the rule for the conduct of the said Inspectors.

5. And be it enacted, that the said Attorney General, Protector of Negroes, shall appoint an office for registering all proceedings relative to the duty of his place, as Protector of Negroes, and shall appoint his chief Clerk to be registrar, with a salary not exceeding ———.

6. And be it enacted, that no Negroes shall be landed for sale in any but the ports following; that is to say, ———; and the Collector of each of the said ports severally shall, within ——— days after the arrival of any ship transporting Negroes, report the same to the Protector of Negroes, or to one of his Inspectors; and the said Protector is hereby authorized and required to examine, or cause to be examined, by one of his Inspectors, with the assistance of the said Collector, or his Deputy, and a Surgeon to be called in on the occasion, the state of the said ship and Negroes; and upon what shall appear to them, the said Protector of Negroes, and the said Collector and Surgeon, to be a sufficient proof, either as arising from their own inspection, or sufficient information on a summary process, of any contravention of this Act, or cruelty to the Negroes, or other malversation of the said Captain, or any of his Officers, the said Protector shall impose a fine on him or them, not exceeding ———; which shall not, however, weaken or invalidate any penalty growing from the bond of the said Master or his owners. And it is hereby provided, that if the said Master, or any of his Officers, shall find himself aggrieved by the said fine, he may, within ——— days, appeal to the Chief Judge, if the Court shall be sitting,

or to the Governour, who shall and are required to hear the said parties, and on hearing are to annul or confirm the same.

7. And be it enacted, that no sale of Negroes shall be made but in the presence of an Inspector, and all Negroes shall be sold severally, or in known and ascertained lots, and not otherwise; and a paper, containing the state and description of each Negro severally sold, and of each lot, shall be taken and registered in the office aforesaid; and if on inspection or information it shall be found that any Negroes shall have, in the same ship, or any other at the same time examined, a wife, an husband, a brother, sister, or child, the person, or persons so related, shall not be sold separately at that or any future sale.

8. And be it enacted, that each and every of His Majesty's Islands and Plantations, in which Negroes are used in cultivation, shall be, by the Governour and the Protector of Negroes for the time being, divided into districts, allowing as much as convenience will admit to the present division into parishes, and subdividing them, where necessary, into districts, according to the number of Negroes. And the said Governour and Protector of Negroes shall cause in each district a church to be built in a convenient place, and a cemetery annexed, and an house for the residence of a Clergyman, with ——— acres of land annexed; and they are hereby authorized to treat for the necessary ground with the proprietor, who is hereby obliged to sell and dispose of the same to the said use; and in case of dispute concerning the value, the same to be settled by a Jury as in like cases is accustomed.

9. And be it enacted, that in each of the said districts shall be established a Presbyter of the Church of England, as by law established, who shall appoint under him one Clerk, who shall be a free Negro, when such properly qualified can be found; (otherwise a white man) with a salary, in each case, of ———; and the said Minister and Clerk, both or one, shall instruct the said Negroes in the Church Catechism, or such

other as shall be provided by the authority in this Act named: and the said Minister shall baptize, as he shall think fit, all Negroes not baptized, and not belonging to Dissenters from the Church of England.

10. And the principal Overseer of each plantation is hereby required to deliver annually unto the Minister a list of all the Negroes upon his plantation, distinguishing their sex and age, and shall, under a penalty of ———, cause all the Negroes under his care, above the age of ——— years, to attend Divine Service once on every Sunday, except in case of sickness, infirmity, or other necessary cause to be given at the time; and shall, by himself or one of those, who are under him, provide for the orderly behaviour of the Negroes under him, and cause them to return to his plantation when Divine Service, or Administration of Sacraments, or Catechism is ended.

11. And be it enacted, that the Minister shall have power to punish any Negro for disorderly conduct during divine Service, by a punishment not exceeding [ten] blows, to be given in one day, and for one offence, which the Overseer, or his under-agent or agents, is hereby directed, according to the orders of the said Minister, effectually to inflict, whenever the same shall be ordered.

12. And be it enacted, that no spirituous liquors of any kind shall be sold, except in towns, within ——— miles distant of any Church, nor within any district during Divine Service, and an hour preceding, and an hour following, the same; and the Minister of each parish shall and is hereby authorized to act as a Justice of the Peace in enforcing the said regulation.

13. And be it enacted, that every Minister shall keep a register of births, burials and marriages, of all Negroes and Mulattoes in his district.

14. And be it enacted, that the Ministers of the several districts shall meet annually, on the ——— day of ———,

in a Synod of the island, to which they belong; and the said Synod shall have for its President such persons as the Bishop of London shall appoint for his Commissary; and the said Synod or General Assembly is hereby authorized, by a majority of voices, to make regulations, which regulations shall be transmitted by the said President or Commissary to the Bishop of London; and when returned by the Bishop of London approved of, then, and not before, the said regulations shall be held in force to bind the said Clergy, their Assistants, Clerks, and Schoolmasters only, and no other persons.

15. And be it enacted, that the said President shall collect matter in the said Assembly, and shall make a report of the state of religion and morals in the several parishes from whence the Synod is deputed, and shall transmit the same, once in the year, in duplicate, through the Governour and Protector of Negroes, to the Bishop of London.

16. And be it enacted and declared, that the Bishop of London for the time being shall be Patron to all and every the said cures in this Act directed, and the said Bishop is hereby required to provide for the due filling thereof, and is to receive from the fund in this Act provided, for the due execution of this Act, a sum not exceeding ——— for each of the said Ministers, for his outfit and passage.

17. And be it enacted, that on misbehaviour, and on complaint from the said Synod, and on hearing the party accused in a plain and summary manner, it shall and may be lawful for the Bishop of London to suspend or to remove any Minister from his cure, as his said offences shall appear to merit.

18. And be it enacted, that for every two districts a school shall be established for young Negroes, to be taught three days in the week, and to be detained from their owner four hours in each day: the number not to be more or fewer than twenty males in each district, who shall be chosen, and vacancies filled, by the Minister of the district; and the said Minister shall pay to the owner of the said boy, and shall be

allowed the same in his accounts at the Synod, to the age of twelve years old, three-pence by the day; and for every boy, from twelve years old to fifteen, five-pence by the day.

19. And it is enacted, that if the President of the Synod aforesaid shall certify to the Protector of Negroes, that any boys in the said schools (provided that the number in no one year shall exceed one in the island of Jamaica, and one in two years in the islands of Barbadoes, Antigua, and Grenada; and one in four years in any of the other Islands) do show a remarkable aptitude for learning, the said Protector is hereby authorized and directed to purchase the said boy at the best rate, at which boys of that age and strength have been sold within the year; and the said Negro so purchased shall be under the entire guardianship of the said Protector of Negroes, who shall send him to the Bishop of London, for his further education in England, and may charge in his accounts for the expense of transporting him to England: and the Bishop of London shall provide for the education of such of the said Negroes as he shall think proper subjects, until the age of twenty-four years, and shall order those, who shall fall short of expectation after one year, to be bound apprentice to some handicraft trade; and when his apprenticeship is finished, the Lord Mayor of London is hereby authorized and directed to receive the said Negro from his master, and to transmit him to the island, from which he came in the West Indies, to be there as a free Negro; subject, however, to the direction of the Protector of Negroes, relatively to his behaviour and employment.

20. And it is hereby enacted and provided, that any planter or owner of Negroes, not being of the Church of England, and not choosing to send his Negroes to attend Divine Service in manner by this Act directed, shall give, jointly or severally, as the case shall require, security to the Protector of Negroes, that a competent Minister of some Christian church or congregation shall be provided for the due instruction of

the Negroes, and for their performing Divine Service according to the description of the religion of the master or masters, in some church or house thereto allotted, in the manner and with the regulations in this Act prescribed with regard to the exercise of religion according to the Church of England.

Provided always, that the marriages of the said Negroes belonging to Dissenters shall be celebrated only in the Church of the said district, and that a register of the births shall be transmitted to the Minister of the said district.

21. And whereas a state of matrimony, and the government of a family, is a principal means of forming men to a fitness for freedom, and to become good Citizens; Be it enacted, that all Negro men and women, above eighteen years of age for the man, and sixteen for the woman, who have cohabited together for twelve months or upwards, or shall cohabit for the same time, and have a child or children, shall be deemed to all intents and purposes to be married; and either of the parties is authorized to require of the Ministers of the district, to be married in the face of the Church.

22. And be it enacted, that from and after the ——— of ———, all Negro men in an healthy condition, and so reported to be, in case the same is denied, by a Surgeon and by an Inspector of Negroes, being twenty-one year's old or upwards, until fifty, and not being before married, shall, on requisition of the Inspectors, be provided by their Masters or Overseers with a woman not having children living, and not exceeding the age of the man; nor in any case exceeding the age of twenty-five years; and such persons shall be married publickly in the face of the Church.

23. And be it enacted, that if any Negro shall refuse a competent marriage tendered to him, and shall not demand another specifically, such as it may be in his Master's power to provide, the Master or Overseer shall be authorized to constrain him by an increase of work, or a lessening of allowance.

24. And be it enacted, that the Minister in each district

shall have, with the assent of the Inspector, full power and authority to punish all acts of adultery, unlawful concubinage, and fornication, amongst Negroes, on hearing and a summary process, by ordering a number of blows, not exceeding   for each offence; and if any white person shall be proved, on information in the Supreme Court to be exhibited by the Protector of Negroes, to have committed adultery with any Negro woman, or to have corrupted any Negro woman under sixteen years of age, he shall be fined in the sum of ———, and shall be for ever disabled from serving the office of Overseer of Negroes, or being Attorney to any Plantation.

25. And be it enacted, that no Slaves shall be compelled to do any work for their masters for [three] days after their marriage.

26. And be it enacted, that no woman shall be obliged to field-work, or any other laborious work, for one month before her delivery, or for six weeks afterwards.

27. And be it enacted, that no husband and wife shall be sold separately, if originally belonging to the same master, nor shall any children, under sixteen, be sold separately from their parents, or one parent, if one be living.

28. And be it enacted, that if an husband and wife, which before their intermarriage belonged to different owners, shall be sold, they shall not be sold at such a distance as to prevent mutual help and cohabitation; and of this distance the Minister shall judge, and his certificate of the inconvenient distance shall be valid, so as to make such sale unlawful, and to render the same null and void.

29. And be it enacted, that no Negro shall be compelled to work for his owner at field-work, or any service relative to a plantation, or to work at any handicraft trade, from eleven o'clock on Saturday forenoon until the usual working hour on Monday morning.

30. And whereas habits of industry and sobriety, and the means of acquiring and preserving property, are proper and

reasonable preparatives to freedom, and will secure against an abuse of the same; Be it enacted, that every Negro man, who shall have served ten years, and is thirty years of age, and is married, and has had two children born of any marriage, shall obtain the whole of Saturday for himself and his wife, and for his own benefit; and after thirty-seven years of age, the whole of Friday for himself and his wife; provided that in both cases the Minister of the district, and the Inspector of Negroes, shall certify that they know nothing against his peaceable, orderly, and industrious behaviour.

31. And be it enacted, that the Master of every plantation shall provide the materials of a good and substantial hut for each married field Negro; and if his plantation shall exceed ——— acres, he shall allot to the same a portion of land not less than ———: and the said hut and land shall remain and stand annexed to the said Negro, for his natural life, or during his bondage; but the same shall not be alienated without the consent of the owners.

32. And be it enacted, that it shall not be lawful for the owner of any Negro, by himself or any other, to take from him any land, house, cattle, goods or money, acquired by the said Negro, whether by purchase, donation or testament, whether the same has been derived from the owner of the said Negro, or any other.

33. And be it enacted, that if the said Negro shall die possessed of any lands, goods, or chattels, and dies without leaving a wife or issue, it shall be lawful for the said Negro to devise or bequeath the same by his last will; but in case the said Negro shall die intestate, and leave a wife and children, the same shall be distributed amongst them, according to the usage under the Statute, commonly called the Statute of Distributions. But if the Negro shall die intestate without wife or children, then, and in that case his estate shall go to the fund provided for the better execution of this Act.

34. And be it enacted, that no Negro, who is married, and

hath resided upon any plantation for twelve months, shall be sold either privately, or by the decree of any Court, but along with the plantation, on which he hath resided, unless he should himself request to be separated therefrom.

35. And be it enacted, that no blows or stripes, exceeding thirteen, shall be inflicted for one offence upon any Negro, without the order of one of His Majesty's Justices of Peace.

36. And it is enacted, that it shall be lawful for the Protector of Negroes, as often as on complaint and hearing he shall be of opinion that any Negro hath been cruelly and inhumanly treated, or when it shall be made to appear to him that an Overseer hath any particular malice, to order, at the desire of the suffering party, the said Negro to be sold to another master.

37. And be it enacted, that, in all cases of injury to member or life, the offences against a Negro shall be deemed and taken to all intents and purposes as if the same were perpetrated against any of His Majesty's Subjects; and the Protector of Negroes, on complaint, or if he shall receive credible information thereof, shall cause an indictment to be presented for the same; and in case of suspicion of any murder of a Negro, an inquest by the Coroner, or Officer acting as such, shall, if practicable, be held into the same.

38. And in order to a gradual manumission of Slaves, as they shall seem fitted to fill the offices of freemen, Be it enacted, that every Negro Slave, being thirty years of age and upwards, and who has had three children born to him in lawful matrimony, and who hath received a certificate from the Minister of his district, or any other Christian teacher, of his regularity in the duties of religion, and of his orderly and good behaviour, may purchase, at rates to be fixed by two Justices of Peace, the freedom of himself, or his wife or children, or of any of them separately, valuing the wife and children, if purchased into liberty by the father of the family, at half only of their marketable values; provided that the said

father shall bind himself in a penalty of ——— for the good behaviour of his children.

39. And be it enacted, that it shall be lawful for the Protector of Negroes to purchase the freedom of any Negro, who shall appear to him to excel in any mechanical art, or other knowledge or practice deemed liberal, and the value shall be settled by a Jury.

40. And be it enacted, that the Protector of Negroes shall be and is authorized and required to act as a Magistrate, for the coercion of all idle, disobedient, or disorderly free Negroes, and he shall by office prosecute them for the offences of idleness, drunkenness, quarrelling, gaming, or vagrancy, in the Supreme Court, or cause them to be prosecuted before one Justice of Peace, as the case may require.

41. And be it enacted, that if any free Negro hath been twice convicted for any of the said misdemeanors, and is judged by the said Protector of Negroes, calling to his assistance two justices of the Peace, to be incorrigibly idle, dissolute and vicious, it shall be lawful, by the order of the said Protector and two justices of Peace, to sell the said free Negro into slavery: the purchase-money to be paid to the person so remanded into servitude, or kept in hand by the Protector and Governour for the benefit of his family.

42. And be it enacted, that the Governour in each Colony shall be assistant to the execution of this Act, and shall receive the reports of the Protector, and such other accounts, as he shall judge material, relative thereto, and shall transmit the same annually to one of His Majesty's Principal Secretaries of State.

Select Bibliography on Edmund Burke

There is a vast literature on Edmund Burke, his life, his thought, and his times. One will find an exhaustive bibliography of it in *Edmund Burke: A Bibliography of Secondary Studies to 1982,* by Clara J. Gandy and Peter J. Stanlis (New York and London: Garland Publishers, 1983).

What is offered here is a small selection of books for the general reader who may want to fill out the background to, and deepen his understanding of, Burke's actual texts. It draws very heavily on the work of Gandy and Stanlis, supplemented by this editor's own knowledge and further help from Professor Stanlis. It in no way pretends to be a guide to the scholarly research on Burke, for which the full Gandy and Stanlis bibliography will be indispensable.

First, however, the reader may want to read more of Burke's writings than are contained in these volumes. The first set of Burke's works was begun during the last years of his life by his disciples and literary executors, Walker King and French Laurence. After his death, they began anew with a set of *The Works of the Right Honourable Edmund Burke* in sixteen volumes, published in London by F. C. and J. Rivington from 1803 to 1827. According to Paul Langford, all subsequent editions of Burke's works, until the one of which Langford is now the general editor, derived essentially from this Rivington edition. The best and most readily available of them are the eight-volume set published in London by Henry G. Bohn in 1854 and the twelve-volume one published in Boston by Little, Brown in 1901.

All of these editions are being replaced for scholarly work on Burke by *The Writings and Speeches of Edmund Burke,* under Paul Langford's general editorship, which commenced publication by the Clarendon Press in Oxford in 1981 and is not yet complete at the time of this writing. Similarly, all previous publications of Burke's correspondence have been replaced by *The Correspondence of Edmund Burke,* published in ten volumes, under the general editorship of Thomas W. Copeland, by the University of Chicago Press and the Cambridge University Press from 1958 to 1970.

Those wishing to get a better acquaintance with the world in which Burke lived and wrote also have a vast literature at their disposal. To mention but a few examples, there are Peter Laslett's touching *The World We Have Lost, Further Explored* (London: Methuen, 1983), which describes life as it was in seventeenth-century England and as it remained without great change into Burke's lifetime, and Dorothy Marshall's *Eighteenth-Century England* (New York: D. McKay, 1962). The aristocratic society that was Burke's political milieu is described by authors whose feelings about it range from left to right: M. L. Bush, *The English Aristocracy* (Manchester University Press, 1984); John Cannon, *Aristocratic Century* (Cambridge University Press, 1984); and G. E. Mingay, *English Landed Society in the Eighteenth Century* (London: Routledge and Kegan Paul; Toronto: University of Toronto Press, 1963) and *The Gentry* (London and New York: Longman, 1976).

Biographies of Burke are rather few in number, and their authors were limited in access to source materials prior to 1949 and the early 1950s, when the Earls Fitzwilliam, the heirs of Burke's political patrons, put a large collection of Burke's previously unpublished papers in the Sheffield Central Library for use by scholars.

The best of the nineteenth-century biographies is Sir James Prior's *Memoir of the Life and Character of the Right Honourable Edmund Burke,* which had five editions, the last of them reprinted in 1967 by Burt Franklin in New York (but the second edition of 1826 is the best one). In the latter half of the nineteenth century, the most influential biography was John Morley's *Burke,* in the English Men of Letters Series, which established the dominant utilitarian interpretation of Burke's thought until after World War II; first published in 1879, it has been several times republished (e.g., London: Macmillan, 1936).

Written in the first half of the twentieth century, *The Early Life, Correspondence and Writings of Edmund Burke,* by Arthur P. I. and Arthur Warren Samuels (Cambridge University Press, 1923), is still useful for this period of Burke's life. Bertram Newman's *Edmund Burke* (London: Bell and Sons, 1927) is not a great biography, but it is serviceable. The best political biography of Burke is Carl B. Cone's *Burke and the Nature of Politics:* vol. 1, *The Age of the American Revolution;* and vol. 2, *The Age of the French Revolution* (Lexington: University of Kentucky Press, 1957, 1964). Russell Kirk's *Edmund Burke: A Genius Reconsidered* (New York and New Rochelle: Arlington House, 1967) is a more popular biography. Charles Parkin's article "Edmund Burke" in the *New Encyclopaedia Britannica* (15th ed., 1980) is a brief but excellent scholarly biography. A new biography that surpasses all previous ones in exhaustive research and wealth of detail is *Edmund Burke,* by F. P. Locke, volume 1 of which was published in 1998. Volume 2, at the time of this writing, was still being written.

Interpretations of Burke's thought, which encompasses not only his political principles but his much broader philosophical and theological views, vary widely. Those who wish to get an idea of the broad scope of these variations may read the introduction to chapter 5 of the Gandy and Stanlis bibliography. To simplify the matter here, however, we may say that the dominant and largely British interpretation focussed on Burke's emphasis on concrete historical facts and developments, on contingency in human affairs, and on "expediency" and practicality in political judgment. In this interpretation, Burke emerges as a utilitarian who ejected from political thought "metaphysics" and natural law in the form of natural rights. After World War II, a school of interpretation arose, mainly on the American side of the Atlantic, that held that Burke had inherited a classical and Christian conception of natural law that furnished him with his view of the world, of man, and of the supreme norms of politics.

There are those who deny that Burke's thought deserved to be called a political philosophy. One example, despite the title of his book, is Frank O'Gorman, *Edmund Burke: His Political Philosophy* (Bloomington: Indiana University Press; London: Allen and Unwin, 1973). O'Gorman, a Lecturer in Modern History at the University of Manchester when he wrote the book, sees Burke as no more than an ideologist for the Rockingham Whigs. A more recent example is Isaac Kramnick's *The Rage of Edmund Burke* (New York: Basic Books, 1977), which psychoanalyzes Burke as a frustrated bourgeois with a love-hate relationship with the aristocracy whom he served, and perhaps a self-suppressed homosexual. Another highly psychological examination of Burke is Conor Cruise O'Brien's *The Great Melody* (University of Chicago Press, 1992).

In the nineteenth century, works by Henry Buckle, Sir Leslie Stephen, and William Lecky placed Burke in the empirical, pragmatic, and utilitarian school of thought. We may take John Morley's *Burke,* already mentioned, as the most influential example of this school. Burke, he says, overthrew "the baneful superstition that politics . . . is a province of morals." John MacCunn, in *The Political Philosophy of Burke* (London: Edward Arnold, 1913; New York: Russell and Russell, 1965), emerges from this tradition by bringing out the higher and wider dimensions of Burke's thought, including his belief in a higher moral law.

In the post–World War II period, Charles Parkin pointed

out the connection in Burke's political thought between natural-law morality and politics in *The Moral Basis of Burke's Political Thought* (Cambridge University Press, 1956). In 1958, there appeared a full-length account of the role played in Burke's thought by the classical and medieval conception of natural law: Peter J. Stanlis's *Edmund Burke and the Natural Law* (Ann Arbor: University of Michigan Press; now available from the Intercollegiate Studies Institute, Wilmington, Del.). It was followed by Francis Canavan's *The Political Reason of Edmund Burke* (Duke University Press, 1960), which argued that Burke's insistence on the concrete, experiential, and variable elements in practical political judgment was fully compatible with the older doctrine of natural law, because that doctrine included the Aristotelian and medieval understanding of practical reason and prudence. Burleigh T. Wilkins wrote a critical review of the clash between the utilitarian and natural-law interpretations of Burke's thought in *The Problem of Burke's Political Philosophy* (Oxford: Clarendon Press, 1967), and came down on the natural-law side.

Along the same line are works by Canavan, *Edmund Burke: Prescription and Providence* (Durham, N.C.: Carolina Academic Press, 1987); Stanlis, *Edmund Burke: The Enlightenment and Revolution* (New Brunswick, N.J., and London: Transaction Publishers, 1991); and Joseph L. Pappin III, *The Metaphysics of Edmund Burke* (Bronx, N.Y.: Fordham University Press, 1993).

While one cannot identify Gerard W. Chapman simply with either the utilitarian or the natural-law school, his *Edmund Burke: The Practical Imagination* (Harvard University Press, 1967) is a valuable examination of the way in which Burke's mind worked in making practical and prudential political judgments.

Critiques of Burke's criticism of the radical democratic ideology of the age of the French Revolution may be found in R. R. Fennessy's *Burke, Paine, and the Rights of Man* (The Hague: Martinus Nijhoff, 1963) and Michael Freeman's *Ed-*

mund Burke and the Critique of Political Radicalism (University of Chicago Press, 1980). Daniel E. Ritchie has edited a collection of essays on Burke's thought from different points of view, including major chapters from a number of the books in this bibliography, in *Edmund Burke: Appraisals and Applications* (New Brunswick, N.J., and London: Transaction Publishers, 1990).

Monographs on the major areas of Burke's political concern that are addressed in the documents included in this set of volumes are surprisingly few. We do have Thomas H. D. Mahoney's *Edmund Burke and Ireland* (Harvard University Press, 1960), but there is no monograph covering Burke on America, on India, or on France.

Harvey Mansfield, Jr., has furnished useful background to *Thoughts on the Cause of the Present Discontents* in his *Statesmanship and Party Government* (University of Chicago Press, 1965), and James Boulton has a chapter on that document in his *The Language of Politics in the Age of Wilkes and Burke* (London: Routledge and Kegan Paul; Toronto: University of Toronto Press, 1963). George H. Guttridge's *English Whiggism and the American Revolution* (Berkeley: University of California Press, 1942) performs a similar function for Burke's speeches on American taxation and conciliation with the colonies, as does Stanlis's *Edmund Burke on Conciliation with the Colonies and Other Papers on the American Revolution* (Lumenburg, Vt.: The Limited Editions Club, Stinehour Press, 1975).

Sir Ernest Barker has essays on Burke and Bristol and on Burke and the French Revolution in his *Essays on Government* (Oxford: Clarendon Press, 1951). Steven Blakemore has edited essays on *Burke and the French Revolution* (Athens and London: University of Georgia Press, 1992), and Peter Stanlis edited *Edmund Burke, the Enlightenment and the Modern World* (University of Detroit Press, 1967), which contains essays on Burke and the American and French revolutions. Boulton's *The Language of Politics* has a chapter on Burke's *Reflections on the Revolution in France.*

Select Bibliography on Edmund Burke

The Gandy and Stanlis bibliography is of the opinion that "perhaps the best general treatment of Burke and India" is in vol. 2, pp. 95–139 and 154–256, of Carl Cone's *Burke and the Nature of Politics,* and that the most authoritative text on it is vol. 5 of *The Writings and Speeches of Edmund Burke.*

There is no one book devoted to the subject of Burke and France, nor any single book in English on Burke and the French Revolution. There are almost innumerable periodical articles, however, and introductions to the numerous editions of Burke's *Reflections on the Revolution in France.* For background, one may consult Frank O'Gorman's doctoral dissertation, *The Whig Party and the French Revolution* (London: Macmillan; New York: St. Martin's Press, 1967), which sets Burke's attack on the French Revolution in the British political context of that time. But all books on Burke's political theory must treat his criticism of the Revolution in some depth.

The only monograph on Burke's economics is Francis Canavan's *The Political Economy of Edmund Burke* (Bronx, N.Y.: Fordham University Press, 1995), but there is a large periodical literature on the subject. For background to the *Speech on the Representation of the Commons in Parliament,* the reader may consult George Stead Veith's *The Genesis of Parliamentary Reform* (London: Constable and Co., 1913; Hamden, Conn.: Shoestring Press, 1965) and John Cannon's *Parliamentary Reform, 1640–1832* (Cambridge: Cambridge University Press, 1973).

There is a large literature on Burke's influence on subsequent thought, a subject too large to enter here, but Russell Kirk's *The Conservative Mind from Burke to Eliot,* 7th rev. ed. (Washington: Regnery Gateway, 1986), should be mentioned for its examination of Burke's impact on American thought, as should G. P. Gooch's *Germany and the French Revolution* (London: Longmans, Green and Co., 1927) for that country.

The typeface used for this book is ITC New Baskerville, which was created for the International Typeface Corporation and is based on the types of the English type founder and printer John Baskerville (1706–75). Baskerville is the quintessential transitional face: it retains the bracketed and oblique serifs of old style faces such as Caslon and Garamond, but in its increased lowercase height, lighter color, and enhanced contrast between thick and thin strokes, it presages modern faces.

Printed on paper that is acid-free and meets the requirements of the American National Standard for Permanence of Paper for Printed Library Materials, z39.48-1992. ♾

Book design by Martin Lubin, New York
Composition by Tseng Information Systems, Inc.,
Durham, North Carolina
Printed and bound by Worzalla Publishing Co.,
Stevens Point, Wisconsin